THE NEIGHBORHOOD HAS ITS OWN RULES

The Neighborhood Has Its Own Rules

Latinos and African Americans in South Los Angeles

Cid Gregory Martinez

NEW YORK UNIVERSITY PRESS
New York

NEW YORK UNIVERSITY PRESS
New York
www.nyupress.org

References to Internet websites (URLs) were accurate at the time of writing. Neither the author nor New York University Press is responsible for URLs that may have expired or changed since the manuscript was prepared.

Library of Congress Cataloging-in-Publication Data
Names: Martinez, Cid Gregory, author.
Title: The neighborhood has its own rules : Latinos and African Americans in South Los Angeles / Cid Gregory Martinez.
Description: New York : New York University Press, [2016] | Includes bibliographical references and index.
Identifiers: LCCN 2016001629 | ISBN 9780814770405 (cl : alk. paper) | ISBN 9780814762844 (pb : alk. paper)
Subjects: LCSH: Los Angeles (Calif.)—Race relations. | Ethnic neighborhoods—California—Los Angeles. | Ethnic conflict—California—Los Angeles. | Neighborhood government—California—Los Angeles. | African Americans—Relations with Hispanic Americans. | African Americans—California—Los Angeles. | Hispanic Americans—California—Los Angeles.
Classification: LCC F869.L89 A2547 2016 | DDC 305.8009794/94—dc23
LC record available at http://lccn.loc.gov/2016001629

New York University Press books are printed on acid-free paper, and their binding materials are chosen for strength and durability. We strive to use environmentally responsible suppliers and materials to the greatest extent possible in publishing our books.

Manufactured in the United States of America

10 9 8 7 6 5 4 3 2 1

Also available as an ebook

CONTENTS

Introduction

Managed Violence

At lunchtime, two male youths, one African American and the other Latino, each around 17 years old, swung at one another in a fist fight. Someone had thrown a milk carton, which had hit a Latino boy in the head. Like the other boys, he wore Dockers khaki pants and a white polo shirt, which was the dress code at the charter school. The Latino boy confronted the African American boy and asked why he had hit him. The confrontation escalated into an angry verbal exchange. In a flash, they circled around one another, swinging at each other, as a mob of mostly Latino and African American youths cheered them on. The eating area was outdoors in the back of the school. It consisted of a set of benches placed next to each other, set on black asphalt and covered with a light aluminum roof for shade. A chain-link fence surrounded the back of the school and lunch area, and it was common here for youths from rival gangs to hang out, blaring music and staring at other students to intimidate them.

The heat from the day heightened the smell of the asphalt outdoors. The crowd got louder and louder, and one could hear yells from the mob of students, such as "fuck him up," "kick that punk's ass," "get that fucking puto." The fight was eventually broken up, but had nearly escalated into an all-group conflict as Latino and African American youths began to divide along racial lines in the lunch area. They yelled back and forth, and it seemed like the situation might turn into a riot, not uncommon since there had been numerous school riots in South Los Angeles (South LA) between Latinos and African Americans in 2003, the year I conducted my fieldwork.

It was my first day on the job as a teaching assistant, and I had been in the middle of the fight, trying to separate the two boys. I kept trying to grab them but they kept moving into the crowd, and the other students got in my way. Finally, a female schoolteacher on yard duty dove in and caught one of the boys by the leg. I was then able to hold off the other boy.

Once the boys were separated, they were whisked away to the principal's office. The racial division, however, continued in the classrooms after the fight. In my classroom, it was noticeable that black and Latino students avoided one another—they did not sit near each other, nor did they speak; occasionally, they looked at one another with blank stares. Then, during class, two boys, one African American and the other Latino, each considered leaders by many, sat together in the corner and began talking as if they were having a business meeting. There was little emotion and very little superfluous conversation. I learned later that the Latino youth, named Skeloe, was considered a leader of one of the Latino gangs on campus. The African American youth was considered the leader of a black gang. Their meeting in the classroom seemed to be a form of negotiation. Later, one of the Latino youths, Damosque, considered to be second in charge of the gang and who later became a close friend of mine, told me what had happened. "They worked it out, Cid. The school couldn't do shit. We just told them what they wanted to hear, but we were going to handle it ourselves." "Is that what Skeloe was doing?" I asked. "Yeah, he handled it with the black dude."

Although the school had tried to mediate the conflict by bringing in counselors to talk with the students, nobody would say anything. As one of the teachers asked the class that I was in, "What is wrong with you guys? We are trying to help you guys, but nobody says anything." Both black and Latino youths understood that there were informal rules for handling disputes that operated outside the control of the school administration and kept violence from escalating.

Just as the youths described in this vignette must cope with violence, other residents find a variety of ways for responding to violence in South LA. An examination of the other common institutional settings reveals a more holistic picture of the dangers and violence that residents face on a daily basis.

One institution at the heart of the South LA area is the Catholic Church. Located in the center of South Los Angeles for nearly 100 years, St. Joseph Parish[1] (known as "St. Joseph's") plays an important role in helping residents cope with violence. Many residents who attend the church live within blocks of the parish, which is located in the poorest part of Los Angeles. To the south of the church is a shopping center that was built to replace an area burned down during the Watts Riots of 1965. To the west are a library and a closed fire station, and caddy-corner is a small public housing project. The church grounds take up more physical space than any surrounding commercial or residential areas, and include the sanctuary for worship and an adjacent residential facility where the priests reside. Behind the grounds are a church-run elementary school and a large open space of black asphalt, nearly a quarter of an acre in size. Finally, the church grounds are enclosed by large, black iron gates that remain open during the day and are closed during the evening. The grounds resemble a self-contained world, nestled within a poor urban landscape. According to some, the intersection in front of the church is the largest marijuana bazaar in South LA, and drug deals occur there on and off throughout the day.

Comments by Father John, the church's lead priest, illustrate the relationship between the parish and the surrounding community:

> Beyond this world [the church], there is no other. The kids don't go to the beach, or travel anywhere. Their world is here. I talked to a woman, a parishioner, who works in a factory; she makes $200, or sometimes, $120 a week. She does piecework and is undocumented. She has no defense. The undocumented don't complain. A lot of people here don't eat meat, food that we take for granted. There is a lot of poverty here. I don't notice depression, though. There is the poverty. But I think they are strong in faith. There are gangs and killings. Recently, a woman of the church lost her son [who was shot to death]. She came to the mass the day her son died because maybe it's their only refuge.

The priest's comments highlight the way parishioners view the church as a refuge from potentially threatening forces immediately outside its walls, such as neighborhood violence and exploitation in the workplace. This social space also acts as a form of refuge from other potentially threatening forces, such as the Immigration and Naturalization Services (INS). Being deported by the INS is a constant fear for many members of the church. In several interviews and interactions, this fear was emphasized, and many parishioners had been told that the INS would not be allowed into the church to detain individuals. Thus, the church takes on the role of an informal institution that provides Latino residents with a safe environment.

The area that I focused on for this book not only has the largest concentration of poor people in Los Angeles, it also has the largest number of public housing facilities in the city. The South LA area has a total of four separate housing projects, two of which are among the largest in Los Angeles, less than one mile from each other. Each public housing unit is a world within a world. I spent many months getting to know people in public housing, initially through my involvement in the City of Los Angeles Neighborhood Councils. I learned from talking to residents in public housing how neighborhood life is shaped by informal rules that run counter to those of mainstream society, as in the following comments by an African American male in his early 20s from the Downing Housing Project:

> CID: It seems like there is street justice and legal justice. One is the law and one is unstated, and one just knows. Are there two types of law that operate here?
>
> LBM: Yeah, there are definitely two types of laws. The street law: more of a "just us," it's street just us in comparison to the judicial system.

Such comments illustrate the existence of an alternative form of justice that operates outside the scope of formal law, real and widely understood by residents of public housing and the wider community of South LA. How is it that both formal and informal laws emerge in modern urban America? How do the informal rules shape daily life for both African Americans and Latinos?

The anecdotes included here sketch out a social structure in which Latinos and African Americans increasingly go underground to alternative worlds where religious institutions and street life provide competing forms of social order. Understanding these alternative worlds is key for answering the central question addressed in this book: how do poor, urban institutions respond to violence?

Doing Ethnography in South Los Angeles

To answer my question about the relationship between alternative worlds and violence, I moved to South Los Angeles in August 2003 to conduct an ethnography of the area. I felt that living in the community, and going beyond the shotgun interviews that are a common practice among sociologists, was critical for understanding residents and their experiences. In addition to becoming a resident of South LA, I volunteered and attended meetings of the Neighborhood Councils, worked as a teaching assistant at a local charter school for youths kicked out of school for gang-related behavior, and volunteered and taught religious classes at a Catholic church.

Gaining entry into the church and gang settings started with my affiliation with the Neighborhood Councils. After conducting preliminary fieldwork in the area, I decided that the Neighborhood Councils would be a good place to get connected with the community. More importantly, the Neighborhood Councils would allow me to see how residents used formal political institutions to address local issues, such as violence and crime. I was quickly accepted by many members of the South LA community; while some viewed me with deep suspicion, most were welcoming. The suspicion was understandable. Dating back before the 1965 Watts Riots, residents felt betrayed by the police, city officials, and journalists. Although most people embraced me, the distrust I encountered made me realize I needed to blend in more. I became good friends with a Neighborhood Council managing coordinator, a Latino male in his mid-30s, who was responsible for overseeing most of the Neighborhood Councils in South Los Angeles. He was surprised to find me attending meeting after meeting in some of the roughest parts of South LA. Most people from outside the area would not dare to traverse some of the rough neighborhoods where the meetings were held. This man's friendship was invaluable. He helped me get connected to key local community members. Shortly thereafter, I became a volunteer with the City of Los Angeles Department of Neighborhood Empowerment (DONE). I became well acquainted with others from the staff at this department, and I visited the office as if I worked there. I started to attend meetings now as a DONE volunteer. My role as a volunteer was important because it gave me an identity. It provided me with a legitimate reason for attending meetings and being involved in the community.

After attending the meetings regularly, I became more familiar with key institutions and organizations in the community. One day while working in a DONE satellite office, located in one of the roughest and poorest parts of South LA, I decided to pay a visit to the Catholic church conveniently located right across the street. I met with the priest of this church and explained my research to him, which at the time was about black and Latino relations. He looked at me and said, "That sounds fantastic! This is the kind of thing that, as a pastor, I am trying to figure out. The church used to be predominantly African American and now it's mostly Latino. We have gone through many changes and your work sounds very useful for me. I will help however I can."

Later, he would use me to help with the church in various ways. I was surprised when one day he said, "Oh Cid, I forgot to tell you, you are going to teach confirmation class for the youth, the teacher is pregnant and now she is ill. So you will have to take over. You start next week." At this parish, I sometimes attended church three to four times on weekends.

Eventually, I realized I needed to get closer to the residents to see what life was like for parishioners outside of the church in their own neighborhoods. I informed the priest that I needed a place to live. He told me that he would ask around for me. Later, I learned that I would be living with a parishioner who resided about four blocks from the parish. This setting allowed me to see what life was like for parishioners inside church and outside in their day-to-day lives. After this arrangement had continued for a few months, I was then assigned to live with another parishioner who also lived near the church.

I considered living with the parishioners in their residences as my third field site—as a resident, I gained firsthand insight into what neighborhood life was like. Furthermore, I got to see life on a daily basis during the week and on the weekends. Doing this informed me about neighborhood dynamics, such as violence, and about the roles that were played interracially between residents. More importantly, living in the neighborhood of South LA allowed me to see the interplay of street life, such as gang life, and its relationship with the church.

Finally, I was able to observe youths who were involved in gang activity by volunteering and eventually working at two charter high schools in South LA. The schools' student bodies consisted primarily of Latino and African American youths between the ages of fourteen and eighteen. These charter schools were founded by a Catholic-affiliated foundation for youths who had been kicked out of Los Angeles Unified School District for a variety of reasons, many for their gang affiliations. At the schools, kids were screened before admission to determine their gang affiliation so that conflict and violence could be minimized. Many of the youths had nowhere else to go; their behavioral history had put them in a position where they could not attend school anywhere else. For many of these youths, dropping out was their next option if they could not cut it at the charter school.

I started as a volunteer teaching assistant at a campus located in the heart of South LA. The campus was originally a Catholic school that had been purchased to now serve high-risk youths, who were evenly composed of Latinos and African Americans. I worked individually with students who needed one-on-one help, assisted teachers with various assignments, and ate lunch with the students.

As the staff began to trust me, I was considered for employment at another satellite campus that served the same at-risk population in the western part of South LA, an area more predominantly African American that had not undergone the same the demographic changes. I was finally hired as a teaching assistant and worked 30 to 40 hours a week at the school. My role as an official employee gave me access to more of an insider perspective than I had had as a volunteer. More importantly, I could better observe the violence the youths were at risk of experiencing before, after, and even during school.

Recruitment and Method

These four field sites became the central lens through which I saw the community. Working and volunteering at the charter school, the church, and the Neighborhood Councils and residing in the neighborhood allowed me to connect with residents and view their daily routines and experiences as they related to issues of violence. Once I became familiar with individuals connected with these institutions, I would follow them out to the broader community in South LA. Unlike most studies, the goal of this one was to view the interrelationships between these various institutional settings, rather than view them as separate, isolated social worlds. In this sense, this book follows in the footsteps of other traditional sociological community studies that attempt to view community in its totality. Each field site from this perspective reflects an important dimension of community life. While there are many aspects of the community I could have focused upon, the classic community studies all recognize that politics, religion, and street life are key elements of community life in general.

I therefore used these sites as the starting points of a snowball sample. The individuals I met would refer me to other individuals of interest. More importantly, as a volunteer and employee, I was viewed with less suspicion, and, over time, residents began to trust me. Most of the data collected were thus field observations based on my interactions with residents.

When the fieldwork was coming to its close in August 2004, however, there were many questions I still had about how residents manage violence. Most of the data collected for this study came from direct observation. During this time, I got to know many of the individuals who are in the study well, so that they were not just subjects, but people that I had established relationships with. While direct observation was my preferred method, there were questions that I felt needed direct answers. Therefore, I conducted exit interviews with the individuals examined in this study. I also felt it was important to gain the perspective of other individuals not directly involved in the institutions that I anchored my observations to. I conducted over 100 interviews with youths from the charter school and with residents who lived in public housing and other residential areas surrounding the institutions of my study.

Violence, Informal Social Control, and Alternative Governance

In many urban poor areas of the United States, such as South LA, local government and formal channels to address crime lack legitimacy and are disconnected from the needs of residents. In their place, I argue that an alternative form of governance has arisen to fill the vacuum.

More importantly, there are multiple and competing types of *alternative* governance that regulate violence. The notion of multiple forms of competing alternative governance, however, has received little attention from scholars.

There are a variety of ways in which neighborhood residents respond to violence according to the sociological literature. The concept of informal social control or some variety of this is often used to explain the way in which neighborhoods respond to violent crime. Informal social control can be defined as the ability of residents to self-regulate activity that is viewed as inappropriate. Neighborhood-watch programs, in which residents organize to address problems such as graffiti and blighted property, are a good example of informal social control.

Conceptually, informal social control can be divided into two categories. The traditional notion of this concept can be traced back to Albert Hunter (1985). According to Hunter, there are three dimensions of social control—the public, the parochial, and the private. The public refers to local government and the community writ large, including law enforcement; the parochial domain consists of the local community, such as stores and churches; and the private domain consists of friendship and kin relations. For Hunter, disorder and crime increase when there is a lack of integration between these dimensions of social control. The clearest example of this would be poor relationships between the police and a given community. In Los Angeles, for example, poor relations between the police and community residents of South LA no doubt undermined the ability to reduce crime. Recent preliminary reports suggest that improved police relations with residents have helped to significantly reduce crime.

Recent work by Patrick Carr (2005), however, suggests that residents can effectively address crime and disorder by a strengthened relationship between the parochial and public orders, with minimal input from the private order. He argues that local government and law enforcement, via the public order, can embolden communities to become more effectively organized and provide badly needed resources to confront neighborhood crime. Thus, Carr emphasizes the importance of the state and local government partnering with communities to effectively solve crime.

While Carr's work advances the concept of informal social control, there are limitations to this approach whereby local government plays a critical role in regulating disorder and crime. First, he assumes that local governments have the resources to aid communities in need to address crime. Local governments, however, struggle now, more than ever, to meet the basic needs of city residents. The anti-tax sentiment pervasive in the United States combined with a struggling national economy poses many obstacles to the generation of badly needed tax revenue. Second, Carr assumes that most communities have positive relations with city government. In many cities, however, poor neighborhoods have long histories of strained relations with local government; Los Angeles is certainly one of these cities. Indeed, two of the largest riots in the 20th-century United States took place in South Los Angeles, rooted in a long history of abuse and neglect by law enforcement and city government.

What emerges from a consideration of the limitations of Carr's analysis is a variable relationship between the state and urban poor communities. More importantly, relations in most US cities between the urban poor and city government have been strained, to say the least. For many urban poor blacks and Latinos, the face of government often becomes associated with the local police.

Recent work by Venkatesh (2006) advances Carr's work in two key ways. First, he demonstrates a type of informal social control that operates with minimal connections to the state. His work focuses on how urban poor Chicagoans attempt to maintain social order and regulate behavior outside the purview of the state, which is necessary due to the ubiquitous underground economic activity of residents who must hustle to make a living. In Venkatesh's model of social control, there is a heightened relationship between the parochial—including community institutions such as gangs—and the private sector, friendship and kin ties in neighborhood settings—concerning the self-regulation of behavior. For example, gangs and residents of Marquis Park hash out the rules about where, when, and how exchange takes place in daily neighborhood life. When rules are violated, violence is used to enforce conformity. In a major contrast with Carr's framework, Venkatesh demonstrates that informal social control in urban poor areas operates with minimal relations with the state and plays a significant role in shaping neighborhood life through the use of violence.

Second, his work demonstrates that there are multiple forms of informal social control that regulate violence, which are not exclusively limited to the street or gangs. Instead, his work focuses on the role of multiple sources of informal social control, namely, gangs and the church.

Venkatesh's findings demonstrate how the church, gangs, and residents negotiate social order by the negotiation and renegotiation of rules in poor neighborhoods through the use of violence. More importantly, however, Venkatesh shows how the church plays the intermediary role of renegotiating the informal rules of the neighborhood when relations break down with a local gang. This work opens the door for further exploration regarding the relationship between competing forms of social order.

Building on this tradition, I introduce the signature concept of this book: alternative governance. This concept starts with the assumption, like Venkatesh's, that there are multiple dimensions of social order in urban poor areas. There are three differences that distinguish this from other works, however. First, this work focuses on the role of interracial relationships in shaping alternative governance. While Venkatesh's work accurately captures how social order is regulated via violence and gangs, he does not explore what this process looks like in more contemporary ghettos, such as South Los Angeles, where urban dwellers are both black and Latino. This is a significant point, since the Latinoization of America's urban areas has greatly accelerated (Small, 2007). As Small argues, we must view modern urban ghettos as heterogeneous rather than homogenous in their makeup.

Second, the institutions outlined in Venkatesh's work are able to structure the lives of urban poor residents via rules and their enforcement through gangs and the church. However, what is the basis of these institutions? Alternative governance answers this question by illustrating the importance of social ties, trust, and a form of reciprocity of giving and taking.

In Venkatesh's observation, church pastors are revered, respected, and provide leadership to urban poor residents. However, why should residents defer to and turn to them for guidance in the first place? Research by Winship and Berrien (1999) provides a clue into the process by which legitimacy operates. They refer to an "umbrella of legitimacy" that pastors acquire through their relationship with residents. In the course of building relationships with residents, pastors develop credibility and legitimacy that can be passed on to local police to address crime. For example, pastors can vouch for police officers as being honest and effective, thereby enhancing their reputation and legitimacy. Building on the concept of an umbrella of legitimacy, I show how legitimacy is acquired. In essence, alternative governance must be established before pastors and churches can wield the role of informal social control agent.

Finally, this work illustrates a dimension not explored by others, namely, how immigrants who reside in urban poor, multiracial communities respond to violence. The concept of alternative governance provides a key insight into this process. Many scholars, such as Robert Sampson (2008) have noted the link between falling crime rates and the increasing presence of Latinos, especially recent immigrants, in inner-city spaces. Yet no work has laid out the processes by which such peace unfolds. Indeed, what has been referred to as the "Latino Paradox," the "protective effect," or "immigrant revitalization" is largely a black box, consisting of many indicators of positive change (Martinez and Valenzuela, 2006) without providing insight into the lived processes by which such protection and revitalization are forged. The concept of "managed violence" compellingly provides insight into such processes, filling a gap in our understanding of urban space, poverty, and violence, and providing the groundwork for a new generation of studies. I suggest that understanding the concept of alternative governance is central to understanding the concept of the protective effect.

To be clear, this book is about the way in which core institutions respond to violence. This work makes a distinct conceptual move by highlighting the processes and strategies used by institutions to respond to violence. Although the institutions examined in this study may not deliberately regulate violence, they nevertheless cope and manage violence. This is a subtle but important difference from the conceptual approach of informal social control, which is too rigid to capture the nuanced response of urban residents to violence, and, instead, focuses on deliberate attempts to regulate human behavior. Thus, alternative governance captures a wider set of practices that includes informal social control types of operation, which regulates behavior, and also daily institutional strategies utilized by residents. Following in the footsteps of Elias (1978) I argue that social organization of violence is at the core of society. In urban poor areas, the varieties of social order are rooted in the notion of alternative governance.

The Book in Context

Two dominant paradigms have shaped the way in which sociologists have examined the causes of violence and disorder in urban poor areas. I refer to these frameworks as the social disorganization and social organization perspectives. The social disorganization perspective assumes that there is a *decline in community* as a result of ecological changes, such as population change, heterogeneity, etc. In contrast, the social organization perspective focuses on the persistence of communities despite ecological changes. The findings from this work make an important contribution to these debates and provide insight into the implications for understanding how residents respond to violence.

Classical social disorganization theorists argue that external factors, such as poverty, ethnic heterogeneity, and population mobility undermine community life, causing neighborhood institutions, such as the family, to break down, leading to disorder, crime, and violence. More contemporary disorganization theorists have argued that deindustrialization, segregation, and the outmigration of the black middle class has led to the further impoverishment of urban blacks, leading to the emergence of the underclass (Wilson, 1987). Thus, the rule of law is undermined in communities that suffer from social disorganization.

One major shortcoming of this perspective is that it assumes that urban poor communities suffer from social pathologies such as high crime, poor health, and low educational attainments. Furthermore, social disorganization is believed to be the root cause of the social pathologies. Wacquant (1997) compellingly notes that the assumption that the urban poor are socially disorganized truncates and distorts our understanding of the urban metropolis. Analyzing the urban poor in terms of deficiencies obscures and overlooks what is central: identifying the principles that underlie its internal order.

In contrast, social organization scholars focus on the institutional form of the ghetto, rather than viewing it as an accumulation of social pathology. There is a long tradition of this perspective dating back to the pioneering work of William Foote Whyte (1943). The perspective was reinvigorated with the work of many scholars (Suttles, 1968) who celebrated the social order and organization of urban poor communities in the 1960s.

Beginning in the 1980s and 1990s, sociologists embarked on several studies that demonstrated the ways in which urban settings are socially organized. Social organization theorists have pursued research in a variety of areas, most prominently focusing on street and religious life.

Continuing in this tradition, Anderson (1999) argues that in economically depressed and high-drug-crime areas of the city, the rules of civil law have been severely weakened and in their place a "code of the street has taken sway." The code consists of a set of prescriptions or informal rules of behavior organized around a desperate search for respect, which governs public social relations, especially violence. These regulate the use of violence and so supply a rationale allowing those who are too aggressive to precipitate violent encounters in an approved way. The rules have been established and are enforced by the street oriented. Knowledge of the code is largely defensive and it is necessary for operating in the public sphere. The terms "decent" and "street" are used to define the status of individuals who live in the ghetto (Anderson, 1999). Street-oriented individuals are those who make up the criminal element and pride themselves on defying the law. In contrast, decent families tend to encourage and respect authority and walk a straight moral line. This strain of thought within the social organization literature focuses on the role of social organization and street life.

While these studies are useful, they offer only a limited perspective by focusing on how social organization shapes the relationship between street life and urban areas. Recent work by Sanchez-Jankowski (2008) has compellingly illustrated how social order is not strictly shaped by the street, but rather by a larger set of community institutions. Sanchez-Jankowski found that barbershops, stores, gangs, and schools create stability and social order. His work is one of the few contemporary studies that examines the role of multiple institutions in creating social order.

Sanchez-Jankowski's work makes an important contribution to the field, but he did not look specifically at the relationship between the church and the street as competing forms of social order; nor did he examine their roles in the regulation of violence. To my knowledge, Venkatesh's *Off the Books* (2006) is the only contemporary ethnography that sheds light on the relationship between the church, the street, and the state. Many urban scholars argue that the church and the street are two of the most important institutions in urban poor areas, yet few studies have examined the relationship between the two. Venkatesh's work documents the role of the street and religion in shaping economic and social relationships in urban poor areas, largely outside the web of economic, political, legal, and law-enforcement structures that dominate mainstream American life. These informal economic relationships encourage extra-legal mechanisms to mediate disputes, thus minimizing the role of the state in effectively controlling the streets.

My study, which revisits the relationship between the church and the street, uses South Los Angeles, rather than Chicago, as the social laboratory for several key reasons. First, South Los Angeles is arguably the largest ghetto west of the Mississippi. Previous studies of the ghetto have focused mostly on Chicago (Venkatesh, 2009). However, sociologists, as noted by Mario Small (2007), should exercise caution in generalizing from the Chicago case to other large urban poor areas.

Following Small's line of thinking, I believe it is important to examine cases that work against this reductive and generalizing tendency. Through the examination of different types of cases, social scientists are able to create new ways of thinking. As Claire Colebrook (2002) notes, concepts should not be amenable to dictionary-style definitions, rather they should be expansive to illuminate the connections that scholars use them to make.

In many ways, South Los Angeles reflects the modern, emerging American urban ghetto, where the increasing presence of the Latino population can no longer be ignored. Thus, this study focuses on a dimension of community life not addressed by the classic and contemporary urban social-organization scholars: how African American and Latino residents respond to precarious situations where both are at constant risk of violence.

This study builds on the work of Venkatesh by outlining the competing, alternative social worlds in which extra-legal mechanisms are embedded. Extra-legal mechanisms are often culturally bound. How do these mechanisms operate in diverse settings? While Venkatesh outlines the process by which the mechanisms operate, he does not provide a framework for examining how extra-legal mechanisms are shaped by interracial relations.

Critics may respond that the issue of interracial relations in urban poor areas has already adequately been addressed. For example, Sally

Engle Merry (1981) has focused on how conceptions of dangerousness are functions of cultural group membership. Merry argues that the lack of social ties between cultural groups enhances crime, as the residents of a community where such ties are absent are less likely to identify criminals and work together to solve crime.

An analytical approach based on the managed violence paradigm goes deeper into the social mechanisms that mediate relations of urban poor residents by sketching a portrait of the alternative social worlds that are utilized as a response to danger and violence. While residents of South LA may be distrustful and suspicious of one another, they do not simply remain anonymous, as Merry points out, but rather they carve out distinct social spaces where they are free to interact without the fear of violence, spaces where they can form intimate social ties with one another. These spaces also contain the potential for the formation of cross-cultural social ties, which are central for managing crime, a theme not thoroughly developed by Merry.

While Merry's work is important, it was conducted in the 1980s, and, therefore, does not reflect the urban changes that have occurred as Latino immigration accelerated in the 1990s. What is needed is a more recent empirical ethnography that informs scholars about the changes in one of America's largest ghettos.

To date, this book is the only intensive, participant-observation study of South LA. Given that it is the first such study of the community, it provides an important understanding of how crime is managed among the urban poor in Los Angeles, and in other cities that are also undergoing an African American to Latino demographic transformation, such as New York and Chicago.

Book Overview

What follows is a portrait of the different dimensions of community in South LA, a portrait that explains how some of the community's key institutions structure how residents respond to violence. I argue that alternative governance has emerged to fill a vacuum, as the state lacks legitimacy and is disconnected from the daily needs of poor black and Latino residents. The key to understanding how residents respond to violence is grounded in the concept of alternative governance.

Governance can be defined as the process by which decisions are made by the authority that underlies it. Implicitly, relationships between groups play an important role in the governing process. Therefore, this book focuses on the role of interracial relationships, relationships that shape the process of alternative governance. Second, I show that alternative governance builds on the concept of patrimonial rule by demonstrating that multiple forms of alternative governance operate simultaneously, and, at times, are in competition to establish order as a response to violence.

In chapter 2, I demonstrate the limited ability of formal legal community institutions in managing violence. I collected data for one year by volunteering and attending City of Los Angeles Neighborhood Council meetings in South LA. In order to gauge the efficacy of formal legal community institutions in combating violence and conflict, the City of Los Angeles Neighborhood Councils were selected as a field site. The second chapter first highlights the institutional strategies used by the Neighborhood Councils. Next, it demonstrates the factors identified for the Councils' inability to manage violence and conflict. These include: (1) low levels of participation, (2) poor outreach, (3) the inability of the City of Los Angeles to mitigate interracial differences, (4) a lack of legitimacy among residents, and (5) the inability of formal legal systems to incorporate noncitizens. Due to these factors, residents did not approach formal political institutions to address community problems, and, instead, resorted to other options.

Chapter 3 introduces the reader to the alternative social spaces that have taken on a new centrality in urban poor areas such as South LA, given the limitations of the state. Furthermore, the church's role as an informal source of social control has become more salient with the influx of Catholic Latino immigrants, many of whom are noncitizens. They, therefore, resort to nongovernmental institutions for refuge and protection—primarily as a result of fear of the state. The findings for this chapter are situated in a well-established body of literature, which establishes that members of religious groups, Catholics, in particular, generate a parallel set of institutions to protect immigrants from hostile forces.[2] Chapter 3 suggests that the Catholic Church continues to maintain this long-standing tradition of protecting immigrants from hostile forces in the United States.

I argue that, instead of protecting immigrants from hostile Protestants as it did in the mid-19th century, the Catholic Church now protects immigrants from the ever-present state and the street gangs. Its social role has been transformed and expanded so that it now acts as a neutral safety zone for both African Americans and Latinos. Furthermore, the Church has been transformed so that it is able to reduce conflict along interracial lines. By managing these risks and conflicts, the Catholic Church shapes the social organization of poor modern urban neighborhoods.

In chapter 4, I demonstrate how the Church acts as an informal social control that manages violence in two key ways. The chapter fleshes out the various strategies used to manage violence. First, the Church proffers its own version of street wisdom that challenges the code of the street. Second, its institutional strategies help parishioners and community members at large deal with violence so that it is manageable for residents. One of the Church's key contributions is in showing how street wisdom is anchored in institutions. The second half of the chapter highlights the ways in which interracial conflict is minimized through deliberate strategies rooted in a narrative of Catholicism.

In chapter 5, I discuss interracial relations between Latino and African American street gangs in South LA. To understand these relations, I conducted the following fieldwork. First, I volunteered and worked in two separate charter schools for high-risk youths who had strong gang ties and histories. Second, I interviewed youths from two of the largest housing projects in South LA. I examined the factors that lead to conflict, cooperation, and avoidance. I argue that informal street norms play a central role in mitigating violence between both groups. Interracial relations are predicated on four key factors: (1) territorial affiliation, (2) control of the illicit underground economy and the neighborhood, (3) gang affiliation, and (4) race. Often it is the presence of a combination of these factors that leads to interracial cooperation, avoidance, or conflict. The dominant outcome, however, is avoidance—the primary way in which interracial conflict is minimized.

In chapter 6, I suggest that a set of informal public norms, rooted in the illicit economy, act as a shared framework for mediating conflict and violence for both gang and non-gang residents in South LA. I term this informal set of public norms "street justice." The negotiation process in the illicit economy between gang and non-gang members is what unites the community under the shared informal public norms—namely, street justice.

The book concludes with a consideration of violence and interracial conflict in multiracial urban poor areas. Researchers who do not consider the new multiracial makeup of urban poor areas and the contemporary forms of informal social control that have arisen with these changes run the risk of advocating inadequate policies. Framing urban violence within a black-and-white paradigm is no longer adequate for understanding how to address urban violence in diverse settings where Latinos and African Americans now share the same neighborhoods.

1

Neighborhood Councils

City Hall Competes with the Street for Legitimacy

Los Angeles recorded 508 murders in 2003 and 516 in 2004—a total of 1,024 murders. According to data collected by the Los Angeles Police Department, each year nearly half of these murders were committed in South Los Angeles (see Table 1.1).

TABLE 1.1. Homicides by Police Division in South Central Los Angeles

	Area (square mi)	2003 Homicides	% of 2003 Homicides	2004 Homicides	% of 2004 Homicides	2003 & 2004 Total Homicides
Los Angeles	503	508		516		1024
South Central	42.7	238	46.85	265	51.36	503
Newton	9.8	46	9.06	45	8.72	91
77th Street	11.3	64	12.60	88	17.05	152
Southeast	9.3	77	15.16	71	13.76	148
Southwest	12.3	51	10.04	61	11.82	112

Source: LAPD

Many of the residents exposed to violence are African Americans and Latinos who live in high-poverty neighborhoods. (Maps 1.1–1.3 reflect the poverty rates and racial makeup of the neighborhoods.)

How do poor residents of South Los Angeles respond to such high levels of violent crime? This chapter answers this question by examining how local political institutions respond to violence. I conducted ethnographic fieldwork in eight separate City of Los Angeles Neighborhood Councils located in South Los Angeles. The Neighborhood Councils were located within the boundaries of four Los Angeles police divisions—Southeast, Southwest, Newton, and 77th Street (known as "the 77th").

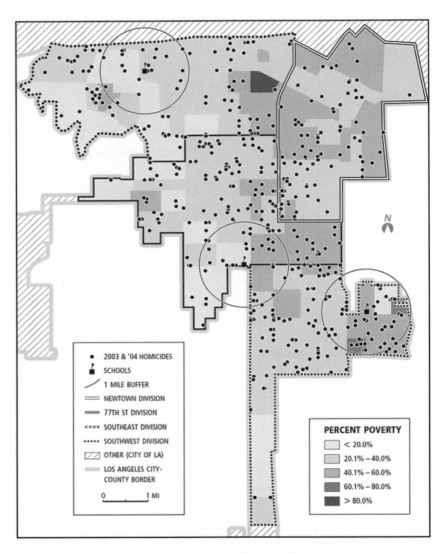

Map 1.1. Percentage of Population in Poverty and Homicides

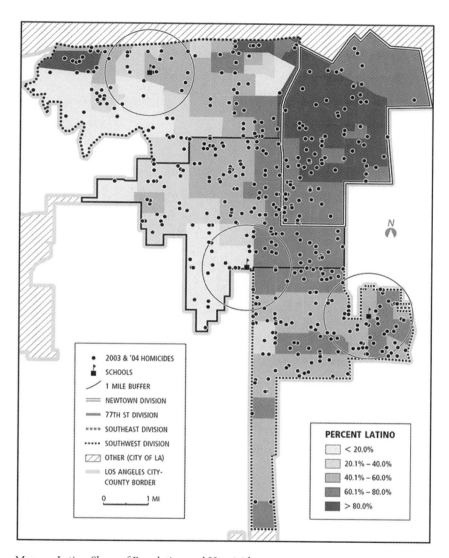

Map 1.2. Latino Share of Population and Homicides

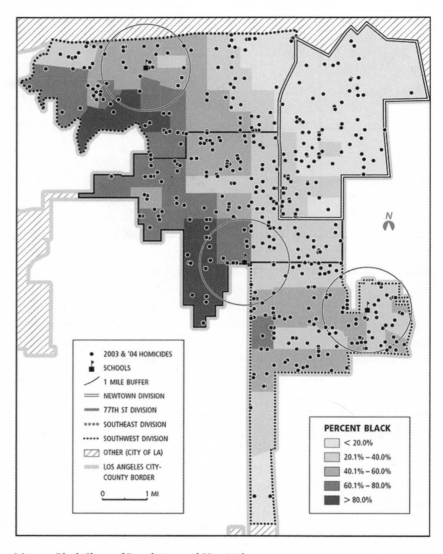

Map 1.3. Black Share of Population and Homicides

A brief history of Los Angeles municipal government is nee place the literature within context. Unlike other major cities in America, the unique form of municipal government in Los Angeles emerged as a result of the reform movement in the 1920s. Fearful that Los Angeles would end up like the "machine-style" political systems of local government in New York and Chicago—which were viewed as corrupt and dominated by ethnic European immigrants—members of the reform movement sought to put an end to this style of local politics.

Beginning in the 1920s, Los Angeles established a style of local government that was designed to maximize participation of the white, middle-class Protestants who migrated to Los Angeles from the midwestern and eastern United States. At the same time, this form of government was meant to minimize the participation and influence of European immigrants, Mexican Americans, African Americans, and other marginal groups who threatened the reform vision of morality. The reform type of local governance became the institutional basis for the City of Los Angeles until the mid-1990s, when the city charter was reformed. Thus, local government in the southwestern United States was run like a business, free of partisan favors, and was never designed for broad inclusion of residents of diverse backgrounds.

What are the consequences of reform types of governance on the modern metropolis of Los Angeles, and how does the governing structure of Los Angeles help us to understand how political institutions respond to violence? To answer this question, it is important to note the impact reform types of government have had on the poor since their inception in Los Angeles. Bridges (1997) argues that the urban poor were better served in the machine forms of government as opposed to the reform types of governing structures. Because machine forms of governance were better connected to residents, they were able to provide direct benefits and were better able to teach them how the political process operates, and, thus, have their voices heard. Therefore, one major and significant effect of reform government was that the ties that connected the local government and the poor communities of Los Angeles became weak and poorly developed.

The organizational structure of reform governance is significant because it shaped the relationship, over time, between Los Angeles municipal government and poor communities such as South LA. Examining the historical relationship between local government and poor communities is a crucial analytical move required to understand how local political governance affects poor communities (Abu-Lughod, 2007). The historical relationship, rather than a period in time, is the key to understanding how local government is likely to respond to crime and rioting. Sociologist Abu-Lughod developed an analytical concept for examining the historical relationship between local government and urban poor communities, which she termed "political culture."

Abu-Lughod argues that much of the urban unrest in cities such as Los Angeles can be attributed to race relations, segregation, and the role of local government and its relationship to poor communalities of color. The key factor, however, is political culture, since it emphasizes the role of local government. Abu-Lughod finds that many of the major uprisings and riots in Los Angeles were affected by the historical legacy of poor ties between City Hall and the poor residents of LA, who reside mainly in South LA and East LA. Beginning with the Zoot Suit Riots of 1943, many Mexican Americans had little political representation to voice their concerns through formal political channels and to address grievances such as housing, job discrimination, and abuse by the police. These frustrations were made manifest in riots between US servicemen and Mexican Americans, including African Americans and Filipinos.

The political culture of Los Angeles also shaped the context for two of the largest riots in America's history. Beginning in World War II, many African Americans were recruited from the South to Los Angeles for industrial work. They were economically integrated through employment, but not politically integrated. Many of these African Americans, through a variety of means, were segregated into the southern part of Los Angeles to form the largest ghetto west of the Mississippi, in what became known as South Central Los Angeles. Poor relationships between the Los Angeles Police Department and residents of South LA became the norm. The inability of City Hall to address these grievances set the stage for the 1965 Watts Riots.

The 1992 riots were precipitated by many of the same factors as the riots of 1965 (Abu-Lughod, 2007). Although a black mayor, Tom Bradley, had been first elected in 1973 and was still in office, many of the problems of the 1960s had never been addressed—for example, abuses by the police and housing discrimination. Instead, many of the problems were amplified: unemployment, which was spurred by white flight after the 1965 riots, and deindustrialization, as a result of the global economy. The inability of City Hall to address these issues set the stage for the largest riot in the United States since the 1960s.

The disconnect between city government and residents of Los Angeles came to a head following the 1992 riots, when many Angelenos began to consider splitting the city into two parts, in what became known as the secession movement. Like the previous periods of unrest outlined thus far, the major motivating factor for splitting the city was that it was out of touch with the needs of residents. Residents from the Valley and Westside complained that City Hall did not address the unique needs of their segments of the city. So, the idea that City Hall was out of touch and disconnected was not exclusive to the poor, but was viewed by Angelenos from different parts of the city and from different backgrounds as a major problem.

Fortunately, the city was spared from division by a charter reform measure that would help to make government more responsive to the needs of Angelenos. There were several key features in the newly formed city charter, but the one element that would bring government down to the communities was the creation of what would be known as the Neighborhood Councils. Essentially, the new charter created a three-tiered government: mayor, City Council, and Neighborhood Councils. The Neighborhood Councils were, in theory, supposed to represent the needs of a small number of neighborhoods and a considerably smaller number of residents. Thus, the new charter created a mandate for a new type of local governance that was decentralized institutionally.

My analysis picks up where Neighborhood Councils entered the picture. The questions that many scholars now must consider are: How much more effective is a decentralized form of government in addressing issues such as violence? Is it able to overcome the weak ties and disconnect that characterized the previous relationships in the reform style of government?

A burgeoning literature is emerging that attempts to examine the effectiveness of decentralized government in addressing issues such as crime and violence. Berry, Portney, and Thomson (1993) argue that decentralized forms of government, which include the Neighborhood

Councils, can effectively enhance democracy at the neighborhood level to address the issues of crime and violence. Archon Fung (2004) advances this body of work by highlighting the importance of "deliberative practices" in decentralized government settings. For Fung, decentralized governments are not sufficient to make local government responsive to community needs. Instead, institutionalized, deliberative practices are needed to overcome the challenges that decentralized governments face, for example, heterogeneity, poverty, and interracial differences.

Important conclusions can be drawn about the effectiveness of LA's municipal government if one considers the implications of the research conducted by Berry et al. and Fung. Although the governing structure of Los Angeles has transitioned into a more decentralized form of governance, the preconditions necessary for a more effective government, which would make City Hall more responsive, are lacking in two serious ways. First, LA's Neighborhood Councils have only advisory power in zoning decisions that may affect residents. According to Barry et al. however, for decentralized forms of government to be effective they must have autonomous power to make decisions regarding issues that impact the community. A second issue that undermines the ability of LA's newly formed decentralized government, according to Fung's framework, is the absence of "deliberative practices" that keep decentralized domains of government, such as Neighborhood Councils, from slipping into conflict, disorderliness, and dominance by local elites. Fung argues that without institutionalized, deliberative practices, decentralized governments run the risk of slipping into what he calls a free-for-all form of laissez-faire. Finally, Fung argues that for municipal government to be effective it must be bottom up, where citizens play an active role directing services. However, in LA's newly revised, decentralized municipal government, many policy decisions continue to be top down.

Building on these insights, I argue that although the newly formed, decentralized municipal government of Los Angeles is making progress toward connecting citizens, the legacy of the Reform Era continues to shape the relationships between poor communities, in particular South Los Angeles and City Hall. I illustrate how many of the same problems that emerged from those weak relationships, for example, the criminalization of African Americans and Latinos and the inability to provide adequate services to address issues such as violence, continue to plague residents in South LA.

What the research on urban politics has demonstrated is that reform government tends to have weaker ties to residents, making it difficult for local government to respond to local issues such as crime. The contemporary literature on urban politics, however, is more optimistic about the possibility of overcoming the weaknesses in traditional forms of government through decentralized municipal governance.

However, this work adds another dimension to the literature that has not yet been addressed. I demonstrate the new challenges that LA's decentralized forms of governance face by examining the Neighborhood Councils. I suggest that LA city government must now compete with alternative forms of governance that have arisen because of the vacuum created by a lack of services. More specifically, the Los Angeles case shows how the authority of local government is challenged by alternative forms of governance, which emerged in the absence of good relationships between City Hall and South Los Angeles. I focus on two elements of this alternative governance. First, I show how City Hall must compete with the street for legitimacy. Second, I demonstrate that an important dimension of alternative governance in South LA is the emergence of a divided community, where interracial relations act as a division between what are actually two communities that coexist in the same social space. The result of this competing form of governance weakens the ability of government to effectively address issues of violence at the local level.

The ghost of Reform Era practices and the emergence of alternative governance, rooted in the criminal underground, present new challenges that undermine the legitimacy of City Hall and thus its effectiveness in addressing violence in South LA.

The Ghost of the Reform Era: The Criminalization of and Governmental Disconnect from the Urban Poor

In this section, I outline two main strategies used by participants in the Neighborhood Councils to manage violence: (1) directing services and (2) holding local law enforcement accountable for their policies. Focusing on the strategies utilized by community residents is significant for two reasons. First, these strategies illustrate the agency of actors and the role that the Neighborhood Councils have in responding to violence. Second, and, more importantly, they show the structural limitations of municipal government in addressing violence through formal, political, institutional means.

This chapter illustrates how these strategies were undermined by poor relations and weak social ties between City Hall and residents of South LA. Furthermore, it illustrates how residents continue to feel criminalized through the suppression tactics of law enforcement. However, the newly formed Neighborhood Councils add a layer of government to connect citizens in a manner that did not exist in the past. I suggest that although City Hall is making progress in connecting residents, serious obstacles rooted as far back as the Reform Era persist.

Directing City Services to Combat Violence

A primary strategy utilized by members of the Neighborhood Councils was to direct city services to areas that residents perceived to have high crime and violence. Neighborhood Councils brought together community residents from various backgrounds; however, the Neighborhood Councils mostly consisted of African American homeowners, nonprofits, church leaders, and a handful of Latino business owners. Homeowners who were not affiliated with churches, nonprofits, or block associations would often engage in their own strategies to manage violence, which were centered on mobilizing city services.

Neighborhood Councils provided a forum where ordinary citizens could have an open dialogue with law enforcement and city service agency representatives regarding crime and violence in their respective neighborhoods. At almost every Neighborhood Council meeting, a representative of the LAPD or the LA County Sheriff's Department was present. They often stood in the background, at times gave presentations to the Councils, and, at other times, they would meet residents in private somewhere inside the meeting space or directly outside to discuss their individual concerns. In addition, representatives from various city agencies gave presentations or updates regarding their activity in the area.

The individual comments from residents, during the general comments or the public safety portions of the meetings, usually gave rise to a larger discussion of how to respond to crime and violence in the area.

The following represents a typical interchange by residents and officials at the Neighborhood Councils in addressing an incidence of violence in the community.

> On a weekday evening, at around 7:00 p.m., 20 residents attend a Neighborhood Council meeting located in the central part of South LA. The people in attendance are almost all African American and range in age from 50 to 60 years old. An even distribution of males and females attend the meeting.
>
> Joe Ramirez, head of the City of Los Angeles gang prevention unit, LA PATH,[1] addresses the Neighborhood Council regarding recent shootings in the area. He states that, whenever there is a shooting in the area, his agency intervenes by providing case management services. He discusses the two organizations that the city contracts with to provide gang intervention services: No Weapons and Solidarity.
>
> Jason Jones, the president of the Neighborhood Council, listens closely to the comments from Ramirez and to the chatter of residents who grumble and listen with suspicion. Residents can be heard reiterating the idea that programs like these do nothing.
>
> Jones: "What is No Weapons doing about the shootings? I haven't heard anything. I live in this area and I know the parents and kids who were involved in the shooting and they tell me that nothing is going on. Can you explain to me what LA PATH is doing?"
>
> The crowd sighs and comments as if in support of what Jones has said. The room becomes filled with energy and people are attuned to the discussion.
>
> Ramirez: "The contractors are supposed to provide case management services and intervene. There is supposed to be a two mile radius drawn around the area of the shooting. This is where the intervention is supposed to occur."
>
> A Council member gets angry and states, "There is no visible sign of LA PATH in the neighborhood. What about outside the two mile area? Can we provide services outside the area? If the program is not working, what can we do? What is the success rate of LA PATH? Because, if it's not working, then the money can be spent on a program that is worthwhile."
>
> Many of the other Council members also seem skeptical about the effectiveness of LA PATH for deterring gang activity and violence. An African

American Council member in her 50s states that the gang programs don't provide decent jobs that allow people to support their families. She states, "Jobs given to gangs need to be higher paying, quality jobs, because gang members will go right back to doing what they did before."

Another Council member states that LA PATH needs to do more outreach to the local recreation center where there are high-risk youth.

Mr. Ramirez fields question after question regarding the inadequacies of the program. Even when residents are not recognized to speak, they talk out of turn or with other individuals sitting next to them, expressing their frustration with the program.

These observations illustrate how residents used the Neighborhood Councils as forums to direct city services. First, Council members raised several questions about the effectiveness of the city's gang intervention program, LA PATH. In many Neighborhood Council meetings in South LA, residents asked tough questions and demanded answers. Having volunteered with the Department of Neighborhood Empowerment (DONE), I became well acquainted with its staff, who would often tell me in private that many of the Neighborhood Councils in South LA were such difficult environments that, in fact, city officials often dreaded visiting them, because the officials knew they would be thoroughly grilled and, in some instances, publicly scolded by neighborhood residents. The public condemnation made city officials take notice of the residents' demands, and often prompted them to action.

Participants in the Neighborhood Councils did have some success in directing services, as a result of these types of interactions. LA PATH eventually did do follow-up work, long after the shootings. The agency finally followed up with its contractors, who eventually did provide case management services in the area. Unfortunately, however, by the time LA PATH acted, another shooting had occurred in another area, and its contractors were not able to keep up with the demands of the violence.

Second, while participants in the Neighborhood Councils tried to sway city officials to respond to violence, many residents did not believe that city programs such as LA PATH could effectively address the volume of violence. As the observations reflect, many residents wanted the LA PATH program scrapped and replaced altogether. Given the limited funds in the city budget dedicated to respond to violence and gangs, it seemed that any intervention program would face an uphill battle in directing services to violence in the area. There were thus strong structural limitations that undermined the civic engagement of residents.

A major obstacle that undermined an effective response to the violence was the disconnect between city services and the needs of community members. The field observations highlighted earlier illustrate how residents felt that the city was out of touch in its response to the high volume of violence. Furthermore, the observations demonstrate how Neighborhood Council members were not directly part of the planning process in responding to violence. Instead, they were passive participants who were not given any meaningful power in coordinating efforts with the city's gang task force, other than grilling officials about their ineffectiveness.

I suggest that the limited role of the Neighborhood Councils is shaped by the decentralized LA city municipal government. In fact, Neighborhood Councils have no real authority other than their advisory role in land use. Their roles and authority are clearly stated in the city charter, which spells out the limits of their power.

So, although Neighborhood Councils provide a forum that brings many elements of the community together, there is no real partnership between the city and community members. City officials visited these settings for informational and educational purposes, occasionally exchanging information that did assist in directing services, but only in a minimal manner.

The limited power of Neighborhood Councils shaped their relationships with City Hall, which undermined the formation of meaningful social ties, which imply equality, reciprocity, and exchange. However, without any real power, Neighborhood Councils were not viewed as equal partners. Therefore, they were unable to hold city programs accountable for the ineffective response to violence.

Directing City Services and Poor Relations

The strategy of directing services, as a way of managing violence, also involved engaging and communicating with high-level city officials. Members of the Neighborhood Councils attempted to address neighborhood violence by bypassing midlevel city officials and going straight to the top. This approach to addressing violence entailed residents of the Neighborhood Councils connecting with city department heads. However, the weak social ties between City Hall and Neighborhood Councils, outlined in the previous section, made it difficult to overcome poor relationships.

Having observed Neighborhood Councils in South LA, I found this approach to be common throughout the area. The following is a description of a Neighborhood Council Ad Hoc Public Safety Committee meeting where this strategy was employed.

> *Several city department heads sit at the front of the room where the Council members sit. The meeting takes place on a weekday evening at 7:00 p.m. I notice that Captain Avila from the LAPD Southeast Division is present, along with the LA City Attorney, Rocky Delgadillo. Several of their assistants are also present, wearing suits and ties. In addition, representatives from the Housing Authority are present, and they sit at the table with the city department heads.*
>
> *After the meeting begins, resident after resident walks up to a microphone stationed in front of the room, near where the department heads and Council members sit. They take notes as the residents angrily state their concerns.*
>
> *An African American wastes no time, and states in a loud and serious tone, "What's going to be done about the rivalry between the two high schools [referring to an ongoing violent feud]? It's only going to get worse! There is also a lot of drug activity in the area!"*
>
> *Jackie Sims [a board member] then takes a turn speaking, "Over 50 people have been accosted and robbed in the Regal Courts housing projects. The only way we are going to solve this problem is by the police and the community feeling comfortable with each another" [referring to poor police relations with residents].*
>
> *Reggie Anthony, a community resident, intervenes and states that it is difficult to build ties with police officers because they are transferred and rotated out of the area frequently.*
>
> *Then, a Latino male in his late 30s walks to the front of the room and states that violence is getting out of control at a local high school, "My son and I witnessed a boy get beat up and robbed for his shoes and shirt on the way to school. It was sad to watch him walk to school like that."*

Next, an African American male in his late 30s says the community is anticipating more violence, "During the summer it gets hot and the only outlet in this area is the pool at the park. Gangs hang around and wait for the kids to get out, and follow them to the shopping center. They take their money or rob them in the stores."

Then, an African American homeowner in his 50s asks demandingly, "What's going to be done for homeowners? We are hearing about people in the projects, but what about us?"

Finally, a representative from Association of Community Organizers for Reform Now (ACORN) states that the gang prevention program, LA PATH, isn't doing anything. He continues, "We are losing kids every day out here."

The City Attorney looks overwhelmed, but confidently states, "I came here to start a dialogue with residents of Pacific Village and with this Neighborhood Council."

An elderly African American Council member interjects, "For the last three years my block club has been trying to get help. LAPD hasn't listened to our needs!"

The City Attorney responds, "Have you contacted our neighborhood prosecutor?" He then mentions the person in charge of the LA PATH program in the Pacific Village area.

These field observations are significant because they illustrate the perception among residents that there was a high level of violence throughout the area. More importantly, though, they show community members of the Neighborhood Councils making an attempt to connect with high-level city officials, for example, the LA city attorney. These types of meetings usually took place because community members requested the presence of top city officials, with the goal of establishing a dialogue and, ultimately, to direct services.

Many residents viewed the City Attorney's Office and the LAPD as not being responsive to their needs, further heightening suspicion and distrust of City Hall, and, ultimately, undermining relations. Indeed, the comments from the Council members and residents reflect the idea that relations between city officials and residents were poor. However, it is significant to note that residents and city officials both desired improved relations, since they were needed for addressing the violence in the area.

Members of the Neighborhood Councils pointed to the constant rotation and turnover of LAPD personnel in the area, which made it difficult to establish ties between residents and the police. Several residents revealed to me that it's very difficult to know whom to contact and whom they could trust to deal with neighborhood violence issues. However, the rotation of police out of the area was only one of many factors that undermined police relationships in South LA.

Distrust and poor relationships with the police are nothing new in South LA. There is a long history of poor police relations going back to the Watts Riots and, more recently, to the civil unrest in 1992. In many ways, the frustration, distrust, and poor relations reaffirm, to residents and law enforcement alike, the ongoing relationship that was framed earlier in LA history.

Poor relationships made it difficult for participants of Neighborhood Councils to direct services that could successfully address violence. It is important to emphasize that poor relationships are not reducible to the police, or, for that fact, the hostility of residents. Instead, the central focus of these poor relations must be the structure of LA's municipal government, which limited the ability of residents to form meaningful social ties, reaffirming poor relationships between residents and the city going back to the Reform Era.

Limited Participation

Participants in Neighborhood Councils also attempted to direct services in a more subtle manner, in which they exchanged information with midlevel law enforcement officials, for example, senior lead officers from the LAPD or the LA County Sheriff's Department. Midlevel officers such as the head beat officers were responsible for specific neighborhoods in South LA. During my fieldwork, I observed that Neighborhood Councils mostly interfaced with lead beat officers in their efforts to address violence. This approach was more targeted, and focused on hot spots where there was a spike in crime.

The following observations from an Ad Hoc Public Safety Committee meeting of the Pacific Village Neighborhood Council, following a rash of robberies that turned into murders near the Metro (subway) line, illustrate how Neighborhood Councils attempted to direct services.

> *The meeting takes place at 7:30 p.m. in a small, rundown neighborhood church behind a large public housing project. The parking lot is mostly dirt, and the complex is surrounded by small, bungalow homes with tall, chain-link fences. One house has two large pit bull dogs roaming the yard. They bark loudly at me and try to climb the fence in an intimidating way. On the other side of the church, there is another chain-link fence holding two large Rottweilers, who also bark loudly and jump up onto the fence when they see me. When I enter the church, it is dark inside and the walls are in need of paint. I am escorted to a room in the back where there are five community residents, many of whom I recognize from the Neighborhood Council. Also in the room are two tall, white, uniformed sheriffs [more precisely, sheriff's deputies], who serve themselves plates of food, which members of the Council have brought for dinner.*
>
> *As Sheriff Reaves states, "We are going to work with the residents of Pacific Village."*

The observation from the Ad Hoc Public Safety Committee illustrates the way in which Neighborhood Council members attempted to address violence by connecting with midlevel law enforcement officials. In this case, the LA County Sheriff's Department exchanged information with residents about the specifics of the murders and robberies in the immediate area. In response, residents were able to direct law enforcement to the places where people were more likely to be victimized. They provided information regarding these places, for example, behind signs. Residents also informed the sheriff's deputies about hot spots of crime, places where young people were robbed on trains.

In response, the deputies took measures to address the concerns of residents. They stated they would place resources in the trains where young people were victimized and in places where residents were ambushed. The deputies also agreed to connect the participants with other city agencies so that they could address violence collectively. In many Neighborhood Councils, I witnessed this type of collaboration between city agencies, where officials from various departments would form relationships and work together to address issues related to violence.

Even though violence was spiraling out of control, there was very little participation in the Neighborhood Council's meeting with the deputies. Only a handful of Council members and neighborhood residents attended the meeting, per the general pattern in most Neighborhood Councils in South LA. Three homicides had occurred off the Metro line within a short period, prompting the meeting. All of the victims were Latino immigrants and were robbed for their paychecks as they returned home from work, according to the deputy's report. This type of violence should have prompted more community involvement, but it did not.

Why did so few people participate in Neighborhood Council meetings despite the murders on the Metro line? I suggest that the structural forces of the municipal government's limited community involvement undermined the ability of the Neighborhood Councils to respond to violence. More specifically, poor relationships and weak social ties undermined faith in city institutions and, therefore, limited community participation through formal political channels. The observations from the meeting reflect the idea that many residents viewed law enforcement as untrustworthy. There are numerous reasons as to why this distrust prevails, which I address later. However, the field notes capture the perception that law enforcement cannot be trusted because residents believed that the police would leak information to criminal elements in the community, who might retaliate, or they believed that nothing would happen if young people called the police when they were victimized. For many residents in South LA, using Neighborhood Councils was not viewed as an effective way to respond to violence.

There were also consequences, which residents had to face, from gangs and others involved in the criminal underworld, if the residents decided to work though political channels such as the Neighborhood Councils. As the deputy noted, gangs increasingly began to claim control of and to regulate activity on the trains. The comments from residents reflect the fact that young people were intimidated by gang members and could not tell their parents, let alone law enforcement, that they were being victimized and robbed on the trains. Given the limited number of transit patrol officers it was difficult for police to protect the young people who rode the trains from school and the adults who commuted from South LA to downtown. What the police and residents were acknowledging was the existence of another major source of social control rooted in the streets.

Residents had a dilemma: they wanted to use civic participation as a means to combat violence, but they also knew that there was a possibility of being retaliated against for cooperating with law enforcement. Ad Hoc Public Safety Committee meetings of the Neighborhood Councils had to balance getting residents to participate in addressing violence, and, at the same time, minimize the possibility that the information would get out to the broader community, which could lead to retaliation. This is why many of the safety committee meetings took place in discrete locations, such as small churches. This is significant because it illustrates the potential risk of pursuing approaches in dealing with violence that utilize law enforcement and city officials. While residents in these meetings were brave enough to meet with law enforcement and provide information and direct services, most residents did not feel the same way because of their fear of the potential consequences.

Doesn't this mean - ppl frm coming/ participating?

Thus, poor social relationships and weak social ties undermined community participation in Neighborhood Councils to address violence. In addition, residents had to weigh the potential consequences of retaliation for divulging information to law enforcement. In the end, many residents thought it was much safer to avoid working with law enforcement. Given the ubiquity of gangs and the failure of most in the community to participate, it is safe to say there was likely a very minimal effect on violence.

Top-Down Governance

A final approach to directing services entailed having an open dialogue with LAPD lead officers during Neighborhood Council meetings. Often the officers would give presentations to residents regarding the amount of crime in the immediate neighborhood. These presentations gave residents an opportunity to speak directly to the police regarding violence in the area.

These strategies are important to note because they illustrate a characteristic institutional feature of LA's municipal governing structure: top-down policies regarding policing. I suggest that the bureaucratic policies of LAPD and City Hall shaped the strategies residents utilized in responding to violence in Neighborhood Councils.

The field notes from a Neighborhood Council in a high-crime neighborhood illustrate how residents used this forum.

> *Approximately 20 people attend a Neighborhood Council in a rundown church. It is in need of paint, and some of the windows are broken. Across the street, to the side of the main entrance, small groups of youth gather in front of bungalow types of homes playing loud music. Cars race up and down the street blasting hip hop music. Across from the main entrance of the church, 10 or 12 men sit in front of a liquor store, drinking large, 40-ounce bottles of beer.*
>
> *Officer Velez: "One of the major problems in the area is the large number of hotels on Guerra Street that lead to prostitution and drugs. These kinds of places become magnets for gangs. The Southeast Division has the most problems with gangs, but we are not too far behind in the 77th Division."*

Several points should be noted from these field observations. First, Neighborhood Councils provided settings in which residents could gain direct information regarding recent crime trends in their neighborhoods. The LAPD used these forums to educate participants about the dangers of various types of crime in the area.

Residents, however, were also interested in directing services and asking for help regarding problems in their neighborhoods, such as school shootings. When they asked sensitive questions about shootings or youths carrying guns in their neighborhoods, the LAPD representatives tended to respond with vague comments such as "We're looking into it." They were not interested in sharing information in a meaningful way, which could have fostered cooperation with neighborhood residents. This type of approach is exemplified by Officer Velez's comments.

I suggest that the limited cooperation between residents and the LAPD is shaped by the Los Angeles municipal government. The response of LAPD to the concerns and issues of residents illustrates a top-down bureaucratic form of governance.[2] The city's new institutional structure may have been decentralized, however, the police and city officials largely remained insulated from the public. These observations from the Neighborhood Council illustrate that residents were not entrusted to develop their own agendas, nor were they allowed to deliberate with public officials in a meaningful way in response to violence.

It is worth noting that LA's decentralized municipal government did give residents more voice and access to city officials, and that the LAPD gradually began to take on a more community-oriented form of policing under Chief William Bratton during the time of my fieldwork. Without question, a reform type of municipal government would not have been any more inclusive and responsive. However, community policing efforts by city government can be inclusive of the general public, and yet still operate in a bureaucratic-management manner (Fung, 2004). *can they?*

The bureaucratic-management arrangement of LA's City Hall implicitly sent a message to residents regarding expectations for civic participation. The field notes demonstrate that residents were expected to be passive-reactive participants who would listen and follow the directives of law enforcement. Residents understood that they were marginal to the decision-making process.

The marginal position of residents reaffirmed the perception of law enforcement as being unresponsive and ineffective in responding to violence. As a result of their marginal position, community residents were reluctant to cooperate with police in providing information regarding neighborhood crime that could lead to arrests. The comments from LAPD reflect the unwillingness of the residents to cooperate with police. What is not noted in the field notes, but what I often observed at these meetings, was the mood of the Neighborhood Councils when police would ask the community to provide support and information to solve crimes. In almost all cases, the room would fall silent at these times, as if a collective nerve had been hit.

LA's top-down municipal structure implicitly sent another message to residents in South LA: addressing violence in the area was not a high priority. The comments from LAPD suggest that violence in South LA did not receive the same attention as violence in affluent parts of the city such as the Valley. A common belief held by residents was that the death of poor, black, and Latino youths did not carry the same weight as homicides in more affluent areas. Many residents viewed City Hall's bureaucratic response to violence in South LA to be insensitive and dehumanizing, given the high volume of homicides in the area and the differential treatment that they received.

City Hall's primary response to violence was largely bureaucratic and top-down. The consequences of this approach were that fewer city resources, such as gang-intervention workers, were likely to be mobilized, for example, nor was there a sense of urgency by the police to find culprits involved in violent crime. The factors outlined earlier in this chapter, such as poor relationships and poor social ties, are likely to have shaped City Hall's limited perspective and its insensitivity to the crime in South LA.

In essence, City Hall accepted the notion that South LA was a violent place and there wasn't much to be done about it. This view was common among most Angelenos and the conventional wisdom was to stay as far away as possible from South LA—never go south of Interstate 10 downtown. Those living in the area south of the freeway were generally thought to be in gangs or associated with violent criminal behavior, and the bureaucratic policies of City Hall reflected the citywide perception of South LA as violent and dangerous.

Thus, the top-down approach was problematic for two reasons: First, it reified the notion that violence in South LA was inevitable and normal, which limited the city's response to crime. Second, it minimized and marginalized residents' participation in addressing violence, further undermining cooperation from residents.

The ghost of the Reform Era continues to overshadow the relationship between City Hall and South LA. Although government decentralization has helped bring City Hall closer to the community, poor relations between City Hall and South LA persist. In addition, the structure of LA's municipal government minimizes the strategies and choices at residents' disposable to combat violence, and, in many instances, undermines them.

Holding City Officials Accountable: Criminalizing the Poor

Another core approach utilized by the residents of South LA to respond to violence was to hold law enforcement officials accountable for their activities. In many Neighborhood Councils in South LA, Council members and participants gained a reputation for not holding back in their criticism of public officials when they believed the police had operated unfairly.

In this section, I demonstrate how South LA residents used the Neighborhood Councils as a forum to hold public officials accountable. However, the poor relationships outlined in the previous section contributed to heavy-handed law enforcement tactics, which many residents viewed as a form of criminalization. I suggest that the criminalization of South LA's residents undermined the community strategy of holding public officials accountable in Neighborhood Councils. The relationship between the city and residents of South LA reinforced the residents' long-standing negative perception of law enforcement and City Hall.

This issue came to the forefront in the spring of 2004, when the LAPD launched an enormous gang raid in one of the largest public housing developments in Pacific Village. Over 100 people were arrested as the LAPD used paramilitary suppression tactics to remove alleged gang members from the housing unit. The following is a description of a Council meeting that followed this event.

> On a weekday evening in the Watts section of South LA, 50 people attend a Neighborhood Council meeting. The meeting is held in a senior-citizen community center. A dominant majority of elected official participants in the Neighborhood Council are African American. Latinos are almost entirely absent from any involvement in the Neighborhood Council. Many of the members who participate in the meetings are homeowners, representatives of churches and nonprofits, employees of the City and County of Los Angeles, and representatives from the local public housing developments.
>
> The Deputy City Attorney responds, "If the police are getting away with harassment and people are getting into trouble, please call my office." He explains to residents that he will talk to Rocky Delgadillo, the city attorney, to clear their names if they are not gang members.

In response to these initial meetings, Neighborhood Council members were able to have a dialogue about what residents believed to be unfair and brutal practices by the LAPD. As a result of this particular meeting, another forum was held to address police department policies and, specifically, the public housing raid. This allowed residents to get more information and demand accountability for the use of force. Thus, by putting pressure on high-level officials, residents forced the LAPD to explain their actions.

The following field notes highlight the interaction of members of the Pacific Village Neighborhood Council and show their dissatisfaction with law enforcement following the implementation of the gang injunction and the police raid in the housing project.

> *Approximately 50 people attend the meeting. Most people who attend are African American. About five Latinos are present. The bulk of the people who attend are older African American women. A handful of African Americans in their 30s are also present. The Los Angeles City Attorney, Rocky Delgadillo, is present along with his aides. They are all wearing suits and ties. In a peculiar fashion, they huddle in a group in the corner of the room, not unlike a football team during a time out, as if they are about to go into battle with the residents. Department heads from the Southeast Division of the LAPD and the LA Fire Department are present, as is Bill Martinez, who oversees gang prevention of the City of LA.*
>
> *Delgadillo begins to look as if he has weathered a beating from residents. He goes around the room talking to people who had questions and comments during his presentation. He gives out his card and talks to individuals, explaining programs available to residents.*

These observations of the Pacific Village Neighborhood Council demonstrate how African Americans tended to view law enforcement's attempt to regulate and manage gang-related activity as a form of harassment and brutality. Many of the residents at the meeting seemed fearful of the police. This view was held by residents of various backgrounds: the elderly, teachers, church leaders, representatives of nonprofits, and former gang members. Only a handful of individuals present at the meeting were affiliated with gangs.

For children, the elderly, and other adults who made up the majority of residents in the Pacific Village area, police policies were seen as excessive and carelessly implemented. The raid on the public housing project was seen as nothing less than terrorizing. According to resident testimonies, the LAPD served people for violating the gang injunction in a paramilitary fashion. They kicked down doors and brandished military-style weapons in front of women and children in the process of detaining suspects. Many residents testified at the public hearing that when the police served individuals for the gang injunction, their actions spilled over to affect ordinary citizens. The result of this was that a wide sector of the community viewed the police and other law enforcement agencies as unfair and abusing their power.

A second segment of the population, who also felt threatened by local law enforcement, were the youths of Pacific Village. In many of the Neighborhood Councils, young people often complained of constant harassment by local law enforcement. As the incidents described above show, young people were not only harassed, but also misidentified as gang members. This had huge implications for them. Once they were misidentified, they were placed in the gang database utilized by the LAPD and the LA County Sheriff's Department; when this happened, they could be prosecuted for a felony simply for congregating in designated public places with other identified gang members. Having the police put your name on a list was considered an extreme form of criminalization by youths. An African American youth representative who was appointed to the Pacific Village Neighborhood Council shared his view about how the police scared many young people in the area:

A lot of youth who need to be at those meetings are not going to attend. The ones who are not in gangs are not going to go because they think they will get locked up just for being there. The ones in gangs won't go at all because they don't trust the police either.

Part of the problem was the LAPD's inability to correctly assess who was in a gang and who wasn't. As one area resident stated, "LAPD thinks that everyone with baggy pants and a white T-shirt is in a gang." Given the poor relations with residents, it was difficult for law enforcement to determine who were actually gang members. The observations from the forum described earlier reflect the fact that many residents believed that the LAPD and the Sheriff's Department did not have the expertise to determine who, in fact, was or wasn't in a gang in Pacific Village. These types of assumptions undermined public perceptions of the competency and effectiveness of local law enforcement.

The suppression tactics of the LAPD also undermined their relationships with many parents and youths in the area. Parents in Pacific Village faced a very difficult dilemma. On the one hand, they were concerned about the safety of their children, who were exposed to violence on a regular basis. On the other hand, many felt that the LAPD and the LA County Sheriff's Department were also a potential threat to their children.

I suggest that the criminalization of South LA residents is, in many respects, a remnant of the Reform Era in local government when City Hall maintained a relationship with South LA that involved weak ties, poor relations, and the criminalization of residents. The two clearest results of this criminalization of South LA residents can be seen in the Watts Riots of 1965 and the 1992 uprisings, both of which were spawned by a long history of police abuse. The modern, decentralized form of LA's government must grapple with similar challenges. As a result of this ongoing perception of criminalization, relations between the LAPD and participants of Neighborhood Councils were heavily strained. The field notes reflect the idea that many residents, working through the proper political channels via the Neighborhood Councils, continued to view the LAPD and City Hall with deep distrust and fear. Thus, just as in the past, residents participating in South LA's Neighborhood Councils struggled to overcome the weak social ties and disconnect from City Hall—a trademark of the Reform Era.

The Neighborhood Council strategy of holding public officials accountable was undermined by the perception of criminalization. Relations were often tense between South LA residents and City Hall. There were two outcomes as a result. First, the public forums became a theater in which the historical abuse and neglect by City Hall were reaffirmed, undermining the legitimacy of City Hall and law enforcement. Second, the accountability strategy created an environment in which residents from the broader community and officials from City Hall were reluctant to work with one another in a meaningful and effective way. On the one hand, residents consistently expressed fear and distrust of law enforcement. On the other hand, city officials, such as representatives of law enforcement and the City Attorney's Office, were hesitant to form meaningful social ties with the South LA community because of the perception that residents were confrontational and critical of their policies in a public forum, which could often be embarrassing and damaging to the reputation of the city department or the official. The result of this was a continued disconnect between City Hall and South LA residents, minimizing any ability to address violence.

The Effects of Parole and Policing on Neighborhood Councils

In Neighborhood Councils throughout the South LA area, many residents viewed law enforcement as a criminalizing force. Ironically, residents were concerned about how to respond to violence committed by those in the criminal underworld, but were equally concerned about the violence committed by law enforcement. Drawing on observations of a Neighborhood Council, which I will refer to as the Beaumont Neighborhood Council, I illustrate how residents spent much of their time focusing on abuses by law enforcement rather than on violence emanating from the streets. Thus, the strategy of holding police accountable was not merely focused on improving services to combat violence, but rather on the abuses of law enforcement and other agencies associated with City Hall.

I turn again here to the matter of how the criminalization of South LA's residents undermined the ability of residents to respond to violence, now focusing in particular on the role of probation and parole in the criminalization process. More specifically, I show what effect overpolicing, combined with a large population on probation and parole, had on the perceptions of participants in Neighborhood Councils.

> On a Wednesday afternoon around 1:00 p.m., approximately 20 residents from the central part of South LA meet at a rundown church. Officer Carson from the LA County Probation Department and the area's lead officer from the LAPD give presentations to the Council. Residents immediately engage the Probation and the LAPD officers regarding their practices in the neighborhood.
> A dead silence hangs over the crowd after his comments.

These observations, from a Beaumont Neighborhood Council meeting, illustrate the common response by South LA residents when the LAPD, probation, and/or parole officials were in attendance at Neighborhood Council meetings. Residents, young and old, male and female, all shared a common perception of law enforcement, including proba-tion and parole officials: they were a potential threat.

More importantly, the observations reflect another source of crimi-nalization not addressed earlier: the combined role of probation, pa-role, and law enforcement. It was not just police that were perceived as a source of harassment by residents, but also probation and parole of-ficers. The overpolicing of the area caused widespread fear that residents would be caught in violation of parole and probation and be sent back to prison. As the African American officer acknowledged, police officers were "paranoid" in their interactions, given the exceptionally high vol-ume of crime in the area, and residents' concerns were legitimate.

Due to the perception of residents that they were criminalized by pa-role, probation, and law enforcement officials, Neighborhood Council meetings tended to focus on abuses by law enforcement rather than on violent crime emanating from the streets. The litany of crimes described by Officer Locket was alarming to residents; however, they were not in-terested in discussing the issue further, and refused to provide police with information to help catch potential criminals or provide strategies to address violence. Rather, residents were interested in using Neighbor-hood Council meetings to gain information regarding police procedures and abuses, and to bring them to the attention of law enforcement. They were also interested in how to minimize the risk of further incarcera-tion, such as having access to public information regarding one's crimi-nal record, in order to avoid receiving another strike.

The composite shows not only how those on parole and probation were criminalized, but also how family members of parolees were in-directly affected, passionately involved as they were in Neighborhood Councils. Participation by family members varied from being elected to positions on the Neighborhood Councils to appointments to an ad hoc committee to something more basic, such as regularly attending meet-ings. The family members of those on parole and probation who were in-volved in Neighborhood Councils were thus in a precarious position, in which they had to negotiate two competing and conflicting interests. On the one hand, they wanted to make sure that family members were not abused by police officers or probation and parole officials. On the other hand, they had civic-minded goals and valued the importance of work-ing with City Hall to address neighborhood issues such as violent crime.

Residents, therefore, took a reserved approach in their dealings with City Hall. This circumspect outlook shaped the way in which residents participated in Neighborhood Council meetings. Fear of the criminal justice system limited the extent to which they formed partnerships and were cooperative with city officials. The result of a limited partnership with City Hall undermined collaborative efforts to effectively address violence in South LA. As in many other Neighborhood Councils outlined in this chapter, the observations also illustrate many residents' unwillingness to work with police to identify criminals or to give other valuable information to address violence.

The perception that probation and parole were criminalizing forces was ubiquitous throughout South LA. The mass incarceration of blacks and Latinos, which skyrocketed in the early 1990s, was one of the key reasons for this perception. I was not able to gain hard data on the number of parolees in South LA, but many law enforcement and public officials shared with me that the area had a disproportionate number of men who were either on parole or on probation. Thus, not only were there a large number of men who were incarcerated, but large numbers of men were periodically released from jail. For example, the director of community empowerment revealed to me that, during the summer of 2004 alone, they were anticipating over 500 people to be paroled back into South LA. According to him, helping them transition back into the community was going to be nothing short of a major undertaking.

Thus, criminalization of residents via law enforcement, probation, and parole ultimately undermined the legitimacy of City Hall. Residents were cautious about the extent of their participation in Neighborhood Councils because of the potential conflicts of interest with law enforcement. They were also hesitant to form partnerships and cooperate with law enforcement because of the potential dangers of doing so. Despite their criminalization, residents were still highly motivated to participate in the Neighborhood Councils. They were not cynical about the political system, but rather knew they had to navigate the dangers associated with City Hall.

My findings add to the literature on the urban poor and violence—one view focuses on the role of culture, while the other focuses on the centrality of neighborhoods. In the first view, cultural outlooks underpin the use of violence and responses to it (Jacobs and Wright, 2006;

Anderson, 1999). Residents of poor urban neighborhoods are either portrayed as "ghetto" or "good" in this framework. "Ghetto" refers to the idea that the urban poor lack middle-class, conventional values, and, instead, embrace a subculture of oppositional values rooted in the street, which is the source of crime and violence. In this framework, there are also the "good" residents, who reflect mainstream middle-class American values.

Recent work by Samspon and Bean (2006) highlights the importance of neighborhood factors in producing violence and the protective factors associated with minimizing it. Moreover, they highlight the centrality of three factors associated with neighborhoods and violence: (1) "ecological dissimilarity" and spatial inequality by race, (2) ethnicity and immigration, and (3) a revised cultural perspective. This perspective emphasizes the link between concentrated disadvantage, segregation, and higher rates of violent crime. Neighborhoods with higher levels of concentrated disadvantage and segregation are believed to have fewer protective factors against violent crime. In contrast, minority neighborhoods with higher numbers of professional or managerial jobholders and immigrants are more protected against violence.

While the common explanations in the literature are significant to note, they have not fully explored a key dynamic that is also at play in shaping the ability of residents to respond to violence: the relationship between neighborhood institutions and municipal government. I have argued that residents do not suffer from a lack of mainstream values, but rather they enthusiastically seek participation in formal political institutions, such as the Neighborhood Councils. In addition, while neighborhood protective factors such as the number of professionals and number of immigrants are significant, the activation of those factors depends in large part on local government. Thus, the ongoing relationship between residents of South LA and municipal government must be considered as an independent force that shapes the ability of the residents to respond to violence.

Under the newly formed Neighborhood Councils, residents in South LA continued to see local government operating in a similar fashion to that of the Reform Era. The two types of criminalization outlined in the preceding sections formed the basis of the perception many residents held of City Hall. This historically informed relationship forms the basis of what Abu-Lughod (2007) refers to as "political culture." In this frame-work, political culture is defined by an ongoing historical relationship between City Hall and community residents. Furthermore, it provides a ready-made framework for agents and institutions to interpret and respond to events.

Although LA's decentralized government is more inclusive and has given voice to many who were not "at the table" in the pre–Neighborhood Council era, it is difficult for residents to view local government in any meaningful way that is significantly different from that of the Reform Era. The implication of this perspective is that the municipal government is not viewed as a legitimate source of rule. This type of relationship made it difficult for LAPD to address violence in the Pacific Village area.

2

Alternative Governance

Latino and African American Interrelations outside of City Hall

The continued criminalization of African Americans and Latinos, combined with the disconnect between large sectors of the poor residents of South Los Angeles and City Hall, poses major challenges for formal authority such as law enforcement to establish legitimacy among residents. More importantly, however, the relationship between City Hall and residents of South LA reinforces a key idea in this chapter: the need for self-governing practices. Given their history of alienation from and poor relations with City Hall, residents created a social order that I refer to as alternative governance. In this section, I provide a brief sketch of this conceptual framework. Two key components of alternative governance are: (1) the role of the street and (2) interracial relations between Latinos and African Americans.

But does this causality exist? He seems to imply that city govs form social order. I don't know tht I agree

Compete with the Street

In this section, I suggest that the emergence of alternative governance plays a central role in the regulation of violence. Moreover, it shapes the way violence is mediated and managed by ordinary citizens. Thus, City Hall must compete with the street for legitimate rule of LA's poor residents. In what follows, I outline a key strategy used by residents in the Neighborhood Councils to manage violence: reshaping neighborhood land use. I illustrate how this strategy was challenged by residents and those associated with the gangs and the underground economy, or what I term "the street."

Weeding Out Crime Spots

One common approach to dealing with violence can be clearly seen in the strategies developed by homeowner groups in South LA. They often identified areas with high levels of crime and blight. Once these areas were identified, they advanced their interests through the Neighborhood Councils. Having spent extensive time residing in the neighborhoods where block groups were active, I was able to observe how their agendas played out in the Councils.

The Jackson Neighborhood Association represents one type of neighborhood organization actively involved in the Neighborhood Councils. I resided in the area of this neighborhood association for six months. I was therefore able to attend the association meetings regularly, as well as attend the Councils in which the Jackson group participated. Thus, I was able to witness firsthand how neighborhood associations crafted policy and how they played out in the Neighborhood Council settings.

The Jackson Neighborhood Association represented an area of about three square blocks. The houses were large, two-story homes that had been built during the early 1920s—palm trees lined many of the streets. One could tell, in its glory, the neighborhood had served an affluent community. I discovered that in the early days of the neighborhood, it was known for being the residence of many African American Hollywood actors. It had also been home to many other wealthy and middle-class African Americans.

Over the years, as South LA became more segregated and abandoned, the Jackson neighborhood gradually became dilapidated, and it finally consisted mostly of poor African Americans. Many of the large homes had been subdivided into rental properties with multiple rooms to accommodate the large number of people who moved to the area. Beginning in the 1960s, the area declined quickly after white flight kicked in, following the Watts Riots. Many of the homes were abandoned and became places of prostitution and of other illicit activity like drug sales. Starting in the late 1990s, the area began to gentrify, with small pockets of white Westside Angelenos moving in. However, the neighborhood, for the most part, remained primarily African American and Latino.

During the time I lived there, gang activity and drug sales were common in the Jackson area. Two gangs controlled the streets: one Latino and the other African American. The Latino gang consisted mostly of youths 14–21 years old. They regularly patrolled the area, and often they would congregate on the steps of apartment complexes where passing residents could see them. They made it a point to let everyone know that they were watching and that they had a presence in the area, sometimes flashing gang signs to people walking or driving by. The Latino gang would also openly sell drugs, using apartment complexes and street corners for their business.

The African American gang members were Crips. In contrast to the Latino gang members, the Crips were older males, ranging in age from the late 20s to early 40s, many of whom were on parole. They congregated on the next street adjacent to the Latino gang. During the day, they could be seen in groups of about 8 to 20 people. They rarely left the street where they regularly congregated.

Finally, there were two houses in the Jackson area where drugs were openly sold. I was able to confirm, through my own observation and information from the LAPD, that they were, in fact, crack houses. From early morning until late at night, there were usually two individuals stationed on the porch of each of the small, bungalow-style houses, ready to provide drugs to customers. I was, at times, amazed at the dedication of the drug dealers, since they were on the porches whatever the weather. I witnessed drug sales frequently from my residence in the area. The Jackson Neighborhood Association had their hands full with gang activity and narcotics sales.

Violence was also very common in the immediate area of the block association. During my six months living in this part of South LA, I calculated that there were approximately six homicides within a six-block radius of where I was living. The violence hit home for me because someone was murdered directly behind where I lived, and someone else was murdered one block away from my home, both within a span of a couple of months. From talking to residents and the LAPD, I discovered that the homicides were gang-related.

Nonfatal violence was endemic in the area. Neighbors would constantly update each other about it. For example, someone was shot exiting a nearby bus stop; a youth, from the Latino gang in my neighborhood, was wounded at a gas station three blocks from where I lived; and the attendant at a neighborhood convenience store was fired upon from an outside window—about 50 yards from my room. The next morning, I visited the scene. The window was shattered and glass was littered all over the sidewalk, plywood was nailed over the broken window, and the store was closed.

Many of the members of the association expressed to me that they felt overwhelmed and frustrated, and were fearful of living in the area. Others told me that they had accepted the gangs and the violence.

Residents attended the neighborhood association meetings as a way of venting their frustration and as a venue to address the gang and violence problems. The majority of attendees were African Americans whose families had resided in the area for several generations. The next largest number of attendees were Latinos who had lived in the area for 20 years or so, and then there were a handful of whites, who had moved more recently into the area from other, more affluent parts of Los Angeles. The members lived in homes within a three-block radius of each other. They ranged in age from 30 to 65 years old, although most were around 50 or older. The observations from one meeting reflect how residents responded to the violence.

> Fifteen people sit gathered in the living room of a Victorian-style home around 7:00 on a weekday evening. The home has much of its original design and is in good shape. Residents sit in the living room as the beat officer from the Los Angeles Police Department details all of the recent crime in the area. The radio around his waist is turned on, and the sound coming from it can be heard. A constant buzz of conversation provides background noise to the discussion.
>
> As the meeting progresses, Allen tells the Block Group that their participation in the local Neighborhood Council has paid off. Allen is an elderly white male in charge of the Neighborhood Association. He informs them that an Ad Hoc Land Use and Public Safety Committee has been approved. Allen states, "The Land Use and Public Safety Committee has been formed to identify crime spots in the area. What I need is for people to email me a list of crime spots each week before the Neighborhood Council meetings. I will then take them to the Neighborhood Councils and forward the list to the city."

The interactions at this meeting show the strategies used by homeowners to address violence. First, there was an organized effort to share information by residents and the LAPD. Second, the block group turned their focus to identifying crime spots and addressing these problems through local political means, via the Neighborhood Councils. Finally, many homeowners felt that municipal land use ordinances could be leveraged to mitigate violence and crime in the area.

When we switch our gaze to the Neighborhood Councils, we get a better sense of the ways in which block groups advanced their agendas in order to combat violence. In this setting, block groups and other participants were able to gain direct access to city services. More importantly, they were able to have a voice in the use of land that they knew was connected to violence. The observations from a Central North Neighborhood Council Public Safety Committee meeting shed light on this process.

> On a weekday night around 7:30, ten people attend the committee meeting in an LA County Social Services building. Most of the attendees are African American homeowners, but there are also a handful of the new, affluent white residents. Attending the meeting are several LAPD officers and other city officials. Residents discuss what they believe to be problems in the area. I recognize Allen from the block group. He goes over a list of crime areas in the neighborhood. He uses a projector to show a building with graffiti and debris surrounding it. The building and property have become a junkyard, with numerous cars stored inside a gated area. Allen then begins to show slides of a building where gangs reside.
>
> LAPD officer, Kyle Jackson: "We have a new commander of the Southwest Division. He is placing a priority on the visible look of the Southwest area. We're citing blighted spots to prevent crime. The appearance of the community is very important. We must hold the community to a standard."

Several observations should be noted here concerning the Public Safety Committees of the Neighborhood Councils. First, participants in the Councils attempted to address violence directly through city services where they were likely to be heard, as opposed to their own individual efforts. As the observations demonstrate, the committee members were able to address violence through the city's CNAP program. The program operates from the City Attorney's Office and is coordinated with three other city agencies—the police, building and safety, and the City Planning Department—to target abandoned structures, nuisance properties, and neighborhood blight. CNAP encourages participation by residents and local area businesses in solving crime issues and addressing problem properties. Using the Neighborhood Councils, residents were able to leverage these city services against high-crime and blighted areas.

Second, although residents were torn regarding who was primarily responsible for the blight, crime, and violence in the area, they acknowledged that the owners of the blighted properties and the gangs played important roles in contributing to crime in the area. Both of these groups were targeted by individuals in the Central North Neighborhood Council. In most of the other Councils, by contrast, residents focused on the properties and crime spots, not on individuals.

Third, the policies for addressing violence were developed, for the most part, by homeowners. In this Neighborhood Council, the members of the Public Safety Committee were African American, Latino, and a few white gentrifying homeowners. There were no Latino-immigrant or African American renters, who made up a large segment of the population in the boundaries of the Neighborhood Council. Thus, the strategies to address violence were developed by a small segment of the population.

↳ maybe not such a good thing?

Consequences of Going After Gangs or Property

There are important consequences for the actors involved and the policies they pursued to combat violence. Although there was debate at the meetings regarding whether gangs or landowners should be targeted using land-use policy via CNAP, residents ultimately targeted both. Having attended numerous meetings, residents in the block group would compile a monthly list of perceived high-crime spots and then lobby to have the Neighborhood Councils approve their choices for the city's CNAP database. It became clear, however, that there were dangers associated with this approach, as reflected in Allen's experience.

Allen would regularly drive around the neighborhood near his residence and within the boundaries of the Neighborhood Council, noting which areas he believed were potentially dangerous. Once he established that the residence or area was dangerous, he would take digital photographs. He revealed his strategy in great detail during and after Council meetings. Allen's practice enraged those who lived in the buildings he targeted, and caused great suspicion among them. In several instances, he was followed and threatened by these same residents. As a homeowner who was not originally from the area, Allen was not fully aware of the conventional wisdom that many in South LA innately understood: be cautious and nonconfrontational when dealing with gangs and individuals in the underground economy. The common practice among most residents was to avoid any dealings with gangs and individuals involved in criminal activity.

During one meeting, the regional coordinator of the City of Los Angeles Department of Neighborhood Empowerment, the agency responsible for overseeing the Neighborhood Councils, went out of her way to communicate to me that what Allen was doing was dangerous.

> REGIONAL COORDINATOR BERNICE: You know Allen, right, he is from the block group that you attend, isn't he?
>
> CID: Yeah, I know him well.
>
> BERNICE: Well, someone needs to talk to him about what he is doing, taking pictures and all that.
>
> CID: What do you mean?
>
> BERNICE: He is going to get himself killed. You can't just go up to people's houses and take pictures of their property. Several residents have told me they have seen what he has been doing, and some of the gangs and other folks have been talking about him. He is going to get himself killed. He needs to watch himself.

What made Allen's situation more dangerous was that he was not only targeting troubled and blighted homes, he was specifically targeting individuals and gangs. Bernice's comments reflect the perception that addressing crime by direct confrontation was a dangerous strategy, given the pervasiveness of gangs in the area. There was roughly a gang on every block in the area of the Neighborhood Council and in the area surrounding the block group. Most of the gangs had been established there for many years. It was not at all unlikely that there could have been harmful consequences for Allen.

[handwritten margin notes: "? He didn't elaborate on leveraging of city services. Land use meaning targeting certain area?"]

In all fairness, Allen was not alone in his approach to managing violence. Many individuals in the Neighborhood Council felt that combating the ecology and environment through land use was a viable strategy to deal with violence. Still, this practice was dangerous if not conducted in a circumspect manner.

This particular approach was successful in some ways, because residents were able to leverage city services through the CNAP program. However, as the example of Allen illustrates, it was not safe to directly confront gangs, and, as Bernice implied, gangs and those in the underground economy should be dealt with indirectly. Thus, efforts to combat violence, for the most part, were limited to going after the urban ecology rather than the actual agents of violence—gangs and individuals associated with criminal activity.

Dealing with Violence Indirectly

The Neighborhood Councils played an important role in shaping land use in a way that very likely did have a positive effect on the quality of residents' lives. However, one glaring issue stood out for residents: why couldn't the Neighborhood Councils confront the major sources of violence, namely, gangs or known criminals directly engaged in violence? Having observed 13 different Neighborhood Councils in South LA for over one year, I was able to document the common responses to violence that the residents utilized. Allen's strategy, illustrated earlier, is in many ways an anomaly. Most residents chose not to use this approach for the reasons outlined above. Allen's story is significant, however, because it illustrates that city institutions must confront another source of power: the street.

In this section, I suggest that participants in the Neighborhood Councils, such as nonprofits and neighborhood associations, were limited in their actions because of the pervasiveness of gangs and the underground criminal world. Residents were torn between city efforts to address violence and crime, and the potential consequences of and obligations involved in competing forms of social control, which I term alternative governance. Thus, managing violence took a peculiar approach in which City Hall had to compete with the street for legitimacy.

While working as an official volunteer for the City of LA's Department of Neighborhood Empowerment (DONE), the organization responsible for managing the day-to-day operations of the Neighborhood Councils, I talked regularly with officials from DONE about the challenges they experienced with residents. I wanted to know about the process involved in establishing the Neighborhood Councils. The local City Council members often assisted DONE with initial outreach to community members when establishing the Councils. Meanwhile, they regularly faced resistance from local gangs. The comments from a representative from City Councilman Bernard Park's office illustrate how there was always a need to restore order in areas that had been overrun by gangs.

> I visit the Constituent Services building in the central part of South LA to speak with staff in Bernard Park's office. Three of Park's representatives meet with me there to discuss the Neighborhood Councils. One of the representatives, Joanne, tells me it is difficult to get people to support establishing Neighborhood Councils.
> Cid: "Why is it difficult?"
> Joanne: "We can't just go into whatever areas we want. We were recently trying to do community outreach in one neighborhood and a group of people came out toward us in a very threatening way. And it wasn't just a few people, I mean we found ourselves surrounded by gangs, who flat out told us: 'Who are you? What are you doing in this neighborhood? And you don't have permission to be here.' They basically told us to leave. We came back a couple of times and got the same response, until one day we explained that we weren't there to take them out but that we wanted to make the community better. They finally allowed us to come in, but we had to get their permission, and they said they wanted to have a voice in the Neighborhood Councils. Do you believe that?"

The comments from Joanne reflect the idea that gangs were an important part of the community who influenced the kinds of activities that were deemed appropriate. In this specific case, the local gang insisted that they have a voice in neighborhood affairs.

This example illustrates that to the extent key segments of the community are excluded and do not have a voice, they are likely to resist attempts to instill traditional types of authority. Joanne had to reiterate to the local gang that the councilman's representatives would be willing to allow them to have a voice in the workings of the Neighborhood Council. It was only after negotiation with the gang that the representatives were able to proceed with setting up the Council.

Patillo-McCoy (1998) documents similar findings in her ethnographic research. She found that dense social networks fostered by residential stability facilitate the informal supervision of neighborhood youths and enhance the activities of formal organizations and institutions. More importantly, however, her findings underscore how the incorporation of gang members and drug dealers into the networks of law-abiding kin and neighbors thwart efforts to completely rid the neighborhood of its criminal element.

A similar experience was revealed to me when I talked with Moses Ramirez. He was the director of a group called Community Empowerment, an organization committed to social and economic justice by addressing crime, violence, addiction, and poverty. Community Empowerment was a major player within the Neighborhood Councils of South LA, and was considered by many to be one of the most influential nonprofit organizations in the area. Moses's comments shed light on the widespread influence of gangs in South LA.

> Organizing the community is not easy in South LA. We went into a large housing complex that is notorious for having shootings in the summer. We were trying to set up a recreation program so kids could stay off the streets in the summer when we get all the shootings around here, and we realized we couldn't get around the gangs. You know they (referring to a large Latino gang) bought up apartment units that are about four stories high, so they could use them as drug houses for the gangs. That's the kind of money they have around here, they can buy buildings if they want. Anyway, we had to get their permission and support before we went in and used the facilities at the housing complex where we were trying to set up the program. That's how things are around here.

Moses's comments illustrate that any attempt to transform the community must eventually confront the pervasiveness of street gangs. Many area residents believed that formal political institutions had little effect on the violence, and they understood that there were consequences for challenging the authority of gangs in South LA. I found this view to be pervasive when visiting and talking with the constituents of one Neighborhood Council.

The same view was held by gang members. I met several active and former gang members who attended Neighborhood Council meetings. On one occasion, when discussing public safety in the community, a former gang member, whom I will call TM, and who was known by several residents at the Main Street Council, told me the following:

> TM: *They are never going to be able to deal with public safety or gangs in these meetings.*
> CID: *Why?*
> TM: *The community is not represented in these meetings because gangs are not represented here.*

Community residents understood the presence of gangs and how intimidation served as an informal way of governing the neighborhood. I gained access to this perspective while working as an assistant to an elected member of a Neighborhood Council in South LA, Juan. He would drive me around his district and introduce me as his assistant. Often, Juan would ask residents how things were going in the neighborhood and ask them to identify problems that he could take up at the Neighborhood Council meetings. Then, he would usually try to convince constituents who were not involved to attend the monthly meetings. Most people showed little interest in attending these meetings. Occasionally, people would explain why they were reluctant to attend them. A Latina homeowner in the area, Sonya, shared her view with us.

> JUAN: *Senora, this man [referring to me] wants to know why you don't go to the Neighborhood Council meetings.*
> SONYA: *Let me tell you why I don't go to meetings around here. My son was getting beat up after school, kids would chase him home and beat him every day. Somebody told me they were going to have meetings at the school to address the problem, so I went. But, could you believe it? The gangs would send spies to the meetings and follow people home on their bikes who went to these meetings. They followed me home on their bikes*

and they threatened to burn my house down if I continued. I told them go ahead, burn my house down, I am not afraid. I come from Mexico and it's tough there, and I am not going to let these guys scare me. Well, I was sort of afraid, but I didn't show it. I started to think maybe they will burn my house down. Well, they continued to follow me home and threatened my son. I thought for sure they were going to burn my house down. One day something did happen. My car didn't work and when my husband checked the car they had poured honey or something like that in my car. My engine was ruined. They didn't burn my house down but they ruined my car and I couldn't even go anywhere. After that I thought, I am not going to waste my time going to any meetings anymore. They can't do anything. What for?

Sonya's comments illustrate how residents understood the dangers in directly challenging the authority of gangs and trying to rid them from the neighborhood.

In some instances, however, participants of the Neighborhood Councils grew tired of the nonconfrontational approach to dealing with gangs. The intimidation of residents also shaped the way in which members of the Councils responded to violence and crime in the area.

At the beginning of a Neighborhood Council meeting one evening, an African American in his mid-50s, who was an elected Council member, expresses his disgust at this pervasive attitude towards gangs. He interrupts the beginning of the meeting and walks up to the microphone sweaty, breathing heavily, and clearly irate. He states the following.

"Sorry, ya all, for the interruption. I am pissed off and I am tired of this! I am late and upset. And you want to know why? Because some youngsters were blocking the street and so I honked. Well guess what happened next? They look at me real dirty and they don't move. So, I tell them to get out of the way. So, this punk walks up to my car and points a gun in my face and asks me if I got problem and if I know who he is. I tell him, you know who I am? I tell him my name and that I am an elected official for the Neighborhood Council in his area. I took off in my car. This guy and his homies are gangsters, everyone on the block knows who they are and what they do. You know people are telling me not to call the police because of pay-

back. Well, you know what, why do we let these people rule our li
You know what? I called the police and they went and picked him up.
And, unfortunately, too many people in this community are afraid to con-
front these people. We need to confront them, but we don't because we are
scared. I know you think I am crazy, but it's time to wake up."

These comments received a mixed reaction from the Council participants. Some applauded the man, but many looked at him as if he was
foolish, because of the potential retaliation. The comments reflected the
frustration with the outlook common among Council participants: don't
confront gangs directly.

Directly addressing crime was a challenge for other reasons as well. In
some instances, participants had relatives, immediate family members,
and friends who were involved in gangs and in the criminal underworld.
Going after gangs posed a dilemma for such Council participants, since
they would be viewed as turning on their own.

My findings are similar to Patilllo-McCoy's (1998): close familial ties
to those involved in the criminal underworld make it difficult for residents to be fully committed to solving crime. However, a key difference
in my argument is this: the criminalization and ongoing negative relations between South LA residents and law enforcement poses a major
obstacle to enforcing formal social control. The background factors outlined in the previous chapter highlight this dynamic.

I gained additional insight into this issue through my attendance at
the Ad Hoc Public Safety Committee meetings held by various Neighborhood Councils. The president of a Neighborhood Council shared his
view in front of the entire Council and residents at one such meeting:

Crime, gangs, all the violence is a major problem in our community. It's bad
here, I am not going to lie. The problem is, we know who is committing a
lot of this crime. Many of these youth and individuals committing crime
are our family members, relatives, and friends. At some point we have to
ask ourselves, what are we going to do about this? Do we want to give up
our loved ones? Are we willing to turn in our own, who are committing
the violence here? I am just saying, y'all, we can't keep pretending like we
don't know. Are we willing to give this information to the police?

hey're not
ufnther heiping

OVERNANCE

h borhood of crime

ANCE | 65

es?

Neighborhood Councils were torn between their
ernment and their ties to their immediate neigh-
ds and family members may have been involved
vorld. Probably only a minority of participants
Nevertheless, these affinities presented a major
ls in attaining a consensus to directly confront
..ore for the violence in the community.

Directly confronting gangs and other criminal elements could also
create situations in the Neighborhood Councils where neighbors would
be pitted against one another, causing conflict. Singling out individuals
as criminals could also affect family members who participated in the
Councils. A former DONE coordinator, who worked in the South LA
area for four years and oversaw the daily functions of the Neighborhood
Councils, shared his view with me.

> If we're talking about South LA, yeah, the main strategy was to go after
> places, not people. People know if you change the environment you can
> affect the crime and violence. So, a lot of times, residents would work
> with the city to shut down alleys and blighted properties. You saw a lot
> of people shutting down alleys a lot. But they weren't going after indi-
> viduals. Why did they do that? Because when you go after people, you're
> pitting neighbors against neighbors, because maybe they have family in
> gangs and now they're going to try to work on the Neighborhood Coun-
> cils? That's gonna create a lot of conflict. They knew that. It's much easier
> to deal with crime and gangs when you take away the face of crime and
> violence. When you take away the face, it's easier to swallow.

Three factors undermined City Hall's efforts to address crime and
violence in South LA. First, gangs wanted a voice at the table, and they
demanded that they be negotiated with when city officials and other
community residents tried to implement programs to reduce violence
and crime. However, many residents and city officials did not believe
the gangs had a right to this. Second, gangs and those involved in the
underground economy used intimidation and the threat of violence as
a means of keeping residents from becoming involved in city programs,
because if the residents did participate, it might undermine the gang's
goals in the community. Therefore, participation in city programs and

snitching, in particular, were not encouraged. Finally, many members of the Neighborhood Councils, both elected officials and neighborhood attendees, had close ties to people who were involved in gangs and the criminal underworld. They were, therefore, torn between their civic duty to the formal law and their obligations to the community, including family, friends, etc. Working with the city and other law-enforcement affiliated organizations could jeopardize the well-being of family members. As a result, alternative governance often trumped City Hall's efforts to manage crime and violence.

Limited Success of Decentralized Government: Nonprofits, Neighborhood Councils, and Violence

A different strategy for addressing violence was utilized by other members of the Neighborhood Councils. They took a broader approach to transform the urban ecology within the Council boundaries, and, at the same time, took a more conciliatory approach with gangs and those in the criminal world. The case of the nonprofit organization Community Empowerment, which operated in the core of South LA, sheds light on this strategy. Their methods were different from other approaches outlined earlier, in subtle but important ways. First, the organization sought to transform major commercial corridors in South LA, not just small residential spaces. Second, they were able to galvanize large sectors of the community to support their initiatives. Finally, the organization had strong ties to local, city, and state government. During the time I worked with Community Empowerment, the founder of the organization, Karen Bass, was elected to the State Assembly. Much of her success can be attributed to the strong base of support cultivated early on by the nonprofit.

Having spent a year volunteering with Community Empowerment, I became familiar with their methods of dealing with the problems of crime and violence. As a volunteer, I could view their objectives and see how these translated into strategies in the Neighborhood Councils. I volunteered with the youth empowerment group, observed their meetings, and followed the young participants around to various rallies, performances, and outreach activities. During this time, I got to know many of the staff members, who had organized a separate group of community activists that focused on adults. Thus, Community Empowerment was unusual in that it had organized two separate contingents of activists: youth and adult.

Community Empowerment traces its origins to the 1992 riots. Following these riots, the organization's founders identified the large number of liquor stores concentrated in the area as a major source of South LA's social ills, from rampant alcoholism and drug use to gang involvement and violence. To combat this problem, the nonprofit organized adults and young people with a major goal in mind: shut down as many liquor stores as possible. To achieve this goal, Community Empowerment brought together a coalition of African Americans and Latinos, working cooperatively within the organization. The nonprofit made it a point to include ordinary neighborhood residents and young people from both ethnic groups.

The headquarters of the organization was anchored in a two-story, industrial-looking, light brown building off of a major South LA commercial corridor that had a great deal of history. Across the street from the headquarters, one could see empty lots surrounded by chain-link fences. The empty lots were the result of the 1992 riots. Palm trees towered in the distance from nearby residential neighborhoods nestled behind the commercial corridors. Community Empowerment was conveniently located adjacent to the City of LA Constituent Services building, which housed the local City Council members and divisions of various city agencies. Down the street, to the south, was a large Nation of Islam building. One could regularly see members at the intersection, wearing suits and bow ties, handing out leaflets to passing cars.

Unlike the homeowners of the block group described earlier, Community Empowerment attempted to transform land use on a much broader scale. Jerry, a committed Community Empowerment volunteer for many years and a devoted organizer, explained to me the organization's strategy.

> JERRY: Look, you have to look at your typical street intersection in some of the big corridors in South LA. They are breeding grounds for drug use, drinking, gangs and crime.
>
> CID: You mean all the liquor stores in South LA?
>
> JERRY: It's not just the liquor stores! Think about this: you have a liquor store, a recycling center, a motel, and a Laundromat all together,

one on each corner. You notice you see them together down here in South LA, right? Well here is what happens. Let's say you need some money, so you get some cans or bottles and go to the recycling center. Okay. Then you go to the liquor store and buy a forty of beer, or dope, whatever, cause that's where you get a lot of drug dealers hanging out. Okay, so now you're high and now maybe you want to get a prostitute. All right, so you buy sex, but now you got pimps hanging around there and drug dealers waiting for customers coming from the liquor store or recycling center. All sorts of stuff can happen, right, with all the criminal elements hanging around together in one area. But, that's not it, though. Say it starts to rain or it gets cold and now you need some shelter from the streets, well, that's where the Laundromat comes into play. A lot of people hang out in the Laundromat for shelter, so they can stay warm and still do their business out here on the corner.

Jerry's comments reveal that Community Empowerment had a clear view of how land use affected crime and violence in South LA. Their approach to managing violence was more strategic and less ad hoc than that of the block association. Moreover, they made an effort to organize the wider community in their efforts to transform the area.

Community Empowerment felt that violent crime was encouraged by the large number of liquor stores, motels, recycling centers, and Laundromats in the area. As Moses Ramirez, the director of Community Empowerment, stated to me in one conversation:

There is a lot crime associated with these kinds of places. The kinds of crime we have found are drinking in public, possession of drugs, having an open container, public drunkenness, and sales to minors. There is also a lot of drug use and sales. Then you get pandering and people urinating in public. But the most common and disturbing stuff is the violent crime. I am talking about assault, homicide, robbery.

When I attended the Neighborhood Council meetings in the area surrounding Community Empowerment's headquarters, I was able to witness how the organization implemented their concerns in local, political, and institutional settings. I would frequently see Jerry attending these meetings. Having spent considerable time observing and volunteering at Community Empowerment, I had developed a good relationship with him, and we were able to talk about how he wanted to advance the interests of the organization.

Jerry not only showed up at the Neighborhood Council meetings in the central part of South LA, where his nonprofit was located, but at meetings all over the area. He always had the same message, regardless of which Neighborhood Council he was attending. He always emphasized the connection between motels, liquor stores, recycling centers, Laundromats, and crime—the official position of the nonprofit he represented. Many other participants at the meetings, including church leaders, community activists, homeowners, block groups, and other nonprofits, shared the vision of Community Empowerment, which made it easier for Jerry to get support for the group's strategy.

After seeing Jerry in action and working with the director of Community Empowerment, it was clear what the strategy was for taking on the land use problems in the area. Community Empowerment tried to get the LAPD and other city agencies, such as the Planning Department, to hold people accountable. Like the block groups, they fought to get the types of troubled areas outlined earlier into the CNAP database.

On one occasion, Community Empowerment was able to mobilize LAPD, the City Planning Department, and City Council members to work cooperatively to close a liquor store in a section of South LA with a long history of crime. Much of this loose coalition was formed during meetings at various Neighborhood Councils throughout South LA.

A description of a public hearing at LA City Hall illustrates what happened when these actors came together to block the owner of the liquor store from getting a renewal license.

About 30 people, mostly African Americans and a handful of Latinos, the majority between 40 and 60, sit in the front of a hearing room at Los Angeles City Hall. The hearing takes place because residents of the Neighborhood Councils and members of Community Empowerment do not want a liquor store to continue its operation. What is startling about the hearing is the level of community support, ranging from homeowners, the LAPD, and the elected LA City Council member from the area, Martin Ludlow.

Councilman Ludlow speaks to the attendees and more directly to the Planning Department representative. He outlines a litany of problems and crimes associated with the liquor store. He is very clear about his position and recommends that the liquor store be closed.

A resident and business owner is then allowed to speak. She states that no matter who the liquor store owner is, there is always crime around the business. As her testimony continues, she states she is a third-generation homeowner and that her home is near the liquor store; everyone who has lived in her house before her has been trying to get rid of the store. The resident asks people who are part of her neighborhood and members of Community Empowerment to stand up. Around 20 people stand, and shout in support.

Resident after resident speaks before the Planning Department representative regarding the liquor store problem in the community.

Finally, two officers from LAPD testify that they have received many more calls for service in that location than they have for other locations, and that there have been numerous violent crimes near the liquor store. They give their complete support to shutting down the liquor store.

The liquor store owner states that it's not just his business that is responsible for the crime in the location, but also the motel across the street where there is drug use.

After the hearing, the representative from the City Planning Department carefully weighed the testimony of the liquor store owner and the broad coalition of people attending who were opposed to the operation of the store. Two weeks later, a decision was mailed out to all interested parties. The Planning Department determined that the business posed a significant danger to residents in the area and its business license would not be renewed. Community Empowerment's efforts seemed to have been successful in utilizing the Neighborhood Council as a vehicle to transform the urban landscape.

What stands out in these observations is the cooperation between the police, the Planning Department, the City Council, block clubs, community residents, and the Neighborhood Councils. By bringing the neighborhood residents and city departments together, the participants were able to have an impact on the land use they believed to be associated with violence.

The collaboration of the different partners in this coalition of community supporters was greatly facilitated by the Neighborhood Councils, which provided a forum to bring together these groups. Furthermore, the Councils allowed all of the parties to dialogue and to develop policy to combat land use that they believed promoted violence and crime.

This dialogue to transform the urban landscape, as outlined in the example above, took place in various Neighborhood Council meetings. Usually, conversations about crime and violence were discussed in the general-comments portion of the meetings, when residents would be allowed to vent about the weekly incidents of violence in their particular neighborhoods. At other times, residents addressed violence more directly in Public Safety Committee meetings. The discussion of how to deal with crime and violence revealed itself even more clearly, however, in the Ad Hoc Public Safety Committee meetings, which generally took place separately from the Neighborhood Councils. In all of these settings, residents discussed and developed their strategies to deal with crime and violence.

While the Neighborhood Councils sometimes facilitated organizations such as Community Empowerment in the achievement of successful outcomes, such as in the example above, these types of victories were difficult to come by, and the Councils and groups such as Community Empowerment faced major challenges in advancing such agendas. It often took a long time to organize residents and connect with city officials to file complaints and to attend hearings. So, while the example of cooperation above was a successful one, this was not the most effective means for combating violence and crime. Furthermore, while Community Empowerment organized broad support, the Neighborhood Councils reflected only a segment of the areas they represented, mostly older African American homeowners, nonprofits, various religious leaders, and long-time community activists. As mentioned earlier, other large segments of the community—renters, Latino immigrants, gangs, and members of the criminal underworld—were largely outside the scope of these proceedings.

The Community Empowerment case illustrates how Neighborhood Councils can act to connect various community actors, as well as shore up ties with different city agencies. The sociological literature refers to this process as "horizontal and vertical ties." The above section suggests that the newly formed, decentralized government is making progress toward connecting citizens to municipal government. However, this section also illustrates that the legacy of the Reform Era continues to haunt the poor in Los Angeles. When torn between obligations and the consequences of turning against their relatives and friends, community residents face great obstacles to embracing efforts by City Hall to address violence and crime.

Interracial Relations: The Second Dimension of Alternative Governance

A second dimension of alternative governance is shaped by interracial divisions between Latinos and African Americans in South LA. Contrary to popular media beliefs, the relationship between these two groups is not based in conflict, but rather is rooted in avoidance, which often translates to divisions and disagreements regarding the appropriate response to violence. The avoidance that characterizes relations between the two populations can be partly explained by the fact that no common institutional affiliations crosscut these interracial lines.[1] Thus, interracial relations are a key part of alternative governance, and, therefore, central to understanding the strategies residents utilized, and the challenges they faced, when responding to violence.

Previous works (e.g., Drake and Cayton, 1993[1945]) have described the ghetto as a city within a city, referring to the parallel world of African Americans established to provide for the necessities not afforded them due to segregation from whites. Given the fact that South LA has historically been considered the largest ghetto west of the Mississippi, this framework has been used by scholars to characterize the area. However, the Latinoization of South LA has created a new type of urban space. The ghetto itself is now divided into two parallel worlds—one black and the other Latino. South LA can be best characterized as two worlds within one space. There are many reasons for this division, which I will explore in subsequent chapters. For now, however, it is important to note that the interracial divisions between Latinos and African Americans make it difficult for the two groups to develop a unified response to violence.

The urban politics literature suggests that decentralized forms of government with ethnic heterogeneous populations face significant challenges. This view emphasizes that participatory devolution will result in the domination of culturally advantaged parties in culturally heterogeneous conditions. The more current literature also suggests, however, that interracial differences do not inevitably lead to conflict and the inability of different groups to work together. Recent work by Fung (2004) illustrates that interracial differences can be mitigated by local government so that residents of diverse backgrounds can effectively work together to address issues like violence and crime. Fung highlights the importance of bottom-up governance by local residents, and the saliency of strong social ties between city governments and communities.

In this section, I show that alternative governance takes the form of interracial avoidance. Moreover, I suggest that the poor ties between City Hall and South LA's residents has created the conditions that cause Latinos and African Americans to be unable to develop a unified response to violence. The inability of City Hall to develop a means of connecting residents of diverse backgrounds has forced residents to rely on ties based on race and kinship as the primary basis of social organization, dividing the two groups when it comes to public safety issues. My observations of various Neighborhood Councils in South LA provide a window into relations between Latinos and African Americans and their contrasting views regarding how to respond to violence at the neighborhood level.

Center Town Neighborhood Council: Distrust of Police

Center Town was one of the few Neighborhood Councils that had an equal number of elected Latinos and African Americans on its board. The representation on the Council reflected the diversity of the area, although Latinos constituted about 70 percent of the residents.

The Center Town meetings regularly took place in a large conference room of a newly built library. The new building stood out on a commercial corridor with many run-down industrial buildings that housed auto service repair shops and recycling centers. The area also included many new Latino stores, such as those selling Mexican meats and foods, known as carnecerias. There were also many liquor stores lining the corridor, around which small groups of men would congregate. Finally, there were many homeless men who pushed carts up and down the street; many of them used the commercial corridor as their home. They slept here and begged for money.

The area was one of the poorest in LA, known for a large amount of crime and violence, and home to numerous gangs, some of which had been in existence for over 40 years. The police division that encompassed the area was notorious for having one of the highest homicide rates in Los Angeles.

Although gang members were only a small part of the population, the reality for most residents was that they had to navigate through one of most dangerous and violent areas in all of Los Angeles. The Neighborhood Council became a tool that residents used to address public-safety issues in their community.

> On one Saturday morning in March, residents meet for the monthly Council meeting. Approximately 12 members of the Council attend, seven Latinos and five African Americans. A translator arrives before the meeting and passes out headphones, so translations from English to Spanish can occur. Three of the seven members only speak Spanish. The city provides translators at the request of the Neighborhood Councils.
>
> As the meeting begins, Ms. Suarez, a Latina Council member, asks the residents in attendance to be quiet while the Council is in session.
>
> Another Council member tells Ms. Suarez, "You are not being fair the way you talk to people. You have no right to tell people to be quiet! That's the job of the president. Public comments are now being allowed. We need to hear from the community!"
>
> The angry interchange seems to affect interactions between Latinos and African Americans. Although both groups regularly interact and group members usually sit near each other, today both groups sit separately.
>
> A Latino male in his early 40s, whom I notice regularly attends the meetings, raises his hand to voice his unhappiness. He states, "We need unity, and today we seem separated. I don't feel part of this community with all this hostility."

As the meeting commences, the Council members and participants stand for the Pledge of Allegiance, which seems to unite everyone at the meeting for a moment.

Following the pledge, however, an older African American male raises his hand, stands up, and states, "I don't feel part of this community today either."

The president of the Council, Raphael Ramirez, apologizes to community residents for the hostility in the meeting. He is aware that a representative from Councilwoman Jan Perry's office is present and that I am observing the Council for a research project. "I will use Robert's Rule's of Order if I have to," he states as he tries to wrestle back control of the meeting.

A translator stands quietly in the back of the room, translating from English to Spanish. Latino Council members hold the headsets close to their ears so they can hear the translation.

Many residents raise their hands and are frustrated that they are not called upon to speak regarding issues. An African American in his late 50s blurts out that the community does not get enough time to participate and voice their concerns.

Ramirez responds, "Public discussion takes place in the Ad Hoc Committees, not necessarily in the Neighborhood Council."

Mr. Rasheed, an older African American male who is actively involved in the Council, states, "We only have the building for a limited amount of time to discuss these things."

Another African American male says, "This is the first time I have been here, but I will not come again if this happens—the outbursts and disagreements are too much."

As the meeting continued, the Council moved to a central item on the agenda—public safety. It was an issue that was consistently addressed or brought up in the Neighborhood Councils that I studied in South LA. All of the Councils established Ad Hoc Public Safety Committees. Neighborhood violence, gangs, and robbery were the most common types of crimes that concerned residents. However, police abuse and mistreatment were also consistently brought up in the meetings I attended in South LA. Residents regularly used the Public Safety Committees to discuss police brutality, which was viewed by many to be just as serious as other types of violent crime.

There were, however, major disagreements between Latino residents and African Americans regarding the role of the police and their legitimacy in the South LA community. The differences between these two groups became clear during one meeting.

> *The chair of the Ad Hoc Public Safety Committee informs the Neighborhood Council that they are planning a Safety Fair in July. He mentions that LAPD's Newton Police Division will be there along with the SWAT team, the captain, and, possibly, the Chief of Police, along with representatives from the local Fire Department. According to the chair, the goal of the fair is to increase safety through education and to connect people with available resources. To hold the event at a nearby park, the cost will be $300 for a city permit.*
>
> *Council Member Ms. Soto states during the discussion that she has brought up the issue of police brutality, but it has been shot down in the past.*
>
> *Her view is echoed by Council Member Alexander, "Until police brutality is addressed, we should not invite the police. We should not pay the $300 to the city either," he states.*
>
> *Many Latino Council members and attendees look surprised by the comments regarding the police.*
>
> *Council Member Philipe fires back at Alexander, "Personal issues should not get in the way of the community coming together."*
>
> *Many African Americans appear disturbed by the Council members' comments. An older African American with a graying beard, who also regularly attends the meetings, responds, "Police should be accountable. When police officers are shot, police pay attention, but when an African American resident is killed, they don't care."*
>
> *Many Latino residents argue throughout the meeting that the police should be more involved with the Neighborhood Council and they should have a presence at the Public Safety Fair.*
>
> *A Latino Council member states, "The police should be harassed because some residents are being harassed by people who live around here," referring to the intimidation of residents by gangs. He continues, "Anyone who uses a firearm should be scrutinized, and someone from the Newton police station should be here to hear these things."*

Police brutality was a major issue in the Council, and the differing views about whether the police should be invited to the Public Safety Fair were split along racial lines when the committee voted—almost all Latinos voted in favor, while all African Americans voted against the measure. ⮑ *Blacks disproportionate mistrust of cops*

It is important to note that the Latinos who were not immigrants and whose families had lived in South LA for many generations tended to have views closer to those of the African Americans. However, the only Latino resident who sided with the African American perspective regarding the role of the police was Ms. Soto, who was a second-generation Mexican American.

Palm Court Neighborhood Council: Distrust of Police and One Another

The weak interracial social ties between Latinos and African Americans and a general distrust of the LAPD's policing tactics further undermined the ability of residents to respond to violence in a unified way. When the LAPD exercised excessive force, it not only revealed how residents were criminalized, but it also provided a window into interracial dynamics between Latinos and African Americans.

Earlier in this chapter, I showed how African Americans continued to feel criminalized by the police, using the example of the raids on the public housing projects. Residents complained of abusive tactics, and that the police were incompetent because they were unable to determine who was actually a violent gang member.

Something more subtle was revealed during the meetings with the LAPD and the members of the Pacific Court Neighborhood Council—that the LAPD was targeting African Americans and ignoring gang violence committed by Latinos. During the Neighborhood Council meeting that I noted earlier in this chapter that occurred after the raids in public housing, I observed something else that illuminated the state of interracial relations between Latinos and African Americans.

> An African American female responds, "You don't know how the community was devastated. Old people and children were traumatized when the raids took place in public housing."

An African American male interjects and tells the City Attorney, "I don't hear you talking about gangs who are Latino! We got about four or five in Pacific Court. Why aren't they pursued?"

Another resident announces to members of the Council that the community task force needs to be reenacted, "I know of five people who had cars illegally searched and impounded. I know five Latinos selling things illegally, but nothing happens to them."

In response, the City Attorney states that none of the Latino gangs have a record of high homicides like the African American gangs targeted in public housing.

The two groups had contrasting perceptions about who was being singled out by law enforcement. As demonstrated above, the Pacific Court Neighborhood Council African American residents believed that African American gangs and non-gang members were being singled out, while Latino gangs were not. African Americans felt that law enforcement operated with two separate standards, one for African Americans and another for Latinos.

Following the raids in public housing, the LAPD started to crack down on alleged gang members who congregated in the housing projects. As a result of the tougher policing practices, many of the gang members, most of whom were African American, began to congregate and conduct their business outside the projects in a neighboring, mostly Latino area. According to Latino residents, the gang injunction described earlier had the unintended effect of causing gang-related crimes to spread from public housing to residential neighborhood settings. A Latina board member of the Pacific Court Neighborhood Council expressed her views on this matter.

The gangs stopped gathering in public housing and committing crimes there after the gang injunction was imposed and cameras were placed there by the City Attorney. They then started going to residential neighborhoods. This is where all the crime was happening. African Americans in the residential neighborhoods accused the police of being racist for going there. The gangs moved from the projects to the Colonia [a residential Latino neighborhood]. Latinos wanted these gangs out of there and African Americans were complaining about this because they felt they were being targeted. Public safety can cause a lot disagreement.

The observations illustrate sharp differences between Latinos' and African Americans' views of the practices the LAPD used to combat violence in public housing. Latinos welcomed the presence of the LAPD in their residential neighborhoods near public housing, while African Americans viewed their presence as another form of criminalization.

Despite the differences in perception regarding the police and their policies among Latinos and African Americans, both were, in general, very distrustful, suspicious, and hesitant to go to the police. In numerous interviews that I conducted, many Latinos and African Americans agreed that going to the police was not an option when there was a problem.

How does one account for the differing views of the police and their policies? I suggest that a lack of community institutions that bring residents together is a major reason for these differing views. Without cross-cultural institutions, which are needed to foster social ties, residents tended to view members of other groups as strangers and were unaware of the experiences of other residents and their experiences with the LAPD and the various forms of law enforcement.

The absence of connecting institutions led to a reliance on race, friendship, and kinship as the primary means of social organization. One outcome of this type of social organization was that residents developed mental maps with boundaries that circumscribed their relationships with others. These cognitive maps informed individuals when and where it was safe to travel, and, equally important, with whom one should interact. In South LA, residents had very defined cognitive maps that defined social space: one for African Americans and the other for Latinos.[2]

Part of the cognitive-mapping process for Latinos and African Americans was to avoid interactions with members of other racial groups and with the police, as well as with any law enforcement type of agency. So why were Latinos more likely to turn to the police than African Americans were? One central reason Latino residents may have welcomed the police presence was because the police were targeting African Americans and not Latinos. Another reason Latino residents may have supported the increased police presence was the fact that the area where the gangs relocated was an almost exclusively Latino neighborhood, and the growing number of African American males congregating there may have led residents to feel threatened. In other words, it was okay for the police to come in "when the other guys" were in their neighborhood. Residents felt that African Americans were in a social space constructed as a Latino area.

The lack of cross-cultural institutions also affected the levels of trust among African Americans and Latinos. Although they resided in the same neighborhoods and in the same public spaces, they mostly remained strangers to one another. Having lived in several neighborhoods in the area surrounding Pacific Courts, I regularly observed little, if any, interaction between Latinos and African Americans, even though they resided in the same area.

The lack of trust between the two groups is likely a result of their mutual anonymity. Merry (1981) points out that "strangers" are perceived as dangerous because of the unpredictable nature of their character, and they cannot, therefore, be trusted. Fear of the unknown is often worse than the reality.

In a manner similar to that outlined by Merry, residents in South LA felt safer when they engaged with people who looked the same, spoke the same language, and who they thus felt could be trusted. The lack of shared institutional settings provided few, if any, opportunities for residents to get to know one another and trust each other.

Finally, the lack of cross-cultural institutional settings in which Latinos and African Americans might come together limited the exchange of information among residents, undermining their ability to work together to respond to violence in the Neighborhood Council settings. Given the lack of trust and the cognitive maps that limited interaction, little or no information was exchanged regarding the types of crime committed and who was committing the crime. Residents, therefore, relied on gossip from members of their own racially bound group as the primary means of making sense of the violence in their respective neighborhoods.

Taken together, the cognitive mapping, lack of trust, and lack of cross-cultural exchange of information formed the basis for the social organization of South LA, which, in turn, led to two separate worlds coexisting in the same space. More importantly, the type of social organization outlined served as the basis of the interracial boundaries that separated the two groups and limited their ability to respond to crime. These dynamics led to differences regarding whether to trust the police or to embrace police practices at the neighborhood level, and to differing perceptions of whether the police were acting fairly or unfairly.

Lack of Connecting Institutions and Interracial Relations

Throughout this chapter, I have argued that the legacy of Reform Era municipal government continues to haunt South LA. One of the unintended consequences of this type of governing structure is that it has created an institutional vacuum where few cross-cultural civic institutions are in place to address issues of crime and violence. In large part, the goal of the Neighborhood Councils was to address this problem.

For Neighborhood Councils to adequately address issues of violence, however, robust participation was required on two levels. First, the Councils required the participation of individuals who reflected the neighborhood demographics. Second, they required a cadre of civic institutions that could bring to bear the interests of the wider community. Mobilizing participants and civic institutions that reflected the needs of both groups proved to be a major obstacle.

During the time I lived in South LA, there were 13 Neighborhood Councils in the area. Judging by my direct observation of the Councils for almost one year, there was virtually no participation by Latinos in most. It was only in the Center Court Neighborhood Council, highlighted earlier in this chapter, that Latinos had equal representation and participation. This held true even in the three Council areas where Latinos comprised a supermajority at the neighborhood level.[3] In neighborhoods where Latinos made up 50–70 percent of the population, they were severely underrepresented in participation and attendance. Finally, in neighborhoods where African Americans were in the narrow majority,[4] Latinos were nonexistent with respect to participation, attendance, and appointment to Council positions.

African Americans, on the other hand, had strong rates of participation in Neighborhood Councils. They were elected to Council positions, appointed to ad hoc committees, and in attendance at general meetings.

Most of the elected Council members were older African Americans who had been active in the South LA community for many years.

African Americans and Latinos were also different with respect to their ties to civic institutions that could advocate for their respective interests. Many of the African American participants in the Neighborhood Councils were members of civic organizations in the community, such as block clubs, community-based organizations (CBOs), and churches. Many of these organizations and churches had direct ties to City Hall and could exercise some limited influence in response to violence. For example, earlier I illustrated how a nonprofit organization was able to work with the LAPD and other key stakeholders to shut down a liquor store. These organizations were an effective means of mobilizing residents to participate in the Neighborhood Councils.

In contrast to African Americans, Latinos had virtually no civic institutions, nonprofits, or homeowners' associations that advocated for them. During the time that I conducted fieldwork, from 2003 to 2005, there was only one nonprofit group that consistently advocated for Latinos in South LA: the Watts/Century Latino Organization (WCLO), which played an important role in addressing issues of public safety and housing.

Two points are worth emphasizing about the institutional landscape of South LA. First, although the Neighborhood Councils were, in theory, supposed to represent a common institutional forum that could bring diverse interests together, the lack of Latino participation severely undermined this goal. Second, there were no institutional settings outside the Neighborhood Councils that fostered cross-cultural social ties. Most churches and nonprofits exclusively served African Americans or Latinos. Thus, the lack of participation of Latinos in the Neighborhood Councils provided little or no opportunity for either group to develop a common agenda to address violence and crime. More importantly, the absence of Latinos in these settings minimized the possibility of developing cross-cultural social ties with African Americans.

The result of this institutional divide was that the social organization of South LA was bounded by interracial avoidance. When it came to developing strategies for dealing with violence, both African Americans and Latinos tended to see crime in a limited way that reflected only the perspectives of their own group. This posed major problems for City

Hall in connecting with the community, since municipal officials usually had to deal with a fractured community. In the end, community attachment trumped the interests of City Hall and other competing visions in responding to issues of violence and crime.

Conclusion

In this chapter, I have argued that Los Angeles's newly formed, decentralized government faces many challenges. There are two important contributions that I seek to make here to the existing literature in urban politics and urban sociology. First, I suggest that the ghost of the Reform Era continues to haunt residents of the city's poorest neighborhoods in South LA. This concept adds to an important theme missing from the contemporary literature in urban studies. In particular, I have shown that scholars must take note of the role of political culture in shaping relations between City Hall and LA's poor residents. Political culture does not exist in a vacuum but is reinforced by institutions, in this case, by municipal government. LA's decentralized government offers more participation, but less power, to residents, and, with its continued top-down bureaucratic approach, City Hall struggles to connect the poor to resources to address issues such as violent crime. While Fung (2004) and other scholars have highlighted the importance of deliberative practices in decentralized municipal government, I have emphasized the structural limitations of LA's municipal government and its role in reinforcing the collective memory among the poor of South LA and in the administration of City Hall.

The second important contribution that I seek to make to the existing urban literature is the focus on what I have termed alternative governance. Throughout the 20th century, when poor blacks and Latinos were disconnected from formal political institutions, they did not resort to a Hobbesian world devoid of social order. Instead, residents of South LA created an alternative social order rooted in the informal codes of the street and in interracial relations. What many urban scholars have failed to note is that alternative governance now challenges and competes with established government, in this case local government, for legitimacy. Increasingly, alternative governance plays a central role in managing violence.

In this chapter, I have provided only a sketch of the concept I refer to as alternative governance and its relationship to City Hall. However, a deeper understanding of this concept is necessary to show its complexity and richness. In the following chapters, I highlight the competing alternative worlds that have arisen in the face of the disconnect between local government and residents in South LA. Understanding these multiple forms of alternative worlds is key to understanding how residents manage violence in South LA.

3

Neighborhood Institutions

Safety from Violence, and the Catholic Church

There are four police divisions in South Los Angeles, arguably the most dangerous area in the entire City of Los Angeles given the consistent high number of murders. My field site was in the core of the Southeast Division, which had the highest number of homicides in South LA in 2003 and ranked second in murders in 2004. To further contextualize the field site used for this study, I looked at the homicide data within a one-mile radius drawn around it. I discovered that 29 individuals were murdered within a one-mile radius of my field site in 2003 and 26 in 2004.

TABLE 3.1. Poverty and Homicide in the Southeast Division

	Area (square mi)	2003 Homicides	% of 2003 Homicides	2004 Homicides	% of 2004 Homicides	2003 & 2004 Total Homicides
Los Angeles	503	508		516		1024
South Central	42.7	238	46.85	265	51.36	503
Newton	9.8	46	9.06	45	8.72	91
77th Street	11.3	64	12.60	88	17.05	152
Southeast	9.3	77	15.16	71	13.76	148
Southwest	12.3	51	10.04	61	11.82	112

Source: LAPD

Most if not all of the residents exposed to the violence are Latinos and African Americans who live in high-poverty neighborhoods. Maps 3.1 and 3.2 illustrate the percentage of Latinos and African Americans in the Southeast Division. Map 3.3 shows the percentage of the population in poverty exposed to violence.

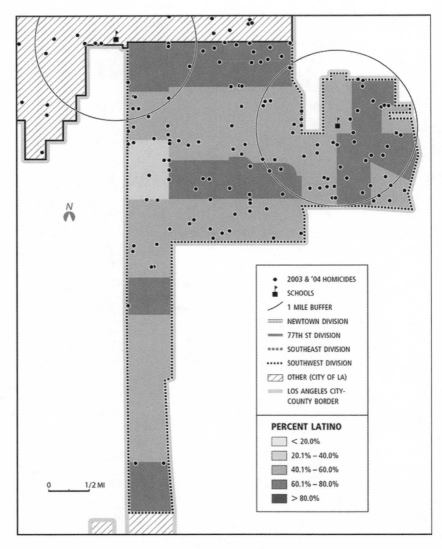

Map 3.1. Latino Share of Population and Homicides in the Southeast Division

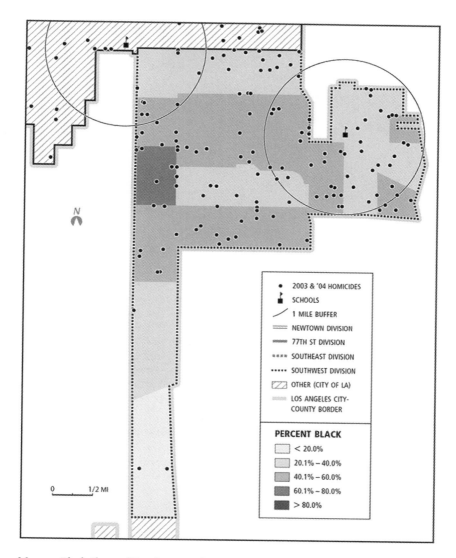

Map 3.2. Black Share of Population and Homicides in the Southeast Division

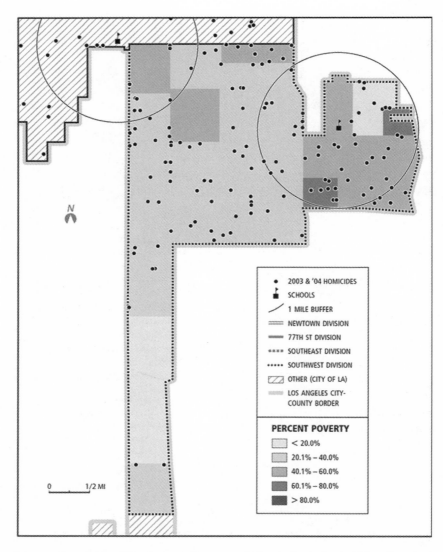

Map 3.3. Percentage of Population in Poverty and Homicides in the Southeast Division

How do neighborhood institutions in poor multiracial neighborhoods respond to violence and manage the risk associated with it? Recent work by sociologists illustrates that organizations have a direct impact upon levels of violence and conflict (Collins, 2008). This chapter follows in this tradition by sketching a portrait of how neighborhood institutions manage risk and potential conflict among the poor black and Latino residents of South Los Angeles. Anderson (1999) shows how a code of the street becomes the primary means by which poor residents manage conflict and disagreements that often lead to violence. In essence, Anderson claims that a code of the street overshadows and trumps the norms of the state. In contrast, I demonstrate how St. Joseph's, a Catholic church located between four housing projects in an area considered to be among the poorest in Los Angeles, acts as an alternative, parallel world that promotes protection and avoidance to minimize conflict. It acts as a competing mediating structure to the code of the street and the formal law of the state. Thus, the church is the center point of a third type of social space that regulates social relations and conflict not documented in the criminology and urban literature. The existence of a third type of alternative mediating structure illustrates that there are multiple forms of competing informal social controls that regulate conflict. I illustrate how this third social space acts as an informal type of social control by protecting residents from state actors, such as US Immigration and Customs Enforcement (ICE); providing an alternative social space, or what I call a "safety zone," for residents from the threat of gangs; and minimizing interracial conflict through the creation of a narrative framework.

St. Joseph's has long been recognized in South LA for serving as a neutral and safe social space where residents are protected from threatening forces. During the Watts Riots of 1965, many buildings were looted, burned, and destroyed near St. Joseph's. *The Tidings*, a Los Angeles–area Catholic newspaper, reported that, following the riot, almost every building surrounding the church was destroyed. St. Joseph's was spared from the destruction and was left virtually unscathed. Many priests and residents have suggested that St. Joseph's was not destroyed because it was viewed with respect and reverence due to its relationship with the African American community in Watts.

St. Joseph's continues to be regarded by residents as a neutral and safe social space. However, its social role has been transformed and expanded so that St. Joseph's now acts as a neutral safety zone for both African Americans and Latinos. Furthermore, the church has transformed so that it is able to reduce conflict between different racial groups. There are, however, distinct differences with regard to whom the church protects, and whom it protects from. The church now protects immigrants from street gangs and from the ever-present state. By managing these risks and conflicts, the Catholic Church shapes the social organization of this poor modern urban neighborhood.

Protecting Immigrants from the State

Today, in South Los Angeles, the Catholic Church protects immigrants primarily from Latin America and Mexico, many of whom are noncitizens. These immigrants' status puts them in constant fear of deportation by agencies such as US Immigration and Customs Enforcement (ICE). Table 3.2 shows the number of noncitizens who live within the South Los Angeles area.

TABLE 3.2. US Census Demographic Profile: 2000
GEOGRAPHIC AREA: South Los Angeles as Defined by Census Tract

Subject Nativity and Citizenship Status	Number	Percent
Total Population	702,288	100
Native Born	449,912	64.1
Foreign Born	252,376	35.9
Naturalized	55,218	7.9
Not a Citizen	197,158	28.1

Nearly 30 percent of all South LA residents are not citizens. These figures suggest that a significant number of Latino immigrants have to deal with the risk of engagement with ICE officials. The figures are even more telling when one considers the extended families of this group's members, such as children, who are also potentially affected by their families' citizenship status. For example, extended family members of those who are not citizens could be directly affected if a loved one, such as a mother, were detained. Children could come home to find their parents missing. The following observations are illustrative of this experience.

On a late weekday afternoon, Father Mike offered me a tour of the parish's elementary school, which is located behind the church. The area is paved with black asphalt and concrete. Children run everywhere and are supervised by school officials. As we walk to the playground, I am introduced to a Mexican male in his mid-40s named Jose, who immigrated to the United States in the early 1980s. I am told that Jose is very active in various ministries throughout the church. In the past, I had noted how frequently he seemed to be involved in church activities. Father Mike tells Jose that I am a graduate student studying in South LA. I ask Jose why Latinos are not more involved with local politics, such as the Neighborhood Council meetings.

Jose tells me, in broken English, that Mexicans do not participate in politics because they are not treated with dignity or respect. "We have no rights in these places. We have no human rights. Here [the church] we are treated like human beings with dignity and respect. Here we have human rights and we are not afraid. We are safe."

These comments capture a pervasive view among Latinos in South LA. First, what Jose says underscores Latino immigrants' constant fear of deportation, and also their avoidance of many formal legal institutions, such as law enforcement and other local government agencies. Many seem to believe that it is wisest to remain as invisible as possible to these institutions, and to avoid any encounter where information could be amassed and collected—information which could be used to detain them in the future.

A second result of the fear of deportation among Latino immigrants is a general perception that they have no rights. This operates in two ways. First, when Latinos do attempt to participate in community affairs, they are often reminded by community members that they are not entitled to do so because they are not citizens. Secondly, Latino immigrants are reluctant to participate in neighborhood civic activities, such as Neighborhood Councils, because they themselves feel they do not have the right to do so because of their citizenship status.

Jose's comments bring to light a more fundamental problem Latino immigrants face, namely, the limited social spaces in which they can maneuver during their daily lives where they are able to feel safe from potential threats and are accorded basic respect and rights. The Catholic Church plays an important role in helping Latino immigrants manage the risk and fear associated with their citizenship status in South LA. The unfolding of events in April 2004 illustrates the way in which the church assists Latino immigrants.

During this time, while I was conducting fieldwork, the INS began a series of raids all over Los Angeles. Parents became increasingly afraid of deportation and of being detained in public places. As a result, they avoided public settings, and many considered not sending their children to school. In addition, parishioners of the church considered not attending services for fear of detention by ICE.

Rumors had spread in the community that ICE would begin raids at Catholic churches in Los Angeles, including in South LA. Having caught word of these rumors, the pastor of the church communicated the following views to me:

> Cid, I have heard about the INS raiding churches. I simply will not have it. I will not allow the INS to come into this church. They are supposed to get permission from the clergy before they come into the premises to do raids on immigrants. Even if they did approach me and ask me for my permission, I would refuse. I don't care. I will have myself arrested if I have to in order to keep the parishioners from getting detained. It's very important to me that parishioners feel safe here.

The pastor's comments reflect a routine institutional strategy utilized by the church in dealing with threats that immigrants face from the state. Based on extensive field observations, the consistent position of St. Joseph's was to protect immigrants at all costs.

During the week following my conversation with the pastor, I attended Sunday mass. Attendance was slightly smaller than usual, and the mood of the parish was tense and uneasy—likely a result of the fear of ICE. The pastor sensed the parishioners' uneasiness, and, in an attempt to reassure them, he stated publicly in the middle of mass that he would not allow the INS to enter church premises to detain Latino immigrants. Parishioners at the mass were relieved, shouting in jovial support and clapping upon hearing their pastor's opposition to INS raids.

In sum, the Catholic Church in South LA has taken on a new significance that contrasts with other institutions of the ghetto. In the past, African Americans were segregated and confined to the ghetto. During the 1965 Watts Riots, the church was likely one of many options that African Americans could utilize as a safe neutral space. Latinos, in contrast, are more limited within the ghetto. Given their citizenship status, a significant percentage of noncitizen Latino immigrants and their extended families are limited in the number and types of social settings and institutions that they feel are safe. The Catholic Church, therefore, plays a significant role as one of the few places that offers protection to this population.

The Threat of Gangs and Violence

In virtually all neighborhoods throughout South Los Angeles, gangs claimed control and regulated the use of social and public spaces. The informal use of many public spaces, such as where and when one could frequent a given neighborhood, was largely under their control. Thus, residents of South LA were physically limited in the social spaces they could maneuver within.

In addition to gangs, the threat of violence in general seemed omnipresent for residents. The perception that South LA was dangerous for residents to maneuver within is substantiated by data from the Los Angeles Police Department. The possibility of violent crime erupting at any time was a daily reality that residents learned to cope with. I suggest that the Catholic Church helped residents to deal with this reality by protecting Latino immigrants from dangerous street gangs and from potential violence in the surrounding area. The churches did this by providing a social space where parishioners felt safe and protected from the threats of the streets.

The experience of local high school students and their parents illustrates the limitations of social space faced by South LA residents. During my fieldwork in South LA, I regularly witnessed many parents and high school youths, who were both African American and Latino, vent their frustration during Neighborhood Council meetings. The meetings were held near the church, so they provided another insight into the inner workings of the surrounding community. During these meetings, representatives of the LAPD and the LA County Sheriff's Department would occasionally provide information about crime trends in the area. Most youths who experienced this fear and intimidation were not involved in gangs. Many of the parents stated that gang activity was so prevalent in the South LA area that youths were afraid to attend public high schools because they felt they would be preyed upon on their way to school—in school—and on the way home. The comments of a Latino parent are telling:

> My son was on his way to school and he gets jumped and robbed for his new tennis shoes right in broad daylight; right in front of a whole bunch of other kids who were on their way to school in the morning. They beat him up, left him on the ground, and then he had to walk to school in his socks. I have talked to other parents and school officials and apparently this happens all the time.

In another public information session held at the Neighborhood Council meetings, a police officer fielded questions from parents who wanted to know what to do if their children were confronted by gangs on their way to school. The officer recommended the following:

> We have been getting a lot of reports of youth being confronted by groups of boys. These groups of boys will ask, "Where are you from?" Shortly after this question, if the wrong answer is given, two things happen. The groups of boys beat or shoot their victim. In some instances, kids are killed. My advice to you is that if anyone asks your kids where they're from, tell them to run for help. It could be life or death.

As a result of these encounters, some parents claimed, many youths did not attend school and dropped out. Officials from the Los Angeles Unified School District listened to parents and other community members plead for a solution. One solution considered was starting up schools in public housing so that youths would not have to walk to school and encounter potential violence and conflict.

The Church's Response to Neighborhood Threats

The threat of gangs and violent crime had a significant impact on the use of social space by residents in the area. As the observations suggest, residents understood that certain social spaces were hot spots and should be avoided altogether. Thus, residents were limited as to what social spaces they felt free to maneuver within. What social spaces provided alternatives? In this section, I suggest that the Catholic Church provided an alternative setting that minimized risk and fear.

A Latina high school student, a parishioner who lives near the church, explained her view:

> It's really dangerous right outside the church. I mean right outside the walls of the church, there are gangs across the street, and things happen to people all the time. As soon as I go inside the church gates, I feel this love from parishioners. The inside of the church walls have a completely different feel than standing outside the church. People seem to be open and welcoming, and you can trust people. Everyone seems easygoing and relaxed inside the church. I feel at peace when I am there. I feel safe.

This comment represents a common view held among parishioners, that the church provides physically and socially safe space, free from neighborhood violence and gang activity. This is reflected in the ways parishioners interact and use the social space of the church. Upon entering the parish grounds, one can observe parishioners of all ages interacting freely. Children run throughout the church grounds and parishioners often socialize in open areas behind the church, in the hall, where tables line the entrance. The church has over 40 ministries, which are utilized regularly throughout the week, providing activities for parishioners of all backgrounds. The frequency of social interaction and the number of activities suggest that residents are not fearful and maintain a level of trust with one another.

I asked several of the clergy why parishioners congregated at the church so frequently. The pastor responded:

> They have nothing to look forward to when they go home. Most of them are poor, and it's not safe to play out in the open where they are from. That's why they stay here. Gangs and violence are common in the area.

In several discussions and conversations with churchgoers, parishioners often expressed that they felt safe from the neighborhood violence inside the church. Most parishioners expressed that they trusted other members of the church. The church was seen as one of the few places in the locality where residents could interact and not be preoccupied with the many problems in the neighborhood, such as crime. The status of the parish as a safety zone was not only recognized by parishioners but by residents in the surrounding area as well.

A priest from the parish described the relationship between the parish and neighborhood gangs. Father Javier, the second in command at St. Joseph's, and I talked in the rectory following a church event. Telling me that many gangs operate right outside the church walls, he stated:

> Many of the gangs in the area hang out all day; they have gotten to know who I am. Despite this, they always seem a little suspicious of me. When I am walking through the area, they seem defensive. As soon as I walk into the church premises, they wave hello or goodbye to me. So it's not a problem that I walk around and see what's going on, as long as I find my way back into the church grounds.

Father Javier went on to tell me that church clergy have become familiar with local residents, many of whom are heavily involved in gang activity. He added that there is an unstated understanding among local gangs, and other predatory individuals and groups, that the church is a neutral place and should be respected. I observed Father Javier's description to be correct. In the year I conducted fieldwork, I did not witness or hear of one instance of violent crime or criminal activity inside the parish grounds. This is striking, given that outside the church was a busy, major street where different gangs from nearby housing projects and residential neighborhoods would frequently pass by and stop. Rarely did they enter the church grounds. When they did enter, they entered as parishioners, were accompanied by members of the parish, or visited with family members who were participants in parish activities. In general, the parish grounds were peaceful and safe during the year I visited the church.

In summation, it is not fair to assume that social order does not exist in poor areas with high levels of crime and violence. Observing only the high levels of violence misses the way in which residents are able to find social order, where stable social settings of interaction can be maintained and high levels of trust are common. Residents find ways of coping with violence through informal means, such as the Catholic Church.

Managing Interracial Conflict

The previous section demonstrates how one Catholic church continues to provide an alternative world in which immigrants are sheltered from hostile forces, just as many churches did in the 19th century. In this section, I suggest that vibrant social institutions in South LA—its churches—play a key role in mediating interracial conflict to make it manageable for its residents.

Beginning in the late 1970s, the St. Joseph's congregation and the population of the parish it serves began to gradually shift from black to brown. By 2000, the church had become mostly Latino. At stake during this change was the soul of a church in existence in the South LA area since 1908. The question that stands out is this: why is there not more interracial conflict between African Americans and Latinos in the area?

The media and many social scientists have anticipated that the Latinoization of South LA would lead to interracial conflict. The fact is, however, there have been few interracial problems. Rather, I show in this section how the Catholic Church has allowed established African Americans and newcomer Latinos to coexist through avoidance—a strategy for managing conflict, too often overlooked, which plays a central role in newly emerging multiracial neighborhoods, such as South LA.

In this section, I demonstrate how day-to-day problems between these groups are diffused and mitigated by the institutional strategies of the church. The section shows the triggers of interracial conflict and the strategies used by the church to quell these triggers. Despite the possibility of interracial conflict, the church is able to keep the differences to a minimum. The ability of the church to successfully navigate these differences is what has allowed the parish to thrive.

The Triggers of Interracial Conflict and the Institutional Response

There are several sources of interracial conflict in multiracial settings such as St. Joseph's. One major source of potential interracial conflict centers on competition for resources.

Competition for Resources

One morning, Father Mike and I talked about when St. Joseph's first experienced large-scale Latino immigration and how this shaped interracial relations.

> Latinos started coming into the area in large numbers in the late 1970s. This was a big change for African American parishioners, who are a very spiritual people. It was around this time that we started having masses in Spanish. I had to reach out to them because there were so many of them.
>
> African Americans resented Latinos; they were coming in very large numbers during this time. They felt like they were being pushed out. It was a tough time for the church. Latinos were also uncomfortable being around African Americans.

The comments from Father Mike reveal the dilemmas faced by institutions in multiracial, poor neighborhoods where Latinos have had an increasing presence. The church attempted to reach out to a new ethnic group, with the unintended consequence of making African Americans feel as if they were being squeezed out.

Several aspects of the parish and its leadership helped to overcome these interracial differences. First, Father Mike's ethnic background aided him in gaining the confidence of both groups and helped him to empathize with their social circumstances. During the early 1970s, Father Mike had come from Ireland to become a priest in South LA. His identity helped minimize mistrust and the idea that the church was favoring one group over the other: "I was an immigrant who came from Ireland. Latinos see me as an immigrant, as do blacks. They both see me as neutral, and not as a favorite for either group."

Father Mike often stated he could relate to both groups because the Irish were often treated as a marginalized group in Europe. His background gave him a unique standing among African Americans, who perceived him as "not being an ordinary white guy." Latinos viewed Father Mike in a similar way, since he is also bilingual and could converse freely in Spanish. Latinos often referred to him as Padre Miguel, indicating that they saw him as one of their own.

A second factor that contributed to minimizing conflict was an institutional strategy—to provide services and ministries to African Americans even though their numbers in the parish had decreased dramatically, something which occurred over time. By 2003, church officials explained to me that they estimated that African Americans constituted 15–20 percent of the congregation. According to Father Mike,

> We could have stopped the English masses that African Americans attended, cold, but we didn't. Instead we continued to have English masses, and we even started having midnight masses for African Americans. It was also important to help the gospel choir grow. We have started to invest even more money in the gospel choir than we did in the past. It has started to now become bicultural, even though it took time.
>
> It was very important for me to let African Americans know we were not turning our backs on them. They needed to know that they are still an important part of this church and they need to be recognized.

By continuing to have English masses and devoting resources to growing the gospel choir, both important to African Americans, the church helped to minimize anxieties that Latinos were taking over. These choices helped to send the message that African Americans were valued parishioners and that their spiritual needs would continue to be addressed.

It is important to note that even though the church made an effort to reach out to African Americans and keep them as part of the parish family, there were unintended consequences. One key result was that African Americans and Latinos ended up attending different masses and participating in different church ministries. Some of this was beyond the church's control. For example, many of the Latino parishioners only speak Spanish and therefore did not feel comfortable participating in English masses or ministries. These Spanish-speaking ministries and services also made some African Americans uncomfortable and had the effect of deterring them from participating with Latinos.

The end result is that Latinos and African Americans avoided each other in most daily interactions at the church; even though they operated within the same physical space, their social space was dictated by other factors. Thus, avoidance rather than conflict was the dominant form of social interaction at the church.

Symbolic Differences

As the ethnic makeup of the church has changed with the influx of Latino immigrants, so has the visual imagery and symbolism in the church and around its grounds. The new Catholic symbols that Latinos value and revere are received with mixed feelings among African Americans. Similarly, Latinos often view the symbols held in high esteem among African Americans with reservation. These contrasting views about which symbols should reflect the parish are also a trigger of interracial conflict. In this section, I show how the parish devised a deliberate strategy to address these differences. More importantly, the parish used these contrasting symbols as a means to promote religious and symbolic interracial unity among Latinos and African American parishioners.

Prior to large-scale immigration into South LA where St. Joseph's is located, the church—with the exception of the clergy—was primarily African American. Today, one can see remnants of the church's old identity in the hall of the main building where worship services are regularly held. Several pictures and symbols of African Catholics appear on the walls of various parts of the church. For example, images of St. Peter Claver are located inside of the church hall and on enormous wall in the back of the church parking lot.

St. Peter Claver is significant for several reasons. First, he is considered the patron saint of African slaves. Claver is known for his service as a Catholic priest, and for declaring that he was "the slave of the black slaves forever" during the 17th century. The image is important because Claver represents a just Catholic who defended those with African ancestry and who respected their plight and history.

The image is also significant because it reflects the history of African Americans who live in South LA. It is no coincidence that many African Americans in Los Angeles are Catholic, since many migrated from Louisiana, where the French influence shaped their religious experience. The symbolism of St. Peter Claver has also shaped the African American ministries at the parish. One of the most active African Americans ministries with the largest number of members, the Knights of St. Peter Claver, borrows its name from him.

In addition, the music in the English masses is unmistakably in the genre of gospel music, found in many other African American churches but uncommon in typical Catholic churches. Most of the choir during the English masses is African American, including its director. The pictures and music are carryovers from the church's predominantly African American past.

Because the number of Latino parishioners has increased, new symbols have emerged at the church; they supplement, and, to some, challenge the traditional African American Catholic imagery. These new symbols are central to a form of Mexican or Latino Catholicism. One crucial symbol for Latino Catholics is the Virgin of Guadalupe.

Before the early 1980s, the Virgin of Guadalupe was not a central figure of the church. As the ethnic population of the church began to change, the Virgin gradually became the most important religious symbol of St. Peter's. Images of the Virgin of Guadalupe can be found everywhere. In front of the church, a large statue of the Virgin is a fixture. Inside the hall, a large flag with the image of the Virgin is on permanent display. Near an inside altar, where candles can be lit, parishioners often pray to a statue of the Virgin. In back of the church, on the wall of the parking lot, is painted a large picture of the Virgin of Guadalupe—the largest image on the parish grounds.

A comment by Alicia, a Latina in her late 30s, and an employee at St. Joseph's for several years, illustrates the significance of the Virgin. I asked her why she prays to the Virgin and not to other saints. She explained:

> I don't know, I have been praying to her since I was very little in Mexico. You just grow up praying to her and don't really question why you do this. I pray to her for favors and she usually helps me out. I keep praying to her because she always helps me.
>
> Mexicans relate to her because she appeared to someone who is *moreno* [dark], and she is also *morena*. So it probably makes it easier for people to relate. She also appeared to someone who was poor in Mexico. You know December 12th, which is the day of Our Lady de Guadalupe, is really big at St. Joseph's. Last year it was on a weekday, and they had

the mass in the morning at 5:30 or 6:00 a.m., before people went to work. Many people showed up. They played and sang *mañanitas*, and brought flowers to our Lady during the ceremony. Father Mike, you know, says that December 12th is actually a bigger deal for parishioners as compared to Christmas, so it is a huge deal. He says more people get involved and participate at the church in the festivities of Our Lady than any other event.

I asked Alicia if Central Americans also participate and connect with the Virgin. She told me they do participate almost as much as Mexicans, but not quite with the same passion.

Alicia's comments are significant for several reasons. First, it is clear that the Virgin is the most dominant religious figure for Latino parishioners. The ubiquity of her images and the festivals celebrated in her honor reflect this. Equally important, however, is the symbolic significance of her image. Alicia's comments illustrate that the Virgin is similar to Latinos in her appearance: being dark skinned. Also, she mentions that the Virgin appeared to a poor person. These factors communicate to Latinos that the Virgin is accessible to people like them: those who are dark skinned and poor. More importantly, the Virgin helps those who suffer marginalization and poverty.

In my conversations with Father Mike, he echoed these sentiments, and his comments shed light on these aspects of the Virgin:

> From my many years here at the church, I can tell you she is popular and they relate to the Virgin because she appeared to a poor Mexican, Juan Diego. As you know, Cid, many of the Mexican immigrants who live here in South Central are some of the poorest people in all of Los Angeles. Also, the form in which the Virgin appeared resonates with the people. The Virgin appeared the way Mexicans look, you know what I mean, right? She is brown just like them. It's fascinating here at the church. People will not come to mass or participate in church activities on Christmas Day, but they will come to mass on December 12th, which is the day of Our Lady, the Virgin [of] Guadalupe.
>
> They come here with this devotion to the Virgin. It's a very powerful devotion. I also think she represents, on a more general level of suffering, being Mexican and goodness. You know, Cid, the parishioners

don't know themselves. That's why they relate to her. I see
mother and I believe the parishioners do as well. They se
protector.

The emergence of Mexican Catholic symbols, such as the Virgin, was
a potential source of conflict among Latinos and African Americans.
The new symbols challenged the traditional African American symbolism at the parish. Many African Americans viewed these symbols as
foreign, alien objects.

Father Mike and I discussed this matter one afternoon, and, as we
walked the church grounds, we were fortunate to run into a long-time
African American parishioner in her early 40s. Father Mike greeted
her and stated, "Go ahead. Tell Cid what you think about the Virgen
de Guadalupe. Be honest now. There is no right or wrong answer." She
responded as follows:

> Honestly, that is a foreign thing to me. I don't identify with that object
> at all. I was brought up in Catholic school not to worship foreign objects
> because they are a form of idolatry. I am not saying that's what it is, but
> it kind of is.

These differences over symbols and their significance to the church's
identity were a constant potential source of conflict. For African Americans, the Virgin of Guadalupe was considered a foreign entity who was
difficult to identify with. She was insignificant in their understanding of
Catholicism. Similarly, Latinos viewed many African American images
as foreign, and not relevant to their experience as Catholics. Members
of this group showed no devotion to those symbols that were central to
African Americans.

Creating Symbolic and Religious Identity: Bridging Avoidance

How was the parish able to overcome the potential for interracial conflict that arose from the differing views over symbolic imagery? I suggest
that the church utilized the contrasting symbols revered by Latinos
and African Americans to create a larger *common narrative framework*
that goes beyond racial identities.[1] This approach helped the church

minimize conflict to a level that was manageable for parishioners, and it allowed St. Joseph's to thrive.

Drawing on the work of Mario Small (2007), I utilize the concept of narrative framework as a lens through which groups make sense of the world. Narrative-related frames consist of ongoing stories, including history and personal experiences. These frames accomplish two things. First, they organize, simplify, and condense perceptions of the world, so that people can selectively punctuate and encode objects, situations, events, and experiences within their environments. Secondly, they shape the way individuals and groups understand their lives as narratives/stories with ongoing and complex plots. Thus, narrative frames become lenses for seeing the world and experiencing others. In what follows, I outline how the parish produced a socially inclusive setting that fostered a common narrative framework.

It is easy to conclude that interracial differences can be addressed by simply diversifying the symbols and imagery of a social setting or urban landscape. But research by urban architects (see, e.g., Hayden, 1995) suggests that acknowledging diversity is not enough to minimize ethnic conflict and maintain a level of cooperativeness—in some cases, it can aggravate interracial tensions. An example of how diversifying symbolic images may backfire can be seen in South LA high schools that have tried this approach. In many high schools throughout the area, conflicts have erupted between Latinos and African Americans on the days schools hold events celebrating Martin Luther King or Cesar Chavez. According to local newspapers, the conflicts were rooted in one or another group's sense that they were being left out or forced to celebrate a cultural event they did not identify with. Why was the outcome different at St. Joseph's? The key difference is that the church was able to enhance social meaning that moved beyond multiple, conflicting ethnic identities.

There were several strategies that St. Joseph's used to produce a socially inclusive setting, which became the basis for a common symbolic framework. First, church officials had a clear understanding that the public space of the church, both inside and outside the parish, was central to creating inclusive membership and cultural belonging.

In June 2000, Father Mike commissioned a mural behind the church that chronicled the lives of parishioners and recognized the political and religious history of each group. In an interview with the *Los Angeles Times*, Father Mike explained his motivation: "The mural is a sign of hope to our community. It is a reminder of our past, and it's the hope that we can bring many groups into the church; we can come together in our diversity" (Garrison, 2000).

These comments reveal that there was a deliberate attempt to utilize public space in a way that created unity by recognizing diversity. On the mural, various types of symbolic images that promote inclusion can be found. There are images of political figures such as Cesar Chavez and Martin Luther King Jr.; images of religious figures such as Peter Claver and the Virgin of Guadalupe; and images of long-time parishioners such as Mary Dudley, who was a church member for over 70 years.

St. Joseph's recognizes the importance of this endeavor and regularly adds new images to the mural, mostly long-time African Americans and Latino parishioners, and clergy who have passed away. Thus, the mural acts as a permanent storehouse of social, religious, political, and historical memories. And the images do even more—representing an attempt to integrate the experiences of parishioners with various religious, social, and political symbols into one distinct Catholic narrative, thus enhancing the social meaning of this public space. It is worth noting that within the mural, the church fused these many diverse experiences into one coherent narrative, both literally and figuratively. By placing the various types of symbols next to each other, the implied message is that all are part of the sacred, and all are on the same spiritual plain.

The church, therefore, through its use of symbolic imagery, nurtured the emergence of a shared narrative with a distinct structure with several dimensions. First, the church selected images that highlight commonalities and similarities rather than differences. For example, the images of Martin Luther King Jr. and Cesar Chavez represent a common theme that both groups strongly identify with, given their histories of discrimination and marginalization: equality and justice. Or, similarly, the image of Mary Dudley represents the theme of service, duty, and dedication to the parish—a theme revered by both groups, not just African Americans.

Second, the narrative structure implicitly communicates to African Americans and Latinos that they are viewed as equals in the eyes of the church. St. Joseph's officials made it a point to equally represent symbols considered significant to each group. Equal representation of symbols throughout the parish helps assuage the idea among African Americans that Latinos "were taking over." During my fieldwork, I found this sentiment to be very common. Contrary to media reports, this did not inevitably lead to conflict between Latinos and African Americans. Rather, those institutions that were able to respond to this sentiment, such as St. Joseph's, were able to minimize conflict among residents.

Other community institutions in South LA, such as the nonprofit Community Coalition, understood the importance of equal representation in the symbols and the ideas considered significant to both Latinos and African Americans. They realized that when one group feels dominated by the other, which could come in the form of numeric dominance, the potential for conflict could emerge. Community Coalition devised a strategy of mutual recognition as a means to achieve black and brown unity.

Church officials at St. Joseph's used a similar approach to the one used by Community Coalition. Given that Latinos comprised over 70 percent of the parish, the perception of ethnic dominance was ever present. Having an equal number of African American symbols in St. Joseph's communicates that although African Americans may be numerically fewer than Latinos, they are viewed as equally important.

Equal recognition of each group is also important because it imparts to parishioners the idea: "we accept you for who you are." The ubiquitous display of images considered significant to each group was a reaffirmation of each group's value. The symbols communicate to the Latino and African American parishioners the message: "your history matters and your community members matter."

A third theme woven into the narrative at the parish, which helps bridge differences between both groups, is the message that God serves those who are marginalized and are poor via intermediary religious figures, such as St. Peter Claver and the Virgin of Guadalupe. Recall the earlier comments of Alicia and Father Mike. Both reaffirmed the idea that the Virgin resonates with Latinos because she is accessible to people like them: those who are dark skinned and poor. She helps those who suffer marginalization. The image and message of Claver is strikingly similar. Claver declared himself to be dedicated in service as "the slave of slaves." Essentially this is the same message communicated by the Virgin, namely, to serve those who are marginalized.

Furthermore, the Virgin of Guadalupe and St. Peter Claver imbue Latino and African American parishioners with the idea that the spiritual is accessible to both groups in distinctive ways. How these symbolic figures appear in the original narrative is significant. Both the Virgin and Claver appeared to dark-skinned individuals: slaves for African Americans and a poor dark Indian for Mexicans. This suggests that although both groups may be marginalized by the wider society, they have equal access to the spiritual world at the parish.

More importantly, by emphasizing the same message through contrasting symbolic imagery, St. Joseph's created a narrative that had broad appeal to both groups.

A final theme woven into the narrative is the idea that the church protects parishioners. St. Peter Claver represents a saint who does more than serve African slaves; he symbolizes a figure who protects. In the mural at the parish, the imagery illustrates Claver shielding slaves with a cross in hand, as if he is protecting them from threatening forces.

It is likely that St. Joseph's, prior to large-scale Latino immigration, played the role of a sanctuary from violence and oppression for African Americans who settled in South LA. This idea, of course, is beyond the scope of this study; however, the fact that the parish was the only structure in the area that withstood damage during the Watts Riots is testimony to its special status among African Americans. St. Joseph's was recognized then as a social space that provided refuge for African Americans, and thus was not to be disturbed. This recognition has continued over the years.

The institutional presence of the Archdiocese of Los Angeles and St. Joseph's Parish during the 1960s provides a clue about the legacy of the church's social role. During the mid-1960s, the archdiocese maintained a noticeable presence in the area by providing social services. According to *The Tidings* Catholic newsletter, there were three Catholic Youth Organizations (CYO) and one Catholic Welfare Bureau (CWB) district, child care centers, and a residence that provided temporary shelter to needy women (*The Tidings*, August 2, 1965).

During and after the Watts Riots, these organizations played a key role in helping residents of the area. The Catholic Welfare Bureau and Catholic Youth Organizations organized committees in public housing to curb the violence during the riots. They also helped organize committees in public housing to provide food and clothing to those affected by the crisis. The intervention and organizing by the church reflects its exceptional status among African Americans as helping and protecting the poor from violence.

Consistent with the image of St. Peter Claver, the Virgin of Guadalupe also represents the theme of protector. As the previous section outlined, she is a motherlike figure who answers prayers when one is in need. Like a good mother, the Virgin is a figure who cares for loved ones and ensures they are safe from hostile forces.

In the previous section, I outlined how the parish protects Latino immigrants from the threat of state violence, via ICE, and from the potential threat of gangs. Thus, the theme communicated by the Virgin of Guadalupe does not merely exist at the symbolic level, but reflects an explicit institutional strategy used by the church to protect immigrants.

Taken in its totality, the parish enhanced social meaning through its use of public symbols and imagery to convey certain key themes: that African Americans and Latinos are viewed equally in the eyes of the church; that they are protected; that they have access to the divine even though they are dark skinned and poor. By expanding social meanings, the church helped forge a narrative framework that allowed Latinos and African Americans to interpret their roles and experiences at the parish as one community. More importantly, this shared framework played a key role in moving both groups beyond their racial identities.

All of these themes helped to overcome the differences between the two groups, and to create an environment that was mutually manageable. In many instances, African Americans and Latinos worked separately in their own ministries. However, rarely was there any noticeable interracial conflict between them.

The Paradox of Avoidance

A third potential source of interracial conflict was centered on two separate but interrelated issues. First, there was a tendency for Latinos and African Americans to fall back into racial cliques. When confronted with a situation that seemed uncomfortable, the safest response was to find comfort in sameness—to seek out people of the same race who spoke the same language. Secondly, the potential for interracial conflict could be exacerbated when African Americans or Latinos felt that they were being forced to interact with one another. In response to these potential sources of conflict, the parish developed a strategy: avoidance. The use of this term has a special meaning within the context of the parish. In this section, I spell out the strategy St. Joseph's used to mitigate the potential for interracial conflict.

Like many settings where people feel uncomfortable around people who are different than they, the easiest thing to do is to stick with those who are the same. The problem with this approach is that when people practice avoidance over time, it can create deep divisions between groups. Avoiding others who were different, based on race, was the most dominant form of social interaction throughout South LA. During my year of fieldwork, and in follow-ups over the years, there was a consistent pattern of interracial relations in South LA: Young children who were African American or Latino could occasionally be seen playing together. This was not uncommon at all. Interracial contact decreased by middle school, although it was still common. At the high school level, however, interracial relationships were almost nonexistent. Adults were even less likely to interact. Clearly, the socialization of race was constructed, and it became more significant as South LA residents matured.

A similar pattern could be seen at St. Joseph's, but there was a noticeable difference and basis for the separation, as my observations and conversations with parishioners after Sunday mass revealed:

> After morning English mass, I get in line in the building where social activities are held. I stand in line with mostly African American parishioners. I pay for my meal and sit at a table with parishioners whom I met playing bingo at the church. I notice that the room is almost exclusively filled with African Americans. There are no Latinos present, even though they can be found all over the parish grounds, participating in other ministries.
>
> An African American altar boy sits next to me as the crowd starts to thin out. I ask the altar boy why there are no Latinos present.
>
> Altar boy: They don't like our food and they never come to our breakfasts. I guess they don't like being around African Americans.

To further explore the issue of group self-separation, I spoke with Latino parishioners. Like African Americans, Latinos also held breakfast fundraisers after mass for their various ministries. The following illustrates the interracial pattern at these events:

> I am urged by Father Mike and the entire congregation to speak with parishioners following the service. When mass ends, I stand in line and notice that only Latinos are present.
>
> I sit next to some parishioners whom I recognize. I glance around the room and there are no African Americans present.
>
> I ask Art, a Latino male in his late 20s, why there are no African Americans present. He states, "Blacks never come to these breakfasts. I guess they don't feel comfortable around Mexicans." Art continues, "It's really not cool, because, hey, they don't help raise money when they don't come. That's what we're trying to do by having these breakfasts."
>
> I tell him that African American parishioners tell me the same thing about Latinos. Art says, "I am not sure why this happens. I think it's the food. Mexicans don't go for sausage, pancakes, and eggs. That is an American breakfast. We want chorizo con huevos and tortillas. Maybe that's why we don't go to those breakfasts."

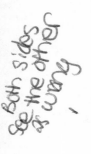

Both sides see the other as the problem

Another source of potential conflict arose when Latinos and African Americans perceived that the church was forcing them to integrate. Both groups would often withdraw from attending and participating in the church when they felt they were being forced to accept religious and cultural practices different from their own. Father Mike explained how this worked:

> I tell you what a trigger of conflict can be: African Americans often feel overwhelmed by all the Latinos and their activities at the church. There are so many of them during Ash Wednesday, when they celebrate the Virgin, Our Lady, and with all the baptisms. It is overwhelming to see all the Latinos.
>
> There were times when we tried to have bilingual masses with African Americans and Latinos, and it was a disaster. We had mariachis play and, oh boy, you should have seen it. The African Americans started looking at each other, and started to walk around the hall during

mass; they looked confused. They started to trickle out of the building little by little. They were overwhelmed! After that, we realized we should have asked the African Americans for their permission. We realized that we have to respect language, respect difference. That is how you get people involved.

These two examples illustrate the potential for interracial conflict, division, and, more importantly, how the loss of parishioners can occur. In response to these triggers of division, the church devised a strategy of avoidance.

While both of the triggers had the potential to undermine interracial relations, avoidance was less volatile than forced integration. Forcing the two groups to interact in church functions essentially brought their latent feelings and negative perceptions out into the open. For example, there was often disagreement between Latinos and African Americans about the interior decoration of the church. Also, during pastoral Council meetings, there was often competition between the two groups regarding the use of church facilities, such as which group would have access on what days.

In contrast, avoidance allowed both groups to be involved separately in the church. Avoidance, in the long run, was potentially divisive, but it was different from integration in two ways. First, with avoidance, conflict did not openly erupt, facilitating conditions in which the groups could tolerate one another. Second, avoidance provided parishioners from each group a social space where they felt comfortable. This was probably the most significant factor, because they were more likely to stay as members and not leave.

The parish leaders had a clear understanding of these interracial triggers, and devised what they believed to be the most practical strategy for dealing with the potential for interracial conflict. Father Mike explained it to me in the following way:

FATHER MIKE: We have to keep some things separate. We have to keep the masses separate; either Spanish or English, but not bilingual. By doing this, we are respecting language, respecting differences. That is how you get people involved.

CID: Aren't you separating people by doing that?

FATHER MIKE: You cannot force groups together. The same philosophy that we use for masses is what we use for ministries. Forced integration separates people. We must respect distinct cultures.

CID: So, this is kind of like avoidance?

FATHER MIKE: Avoidance helps to promote bringing people into the church.

CID: It seems like a paradox, because you are getting both groups into the church. But, because they are in different masses, etc., they're separate.

FATHER MIKE: It is a paradox, but we get them in the door. If you don't do this, they will feel alienated and leave the church. Forced unity is forced division. In the long run, what you do is fish them in, that is a start.

Notice that the strategy of avoidance consisted of several dimensions. Avoidance was perceived by the church leadership as a way of respecting the distinct language and culture of each group. Another dimension of avoidance was the idea that this approach could shape future relations. In the present, St. Joseph's leadership realized African Americans and Latinos were separated. However, they felt that over time this could change. According to the comments of the pastor, the first step toward improving relations was getting potential parishioners from both groups in the door, under the same roof, and into the same church. Father Mike captured this idea, stating, "If I can get people into the same room, that is an accomplishment. Getting people into the same church is the first barrier!"

This strategy was important since bringing Latinos and African Americans into the same social setting was not common, outside of St. Joseph's, in most parts of South LA. Although the two groups lived in many of the same neighborhoods, their interactions were limited. Creating a shared social space where both groups could participate in activities, a space that was not compulsory, such as public school, was a challenge for the church.

Another dimension of avoidance was to nurture cooperation between the two groups through the cultivation of leadership. Church officials believed that if racial groups felt comfortable and respected in their own social spaces, eventually leaders would emerge. These leaders, in turn, would do more for the church, devote more time, energy, and resources, and also mobilize more parishioners to participate regularly.

One key contribution of leaders was their ability to help attract and anchor parishioners. By working directly with respected leaders as intermediaries within the church, parishioners were more likely to develop strong attachments. As these attachments grew, leaders and other parishioners would, hopefully, see commonalities with other racial groups, and, therefore, be more likely to work cooperatively, and eventually integrate within the church. Father Mike made this point clear when he stated: "If the leadership feels respected they will do more for the church and bring more parishioners in. If you don't respect them, and force them to integrate, they will feel alienated and leave the church; eventually this approach helps bring them together."

Observations of St. Joseph's during the initial fieldwork, revealed that most church ministries were managed and guided by leaders who had developed strong ties to the church. Throughout my year of fieldwork, I noticed the same group of individuals making it their responsibility to manage the day-to-day affairs of these ministries. Their leadership had a strong influence on the parishioners.

St. Joseph's strategy appears to have been successful. One visible indicator of improved relations and better integration can be seen in the increasing multiracial makeup of masses and ministries. In English mass, for example, there is an increasing number of Latinos who attend services with African Americans. In various activities, such as the gospel choir, arguably one of the most important African American activities at the church, an increasing number of Latinos participate. While many ministries remain separate, there has been a gradual integration of the two groups in various social settings and ministries throughout the church.

The conventional understanding of avoidance involves separation, and a lack of deliberate social interaction. The concept of avoidance as developed by St. Joseph's officials is distinctly different. In this setting, avoidance is viewed as a long-term strategy, incrementally leading to integration. Avoidance begins as a strategy to simply get Latinos and African Americans into the same building; then it helps them to develop attachments, and, finally, produces integration.

4

Faith Is the Opposite of Fear

The Catholic Church as Alternative Governance

I have argued that the Catholic Church can act as an alternative social space that minimizes interracial conflict and provides a safety zone for residents against threats from gangs and the state. I have emphasized that this space is exceptional in that it represents a third type of social control distinct from the code of the street and the rule of law of the state.

In this chapter, I flesh out the description of this third type of informal social control by outlining two strategies utilized to confront and minimize violence in South LA. Both involve a form of avoidance: street wisdom and the formation of institutional alliances with intralocal parties.

Urban scholars have made two common assumptions about street wisdom and violence. First, they view the streets as the source of a code for dealing with conflict (Anderson, 1999). While Omar McRoberts (2004) has found that churches also proffer their own version of street wisdom concerning how to cope with violence, this observation has received little attention from urban and criminological scholars.

A second assumption is that retaliation is the primary response to conflict. Urban scholars (Anderson, 1999; Jacobs and Wright, 2006) have focused on retaliation as the primary means by which poor urban youths respond to conflict, where one's reputation is paramount. Recently, scholars have challenged this view and have begun to reconsider retaliation. Garot (2009) found that emotions, social networks, and ambivalence can all act as structural inhibitors to violence, and thereby lessen the likelihood of retaliation.

Building on this strain of thought, which challenges the set of assumptions associated with the code of the street, I suggest that St. Joseph's is able to manage violence through two primary strategies. First, the parish proffers its own version of street wisdom. I build on the idea that retaliation is not the only response utilized by poor urban residents when confronted with conflict. In contrast to other works that have addressed these themes, I emphasize the role of narrative in providing a framework to respond to violence—one that does not involve retaliation as a first response to conflict.

Secondly, St. Joseph's utilizes routine institutional practices and tactics designed to manage and minimize violence. Previous studies that have reconsidered retaliation (e.g., Garot, 2009) have not fully explored the role of institutions in managing violence, and, instead, have focused on the role of emotions and social ties.

Intra-parish Response to Violence: Confronting Conflict through Narrative

In what follows, I illustrate a version of street wisdom proffered at St. Joseph's. Key to this street wisdom is what I refer to as a narrative framework, which provides strategies and insights for confronting conflict and violence.

During 2003–2004, when I conducted intensive participant observation fieldwork at St. Joseph's, I gained access to youths by volunteering as a substitute instructor for confirmation classes at the parish, a form of religious instruction for 16- to 18-year-olds. Confirmation classes were regularly held in the Catholic elementary school that stands behind the main church structure. Almost 200 young people attended the classes every Wednesday evening during the fall and spring semesters. Altogether, these classes lasted about nine months.

The following observations from the classes provide a clue about the structure of the narrative framework and how it guides youths in confronting violence:

> On a Wednesday afternoon, I sit in the back of the classroom where the confirmation class occurs. The class is completely Latino, mostly Mexicans, a few El Salvadorans, and one youth who is mixed race. His mother is Mexican and his father is African American. I sit in the back taking notes. Throughout the class, the youth talk about many different themes. Some themes, however, continue to resurface repeatedly among the youth. In particular, neighborhood violence comes up frequently.

The instructor talks to the class about gang violence. A youth raises his hand and asks, "When is it ok to kill someone?" The instructor responds, "What do you guys think?" The class debates the issue for a long time and considers what sort of punishment they will receive from God. After awhile, the instructor intervenes and says, "Where is the love?" He stresses the point that people have to learn to open their hearts and forgive; otherwise they will always live in fear.

At another afternoon confirmation class, similar themes of neighborhood violence and gangs resurfaced. The following is a description of the interaction between the instructor and the students.

VICENTE: These things [fear and guilt] affect our relations with other people. What can you replace fear with?

LATINA 1: Happiness.

VICENTE: What is the opposite of fear?

The class looks puzzled and listens attentively.

VICENTE: Faith is the opposite of fear. What is the opposite of guilt?

The class remains silent.

VICENTE: Trust is the opposite. The first time I moved into South Central, guess what happened?

LATINO 1: You got jacked!

LATINO 2: You got a shotgun?

VICENTE: I put bars on all the windows. Someone knocked on my door. There was no curtain, and I was scared.

LATINO 1: [Points his finger like a gun and makes a "click" sound as if pulling a gun trigger.]

The class laughs, though many do not respond to the sounds made by the boy.

VICENTE: Someone knocked on my door and said that their name was Jerry. I freaked out and turned out the lights. Later that evening someone from Home Depot called named Jerry, who was supposed to do some work at my house. I didn't have trust. I had to learn to trust my neighbors. They are great and take my trash can out for me when I forget. How do you increase faith?

LATINA 1: Find someone. A friend, family member?

VICENTE: Is it easy to trust?

LATINA 2: No. Sometimes we are judged when we do.

VICENTE: Exactly. They will judge. How many people feel they are the only ones with problems? No . . . Yes? Celia hit it right on the head. You have to learn to trust someone. How do you learn to trust God? There is a drive-by shooting. How do you regain it?

Some Latino students make noises that sound like gunshots.

LATINA 2 : Can you find something positive in the tragedy?

VICENTE: Do you cherish what you took for granted?

The conversation about trusting God continues. A talkative Latina interjects.

→PROBLEMATIC

LATINA 3: My mom had cancer. I felt bad. Finally, I just accepted it. You learn to appreciate everything you have.

Some listen. Others chatter in both English and Spanish, or some combination of the two. The conversation between students continues with occasional joking.

VICENTE: Now that you are aware of fear and guilt, how would relations look like with other people? Remember the mind is there to serve the heart. What about gang violence?

LATINO 2: Give the MLK speech. ["I Have a Dream"]

VICENTE: If you commit a sin, you don't tell God. If you do something good, you tell everyone.

LATINO 2: Not if someone does something on the street. Then, you get props.

This confirmation class scene, a typical one, paints a picture of the street wisdom that the church imbued parishioners with. The narrative illustrates two themes that stand in stark contrast to the code of the street.

First, the message to the youth was plain and simple: conti... others, and God, even when confronted with violence. Given the i... level of violence in the area, it was common for residents to be suspicious and distrustful of the intentions of others in South LA. Overcoming distrust required diligence on the part of the parish.

The message of trust, as promulgated by the church, stands in direct contrast to the code of the street, which is premised upon distrust. According to the code of the street, distrust dominates relations among the poor. For example, poor residents are viewed as potential predators and, therefore, should not be trusted. Similarly, law enforcement is viewed with mistrust and is seen as the enemy.

Both of these tenets of the code of the street motivate retaliation. The line of thinking is as follows: other people can't be trusted, and neither can law enforcement; therefore, one must rely on self-help and retaliation to resolve disputes. The observations at St. Joseph's suggest that trust can be nurtured. More importantly, if there are social spaces that reinforce the message of trust, then, by default, retaliation is less likely to emerge.

A second theme that emerges from the narrative is the conditions under which violence and homicide are deemed acceptable. Violence, as a response to conflict, was often discussed among youths. This is evidenced in the observations of the youths when they grappled with the following question: when is it okay to kill? The message from the parish was that an alternative to homicide is forgiveness. Thus, a second key element that emerges in the narrative developed at the parish is to avoid violence, and, instead, forgive others rather than retaliate.

The notion of forgiveness stands in stark contrast to the common response to conflict according to the code of the street: retaliation. The code's framework provides little or no alternative strategy to conflict besides violence. Yet the observations at St. Joseph's illustrate that alternatives do exist and do promote a reconsideration of retaliation. The observations demonstrate that the narrative rooted in the parish coexists tensely with the code of the street. The comments from the youths consistently demonstrate that props and street respect are common strategies for addressing conflict.

A fourth important element of the narrative found at St. Joseph's revolves around the idea of hope. Hope exists on two levels at the parish:

the material mundane and the spiritual afterlife.[1] My interaction with Father John and the parishioners illustrates the significance of hope:

> The pastor of the church and I walk through the church grounds one afternoon. A parishioner—a Mexican woman in her early thirties along with her child—greets Father John. He asks, "Are you afraid to die, senora?" The response: "No, father, I am not afraid to die, as long as I have the Lord."
>
> The scenario repeats itself, over and over, with Father John asking one parishioner after another if they are afraid to die. He asks Latino males and females of different ages. Without hesitation, they respond by reaffirming the idea that they do not fear dying.

These comments help to clarify the significance of hope as it relates to the narrative promoted by the church. They show that even when confronted with death, there is no fear because of how the parishioners believe they will be treated in the afterlife. Implicitly, there is comfort in knowing that the soul will be cared for, and will be in good hands, after death. This suggests that parishioners are able to maintain a hopeful outlook about their existence—even after life is over.

Given the high levels of violence and homicide in South LA, this framework is useful for carrying on with the daily demands of neighborhood life by not allowing fear to impede with these goals. Minimizing fear is thus partly motivated by faith in a higher power. One afternoon, the church held a dinner at which parishioners from South LA and an affluent Manhattan Beach parish from Orange County came together. Outside the church, across the street, loud automatic gunfire could be heard. Immediately, all of the attendees froze. Within seconds, the Latino parishioners went back to their conversing and eating, while those from the affluent Manhattan Beach parish were noticeably shaken up— it took several moments before they went back to talking and eating.

The comments quoted above from the confirmation class further show how the message of hope operates. By emphasizing the importance of reevaluating things such as family members and relationships, and not taking them for granted, parishioners are able to maintain a healthy positive outlook, despite the tragedy and violence endemic to the area.

Finally, parishioners understand that to receive protection in the afterlife, and in the physical world, they must uphold some of the precepts and teachings of the Church. This acts as a motivation to keep parishioners from falling into fatalism or nihilism. As the interaction between the students and instructor show, there are also consequences that one may suffer for "killing" someone else.

The centrality of hope as a constituent element of the alternative form of street wisdom preferred by the Church stands in stark contrast to the code of the street. In the code of the street, fatalism enables inner-city youths to minimize fear and pursue violent retaliation. For example, according to Jacobs and Wright (2006), young people are aware of the consequences of retaliation, yet are able to overcome the fear of payback through fatalism, which they believe to be endemic among the urban poor. Fatalism, as promoted by the code of the street, is the belief that things are beyond one's control and that all is lost. Once this view is embraced, nothing matters, including fear of retaliation.

In contrast, the form of street wisdom illustrated in this study involves a message of resilient hope that was constantly reinforced and imbued to young people and adults alike. It was commonly found not only in youth courses, or in mass, but was prevalent everywhere at the parish. Hope, like fatalism, provides a means of confronting fear. However, when hope is the primary means of confronting fear, it provides an alternative to retaliation through violence. The key difference, when hope is the source of overcoming fear, is that violence is minimized.

The alternative form of street wisdom promoted at St. Joseph's was also reinforced through a variety of different sources. Another strategy used to reinforce the message of nonviolence involved regularly bringing guest speakers to the parish to speak to children and youths about the dangers of violence and gangs. For example, on one occasion a former gang member, who was paralyzed during a gang-related shooting, spoke to 50 elementary school children about his experiences. He described his life in the gang, how he was shot, and what his life is like in a wheelchair, paralyzed. Young people in the parish could relate to these real-life stories and were often mesmerized by such speakers.

The various dimensions of street wisdom illustrated in this section can be viewed as an attempt to create a moral framework, which helps the poor residents of the parish manage potential conflict. This moral framework takes on a central role, given the limitations of the formal law. The pastor explained this as follows:

CID: It must be difficult to get parishioners to follow these ideas.

FATHER JOHN: Well, the Latinos, they are afraid to go to the police because many are not citizens and are afraid of what will happen to them. African Americans also have distrust of the law because of the history of discrimination.

CID: There is also a big informal economy. Doesn't that make it difficult for people to go to law enforcement for conflicts and problems?

FATHER JOHN: Many people here do not go to the police or government when they have problems. And, I can't make them follow the rules or laws. Forget about rules! I try to teach them what is right or wrong. The church becomes a moral compass to help them think about what is right or wrong. I want them to develop a conscience with a good voice and a bad voice.

The pastor suggests that the church makes a concerted effort to nurture a moral narrative framework that acts as an alternative to the formal legal system. This framework is rooted not in formal law, but in a set of deeper religious and moral principles. Given the limitations of the rules of the formal legal system, the narrative developed by the parish helps to fill the void.

During a follow-up interview several years later, I spoke with one of the new priests at the parish, Father Joe, regarding the church's alternative moral narrative. He stated,

> We have a clear message to counter the street culture and violence. We have different teachings about the options they have when they deal with conflict; how to interpret events, such as tragedy, and how to deal with their desires. A lot of times they want material things the fast way. We have to be vigilant, because they are always receiving a different message from the streets.

These comments reveal a lucid awareness of the need to counter the message of the streets. This factor has largely been overlooked in previous research. Urban scholars have attempted to show that social order exists in poor urban areas based on a code of the street, but they have failed to note how other forms of narratives can coexist. Social order, in poor urban areas, can also be anchored in moral frameworks that discourage violence rather than promote it.

Institutional Response to Violence through Practice and Tactics

Several strategies were utilized by St. Joseph's to minimize its parishioners' exposure to the risk of violence. In this section, I focus on two different sets of such strategies—first, those utilized by the church and its parishioners; second, those involving inter-institutional relations with local neighborhood organizations.

One strategy utilized by the church was for the priests to walk some of the meanest streets in South LA. This was intended to show that the parish had a presence in the area and that it challenged the rules of the street in the surrounding neighborhoods. As part of his routine, Father John, and the other priests, would regularly walk through public areas where most parishioners felt intimidated, fearing that they could be victimized by gangs or other predators. Father Joe explained to me:

> I started doing something Father John started, which is to walk where our parishioners have to walk. Our parishioners live in intimidation and fear. They can't allow their kids to play outside freely. They are indoors a lot, with all these bars on the windows, many times crossing paths with the young black gangs, sometimes Hispanic, but mostly black gangs. They feel like they are exercising intimidation on them, as if they are trespassing, telling them this is not their place.
>
> I make a simple statement by going out there and by walking freely through public housing; we are saying this is the proper place people should be able to walk freely; this is your neighborhood, too. When our parishioners look through their doors and windows, and see us walking, they are happy to say hello to us. We are trying to reintroduce that this is a neighborhood, this is a place where families live, and you should have a right to feel safe. And, by doing that, also saying, implicitly to gang members, we know what you're about, but we know what our people have a right to. We are here, too; you want to be a presence, well, we have a presence, too. They know that we are in the game; we are in the mix, too. It's a gesture of solidarity with the people, too, where they feel they don't have much of a voice, especially when they are undocumented.
>
> We won't be intimidated. Because the main source of their force is their guns, they [gangs] are standing on the shoulders of a reputation of violence and intimidation that doesn't need to be exercised. It's an unspo-

ken whisper that is haunting the people. Us going out there, like when we walk the big public housing areas, I see people and groups who are evidently gang bangers. I go up to them and say hello. They are reading it clearly, thinking he's not crossing the street, he's not intimidated. I am doing it for the people. I am letting those guys know it.

One of the results of this is that young Hispanics say, we're not going to put up with this anymore, and they end up doing the same thing as blacks. They form their own gangs, for protection, for respect.

These comments illustrate the way in which the priests' presence disrupted the expected norms of interaction between gangs and residents, many of whom are parishioners. As Father Joe suggests, many areas of South LA are controlled by gangs through force and intimidation. By walking through these places, such as public housing, the priests challenged the terms of the social order of the gangs. They did this by confronting gang members, and by walking freely through areas usually considered restricted.

These regular walks through public housing not only disrupted the rule of intimidation and fear by gangs, but also symbolically weakened the domination of gangs in these areas. This is not a new idea. A century ago, Max Weber argued that types of domination and authority are the result of belief. In this particular case, the type of domination used by gangs is rooted in violence and intimidation. By explicitly and publicly breaking their rules, the priests challenged the gangs' domination. As Father Joe stated, "[W]e are in the game; we are in the mix, too." By challenging the belief system of the gangs, St. Joseph's creates a space for residents to entertain alternatives to a social order predicated on violence and intimidation.

The act of freely walking through these areas should not be underestimated. According to the clergy at the church and neighborhood residents interviewed in public housing, there was a perception that the police and other law enforcement feared traveling into these neighborhoods. During my fieldwork, it was common knowledge among residents that LAPD never traveled into public housing without a minimum of four patrol cars. Given the makeup of some neighborhoods, police stated that they could easily become cornered, and, thus, vulnerable to gangs and other potential predators. Father John explained to me, "If the police are scared of people in South LA, what kind of message does that send to people who live there?" A new priest at the parish gave his view about what parishioners experience and express to him regarding the area:

> They feel completely unprotected living there. The gangs have guns; they [residents] have nothing. Nobody can help them, not even the police. They are defenseless.

The priests, however, were able to walk through these areas, and not because they were simply brazen individuals. The reputation of the Church played a major factor in giving a pass to the priests. Father Guapo gave his account of this:

> The gangs control many areas. Most people have to get permission to go through these areas; politicians have to negotiate with gangs to have programs. The elected leaders in large housing projects often have to negotiate to set up programs. You know one of them, Cid.
> We don't have to negotiate with gangs. Every year we have Los Pasadas in the largest public housing project. Our reputation gives us a pass. The gangs, and everyone, know we are there to help. It's in their interest to leave us alone. Plus, I think gangs are superstitious; they don't want problems with God. We have been in the area for almost 100 years now. We are the oldest institution in the area and have built up a reputation for a long time.

probs True

These comments illustrate the fact that at the same time that St. Joseph's challenges the violent social order of gangs, the church is also recognized as a reputable institution in its own right. Having served many area residents over the years, and having developed relations even with those who were not parishioners, St. Joseph's developed a reputation that grants it special status.

A second institutional strategy utilized by the church was to actively partner with local neighborhood institutions to manage violence—perhaps the most significant example was the Gang Task Force (GTF). The parish's relationship with the GTF provided a window into how St. Joseph's managed violence and risk through a strategy that I refer to in general as "street-level politics."

At the close of 2005, the area surrounding St. Joseph's church experienced 18 gang-related shootings—seven ended in homicides. In response, the local councilperson began to assemble a gang task force with the help of the City of Los Angeles Human Relations Commission (HRC).[2] A former HRC representative gave his perspective on the origins of the GTF:

> The councilperson needed help. The community was coming down on her after all the shootings, and wanted something to be done. She called HRC to help assemble the GTF, so we facilitated some meetings. Luckily, at the time, the captain of the LAPD Southeast Division was open to working with the community, something you didn't see before. We try to get LAPD, the sheriffs, school representatives, gang intervention workers, churches, and other community leaders together to address the violence.

The pastor of St. Joseph's decided that getting involved with the GTF was important for the sake of the church's parishioners for several reasons. First, the church was located in the heart of South LA, where violence was common and the homicide rate consistently ranked number one in the greater LA region. The area also had the highest concentration of gangs in Los Angeles County. This had a major impact on the lives of the parishioners, many of whom lived near the church.

Given the concentration of violence in the area, the parish's leadership concluded it was important for parishioners to get involved with the GTF. Father Guapo explained the reasons St. Joseph's joined the GTF:

> We started to meet every Thursday, after the killings and shootings in the housing developments. We met for a while to try to figure out what we were going to do. There was no clear direction at first. We finally decided our goal would be to protect youth from joining gangs. That is important for our church as well.

According to many of the priests, parishioners, and residents, most of the violence in South LA was gang-related. So the church's position was that if it could help prevent youths from joining gangs, that would go a long way toward minimizing violence in the area.

The parish priests felt that, overall, the GTF was successful in addressing the high level of violence, even though they had mixed feelings about its efficacy. Father John stated his view about the function of the GTF:

> I think it's really useful in some ways. Everyone from the community puts their stuff on the table. City, county, and nonprofits talk about the resources out there, the issues facing the community, and the concerns people have. Having the city officials out there makes the police police themselves.
>
> Having the police there helps, too. They give statistics and let people know about crime trends. Residents vent their feelings and express their needs. The main thing these meetings do is to keep the police and other city agencies accountable.
>
> Also, remember this: without LAPD reaching out, this could not have happened. In the past, LAPD considered themselves a gang. I know because I worked for LAPD awhile ago. And, their view was that we were going to go toe-to-toe with the gangs and that we could outdo them. There were a lot of scandals, you know, and then, after that, things began to change within the LAPD. They have increasingly become more community-oriented. The captain who was here made an effort to reach out and work cooperatively.

Father John's comments reveal the way in which the GTF promoted accountability of local law enforcement. Having an open forum allowed residents to express their needs to the LAPD, and, also, to express how they could work collaboratively to solve problems. Residents understood, better than anyone else could, how to identify local crime problems. Their insights helped LAPD, and other law enforcement agencies, carry out targeted solutions to these problems. Given the weekly GTF meetings, the police knew they would have to demonstrate progress to community members of the task force. Father John's comments also illustrate how neighborhood institutions were able to share resources and information to address neighborhood violence. In many instances, there were services or programs to combat gangs and violence, but most community members did not know of them.

Father Guapo was more adamant about the success of the task force:

FATHER GUAPO: Overall, I would say the GTF is a success. It deals
with crime in an informal way. We have been able to make connections. We learn from alliances with other organizations that are
going through the same thing we are [i.e., violence]. It helps to bring
organizations together.

I met a community leader who was African American, named Joe.
He provided jobs for youths in a nearby public housing project. We
got to know each other and started talking. We realized that many
services tended to serve either Latinos or African Americans, but
not both groups. We decided that we would begin to share resources. We would provide services for African American youths
from the housing developments, and he would try to help our
Latino parishioners.

Joe pledged to attend mass regularly at St. Joseph's. He felt out of
place at first, but was eventually embraced by the parishioners. After
awhile, when he didn't come to mass, people would ask, "Where is
that guy?" As Joe became more involved in the church, he was able
to form relationships, which helped him identify youths who could
benefit from the jobs program.

Hey, they got our kids jobs.

CID: How many?

FATHER GUAPO: A good number of Latino youths got jobs from him.

Father Guapo's comments suggest that the GTF provided more than
the shared resources that Father John described. By actively working
with the GTF, the parish was able to form social ties with other local
leaders and community institutions. These social ties, according to Father Guapo, allowed community institutions, such as St. Joseph's, to
forge alliances that helped to minimize violence in the area.

The social ties and alliances forged at the GTF represent the expan-
sion of a strategy I have previously referred to as street-level politics.
Prior to the formation of the GTF, the church already had strong inroads
into the local housing projects, because many of the church's parishioners resided in those areas. Also, the pastor had formed relationships
with many of the local leaders in public housing. Participating in the
GTF helped forge new relationships with other leaders, such as Joe, who
worked directly to combat the gang problem. The new relationships al-

lowed an exchange of resources and information, and helped [   ]
an ongoing relationship between the parish and the local public hous..
leadership, a relationship that has lasted for years.

Before the formation of the GTF by the local councilwoman, the pastor of St Joseph's had maintained strong ties with the staff from her field office, which was conveniently located right across the street. From the GTF's outset, St. Joseph's was thus in a strategic position to ensure that it had a seat at the table. Also, the prior relationship helped to ensure that the church would be treated with respect, and that its concerns would be taken seriously. Hence, St. Joseph's previous outreach efforts put it in an advantageous position to address gang violence when the opportunity presented itself.

The alliances forged through St. Joseph's participation in the GTF constitute what urban sociologists refer to as horizontal and vertical social ties. Horizontal social ties refer to connections between neighborhood institutions, which help to coordinate and focus existing resources to address neighborhood problems (Kornhauser, 1978; Patillo-McCoy, 1998). Vertical ties, in contrast, refer to connections between neighborhoods and extra-neighborhood institutions, which draw precious resources into the neighborhoods, while presenting neighborhood affairs to a broader public (Bursik and Gramsik, 1993).

St. Joseph's was able to broker both types of social ties. The example of Joe, from public housing, cooperating with St. Joseph's to share resources, information and partnerships, is an illustration of a horizontal social tie. Partnerships between St. Joseph's and city and county agencies, such as the LAPD and the Human Relations Commission, are examples of vertical social ties.

The combination of connections within and outside the community facilitated a communal approach to combating gangs and violence in the area. Although St. Joseph's could develop its own institutional strategies to manage violence, there was a clear understanding that, by building community social ties through street level politics, the church would more effectively address violence in the area.

The social ties developed outside the parish played a role in a third strategy utilized by the parish to manage violence: acting as an intermediary between residents and law enforcement. Through regular attendance and participation, the clergy of St. Joseph's was able to strengthen preexisting social ties with local law enforcement. Prior to its membership in the GTF, St. Joseph's had developed strong ties to the LAPD; Father Guapo had served as a chaplain for the department for over five years. In addition, Father John served a short time with the LAPD as an officer, before resigning to become a priest. These prior relationships helped to strengthen ties with the police department, once the parish made a commitment to participate in the GTF. Father Guapo explained:

> FATHER GUAPO: Because of our relationships with LAPD and with our parishioners, who are mostly Mexican and undocumented, we act as a middleman sometimes.
>
> Recently, LAPD came to us, and told us that a lot of Latino immigrants are robbed and burglarized by gangs and other street people. They do it because they know the Latinos will not go to the police because they are undocumented. The Latinos are afraid to go to the police. It happens a lot, too! So they [the police] came to us because they know there are many Latino immigrants here and they trust us. They wanted to start a program where people could call in anonymously. So, they wanted to know if they could put flyers in the church telling people about the program. I told them they could put the flyers here, and they could even put my name down as a contact person, if the parishioners didn't feel comfortable.
>
> Many times, people will come to me and tell me what happened to them, if they were victimized, you know. Sometimes if they won't contact the police, I will do it myself.
>
> CID: Are there other ways in which you help residents deal with the police?
>
> FATHER GUAPO: Yeah, sometimes I will try to answer questions that they might have about the way LAPD operates. For example, one couple saw a shooting and the body was out there for a while. They thought one of their neighbors was murdered and they thought the police didn't do anything. Well, I have a lot of contacts with LAPD, so I was able to find out what happened on their block. It turns out, the guy lived. If he was dead, there would have been a crime scene, but there wasn't. That's why they thought the police didn't do anything.

But, I think it helps them to have someone who can explain the way in which the police operate. They fear them so much, and this causes a lot of confusion and rumors to spread, and that makes things worse.

These comments reflect the way in which St. Joseph's is able to address issues of violence, by acting as a mediator between residents and law enforcement. Acting as a mediator, the parish is able to function as a link, providing information needed to solve incidents of violent crime. This type of interaction, between the parish and the residents, helps to create coordination with the police, and reduces the potential of violent crime. As Father Guapo stated, "They may be afraid to go to the police, but I am not afraid to act on their behalf."

Yet another strategy used by the church to manage violence was to reach out to members of the parish who were entangled in the web of violence, specifically those who were involved in gangs. Father Guapo explained:

There are some of our parishioners who are involved in gangs. They don't tell us they are involved in gangs, but their parents will occasionally come to us and let us know.

There was one fellow I remember. He used to come to church here when he was younger, and he stopped coming when he got older. His mother told me about him and how he was involved in a gang; I told her to have him call me. I was surprised because, shortly afterwards, he called. He came by the office and we talked. He started attending church. When I talk to him, I try to provide alternatives for him to think about for his life.

We want people who are involved in gangs to know the church is here for them. We try to teach them with a different model than violence. We want them to think about respect and love, instead. We also try to get them connected with some of the resources, like the jobs program, or other social services, we might have to help.

I don't think that guy is involved with the gang anymore. His mom told me he is working and is focusing on his family now. But, you know a lot of youth go in and out with their involvement with gangs. It's hard to break away for many of them.

During my fieldwork, St. Joseph's provided outreach to parishioners who had various levels of involvement with gangs. These ranged from youths who were becoming involved with gangs, those already actively involved in gangs, and still others who were transitioning out of gangs and trying to change their lives. Through its strong social ties with other organizations, such as the GTF, its antiviolence narrative message, and its status as a safety zone, the church was able to offer an alternative institutional setting to gang violence.

The parish's version of what I have called street-level politics is an ongoing strategy that emphasizes the importance of building and bridging social ties throughout the larger South LA community.

One church resource that was highly coveted by community members was St. Joseph's elementary and middle school. In an attempt to reach out to needy residents of the community, the parish, every year, made a concerted effort to recruit students and provide scholarships for African American and Latino children and teenagers from the nearby housing projects. The parish school was overwhelmingly the preference over public schools in the area, where violence and institutional neglect were common. St. Joseph's school, in contrast, was safe, and provided individualized, quality instruction.

St. Joseph's also helped build ties with the community by sponsoring festivals and celebrations. These events were held outside the church proper, in public housing or on the church grounds, and outside organizations' members, many of whom were not Catholic, were invited. Often the clergy would organize events, and foot the bill, for various celebrations in public housing, such as Los Posadas.[3] On one occasion, the church held a special day for mothers who had lost their children to gang violence. Hundreds of people of various denominations attended the event from the immediate area.

The parish also often doled out various goods, when available, for community organizations outside of the church community. According to Father John,

> I was told that the corporate Sees Candy office often donated candy for some organizations. I wanted to get some things for Easter. So, I called them, and the conversation was interesting. You should have heard it, Cid.

I could tell the corporate lady was African American on the phone. At first, she wasn't really warm when I told her I was from a Catholic church, and she could hear my Irish accent. But, then, when I told her I was from a certain part of South LA, her tone changed. I explained we had some of the poorest people in the city of LA, in this part of South LA.

She told me they would send a lot of candy and they did. They sent thousands of dollars worth of candy to our church. A big truck came and there were crates of the stuff everywhere. I decided we should share it with the rest of the community. So, I called some elected leaders from public housing, and they shared it with the residents there.

Well, after awhile everybody in this part of South LA had Sees Candy. You could see children and adults, everyone, walking around the streets with Sees Candy. They didn't give us the cheap stuff either, it was good quality chocolate. Can you imagine that, all the poorest of the poor walking around with high-quality Sees Candy?

Here is what I realized, though: everyone in this area is going to remember who gave it to them. It may have only been candy, but people from public housing will remember that's the church that gave us the really good candy. We give more than candy, but the point is that is how you build relations with people in the community, something we do all the time.

These examples illustrate the way in which St. Joseph's is able to connect to the broader community by sharing its resources. By giving to the wider community, the church is able to nurture a web of social ties, where reciprocity and obligation are forged. Father Guapo expressed a clear understanding of this when he stated,

By sharing our resources and social services, we are helping to connect to the wider community. We are trying to build a community, to create an environment of respect that is counter to gangs and violence.

These comments suggest that building social ties through sharing resources is not an end in itself, but rather part of a larger goal of utilizing community ties to build a community infrastructure and environment that counters the prevalence of violence. The social ties cultivated through the use of resources and reciprocity strengthen the church's capacity to deal with violence. By doling out resources and forging social ties, St. Joseph's is able to leverage other neighborhood institutions, informally, for various resources and community support.

I have purposely used the term "street-level politics" because there are many parallels with the manner in which local politicians operate. Like official politicians, clergy members must gain favor by supplying resources, jobs, and so forth. In addition, they must have stable allies whom they can utilize when moving forward with an initiative. Street-level politics is the strategy that precedes the development of social ties and allows for their genesis.

Church-Based Social Control

In a 2011 interview on NPR, criminologist David Kennedy stated that the rule of law in many of America's poorest neighborhoods has been completely undermined by gangs and the proliferation of the underground economy. This is partly true, but does not tell the whole story. I have suggested here, that while the rule of law may be weakened and undermined, competing forms of social control have emerged to fill the void, and they play a role in managing conflict.

Taken in their totality, the two types of strategies outlined in this section, the alternative frame of street wisdom proffered by the church, and its institutional policy, constitute a form of social control. The term "social control" used in this context refers to the way in which violence, risk, and conflict are regulated by institutions. In this particular case, St. Joseph's plays a major role in providing a framework to interpret violence and conflict. The church's narrative provides guidelines that shape social relationships in South LA.

St. Joseph's institutional policies, the establishment of social ties through street-level politics, helped forge a community alliance to minimize violence in the area. By forging vertical and horizontal social ties, the parish was able to develop a web of relations based on reciprocity and obligation so that it could work with other community institutions informally.

Finally, the parish acted as a source of social control through its role as intermediary between residents and formal legal institutions, like the LAPD. Having strong connections to law enforcement and to other city agencies, as well as to its parishioners, St. Joseph's was able to provide information and resources to both sides to help minimize violence.

The observations and data outlined above illustrate that the church acts as an alternative social space and, also, as a source of social control distinct from two other competing sources of rule: gangs and the formal legal system. St. Joseph's form of social control contrasts with that of the gangs and the formal legal system in several ways.

First, unlike the gangs, the church does not rule through violence and intimidation. Rather, its type of social control is based on cooperation and negotiation, whereby reciprocity and obligations emerge. Furthermore, unlike as with the gangs, violence is discouraged. While gangs also use negotiation and cooperation in their dealings with residents and other gangs, their primary means of settling conflicts and disagreements involves intimidation and force.

Secondly, unlike the formal legal system, St. Joseph's promotes a system of social regulation rooted in a morality of right and wrong, rather than in rules and laws. This occurs partly out of necessity, because many of the parishioners are undocumented immigrants from Mexico and Central America. Their citizenship status makes them reluctant to go to law enforcement when faced with conflict and violence.

The large number of individuals who are involved in the informal economy also makes residents reluctant to go to law enforcement to settle disputes and disagreements. The concentration of poor Angelenos in South LA has created the conditions for a burgeoning informal economy, which many residents and parishioners depend upon for sustenance. Street vending, unlicensed auto repair, and swap meets are common types of informal income-generating strategies throughout the area. Given the illegal nature of such activities, participants in this underground economy refuse to engage in the formal legal system.

Given the limitations of working with law enforcement, and the fear and intimidation of gangs, residents and parishioners look to the parish as an alternative source of social rule. The changing multiracial makeup of poor urban neighborhoods such as South LA has created the conditions in which new social spaces and forms of regulation have emerged.

Drake and Cayton (1993[1945]) convincingly argued that black ghettos were parallel to the white world that excluded them. The Latino experience is similar, but it is fundamentally different from that of African Americans, because Latinos are more limited in the social spaces they can navigate within the ghetto. Their citizenship status not only puts them at risk outside their neighborhoods, but also within them. Latinos, therefore, look to places such as St. Joseph's to provide an alternative social space, which, in turn, provides an alternative form of social control.

Limitations and Challenges of Informal Management of Violence

So far, I have argued that informal social control plays an important role in managing risk and violence in South LA; however, there are limitations and challenges to this approach. St. Joseph's managed violence at the institutional level and at larger, communitywide levels. While the church was able to successfully manage violence in a way that promoted safety and minimized risk for its parishioners, a larger challenge existed at the community level. In this section, I sketch out the various community factors that posed serious challenges to a unified community-form of social control. Two factors were at play, which hindered a communitywide response to managing violence: inadequate inclusive organizational infrastructure and interracial relations.

In order to illustrate the obstacles to informal social control of violence, I focus on the formation of the GTF and the relationships among various members of this organization. Examining this case provides insight into a phenomenon that plagues South LA as the city confronts issues of violence and crime in the area.

Following the 18 shootings that took place in the area surrounding St. Joseph's during late 2005, South LA residents and community activists came together and demanded that their Councilwoman take action. The LA Human Relations Commission (HRC) was contacted to organize and facilitate a meeting with community members to address the violence. A former HRC official, named Al, who worked in the department during the turmoil, explained the challenges the HRC and the community faced at the outset:

> When GTF was forming, it was not organized correctly. HRC never trained people who were selected to serve on GTF. They never clarified what their roles were going to be, either. They never made an attempt to

facilitate meetings with the Latino leadership, either. What HRC did was moderate, not facilitate. There is a big difference, you know.

GTF was formed in an emergency and in a reactionary way. That was what motivated its formation—people, for good reason, wanted something done about all the shootings. As a result GTF was very short-sighted.

The targeted leadership for GTF was not able to look at the broader picture, to move beyond "my neighborhood." Because it was reactive, it was not able to develop targeted leadership. Everyone was in survival mode.

Al's observations reflect a communitywide response to violence that was formed during a period of crisis. This had the unintended effect of shaping the organizational structure of the GTF within a limited scope. As a result, there was little or no vision with respect to the selection of leaders, and no comprehensive solution to violence that considered the needs of the community at large. Thus, the crisis of violence overshadowed the need to reach out to the larger community to combat the problem.

The institutional practices of the GTF shaped the community response in dealing with violence in several key respects. Father John described the challenges:

> The problem with GTF is that it is limited and it doesn't represent the whole community here in South LA. The Latino outreach is limited to our parish and Watts/Century Latino Organization [WCLO]. The task force doesn't represent the new [Latino] population.

A sentiment expressed by three priests at the parish was that the GTF largely ignored the Latino population.[4] Beyond the influence of WCLO and St. Joseph's in the GTF, there were literally no other individuals or delegates of institutions who represented the needs of Latinos in the area.

Although the parish priests and parishioners generally felt that the GTF was successful in addressing the issue of gangs and violence, they also viewed some of its leaders as being out of touch with the needs of the Latino community. The comments of Father Joe reflect this:

I think a lot of African Americans feel that the shootings are black on black and that should be the focus of the task force. But, a lot of the shooting and gang violence is also brown on brown. Also, there are now more Latino gangs popping up as the population increases. They are going to have a major problem on their hands and they are ignoring it. The leaders of GTF are out of touch with the needs of the community and Latinos. They have an older generation of African Americans who were involved in the community in the 1960s. I don't think they really have a feel with what's going on with the new generation. They don't seem to be going anywhere lately; people just complain at the meetings now.

The comments by both priests reveal that the organizational structure of the GTF failed to represent the needs of Latinos in relation to violence. What is striking about the lack of representation is that Latinos constitute an overwhelming majority of the population in the area.[5]

The comments of the priests at St. Joseph's also suggest that many of the leaders at the GTF are out of touch with the needs of African Americans. Certain local activists in South LA who have a long tradition of community involvement have taken on the role of the voice of the community. Yet several community residents echoed the idea that not everyone accepted this older generation as the central voice of the community to represent their needs. Al, the former employee of LA HRC, stated to me,

> You get the self-appointed leaders running the show at a lot of these community meetings. They become the gatekeepers for the community. They don't even represent the needs of African Americans.

Rather than view the lack of representation of Latinos at the table as a purely interracial group problem, the observations and evidence here suggest that the organizational setting played a role in undermining relationships between the two groups, making it difficult to combat violence in a comprehensive manner.

By ignoring the importance of outreach to other key stakeholders, the GTF limited its ability to bridge relationships between various sectors of the community to combat violence. As previous research has indicated, one key factor in minimizing neighborhood violence is the ability of residents to work collectively to develop strategies (Sampson, Morenoff, and Gannon-Rowley, 2002). The ability of Latinos to forge social ties with African Americans was severely limited by their lack of representation and outreach.

St. Joseph's may have had control over its own institutional policies to shape interracial relations and combat violence and risk, but the church was at the mercy of the larger community organizations, such as the GTF, to reconcile these types of problems. Father Guapo, expressed his frustration regarding this situation:

> In the church, our faith brings us together. We make it a point to nurture separate leadership with African Americans and Latinos, and once we have done this, we bring them together. There is nothing like that at GTF. There is no way to nurture Latino groups or leaders separately. That makes it hard for them to deal with community problems like we do.

Thus, a major obstacle to dealing with violence and gangs was the difficulty in developing a unified community response that was inclusive of both Latinos and African Americans. The manner in which interracial relationships were dealt with contrasted greatly between St. Joseph's and other institutions.

A second factor that made it difficult to organize a communitywide approach to confronting violence was the undocumented status of a large Latino population. Father Juan expressed his view:

> Outreach to the Latino community is a big problem, but, when it comes to participation in organizations like GTF, there is a lot of apathy on the part of the Latino community. Being illegal undermines participation.

Father Guapo expressed a similar sentiment:

> Because many Latinos are undocumented, they think they are just in a transitional phase. They think they are going back to Mexico, or they are leaving the area. Some do leave the area, but many of them end up staying here. So they don't get involved with things like GTF. They [Latinos] have to learn to get involved.

The comments from both priests reveal that the undocumented status of Latinos deterred their participation in community organizations, such as the GTF. Fear of being deported, due to citizenship status, compelled many Latinos to avoid all contact with government agencies. The non-citizenship status of Latinos also created the perception that they were only temporarily residing in South LA, and, because of this, they did not see the value of community participation.

Finally, it was a major challenge for the GTF to acquire the resources needed to combat violence. South LA has one of the highest levels of poverty in the greater Los Angeles area, and there was never enough funding available for job training and employment. As Father Guapo stated:

> One of the things we needed to combat gangs was jobs. We had some success getting jobs for our kids at St. Joseph's and in public housing. But, there are only so many jobs that the city and county can help provide. This part of LA has very few jobs, so where are they going to come from?

Despite the efforts by the GTF to organize the community and develop strategies for combating gangs and violence, the task force was crippled by a lack of funding both from within the community and from the outside city, county, and state agencies.

Urban and criminological scholars, who emphasize the role of collective efficacy in mitigating crime and violence, rarely take such factors into consideration. The role of interracial relationships has received little attention in analyses of the ability of residents to work collectively to mobilize against neighborhood violence. Instead, scholars continue to focus on black-white relationships, ignoring the reality that Latinos now constitute the largest number of urban dwellers in the United States. The inability to forge social ties communitywide between African Americans and Latinos is a major obstacle in forging a unified response to violence.

Collective-efficacy scholars have also ignored the role of citizenship status as a major impediment to neighborhood mobilization. Little attention has been focused on the fact that Latino immigrants face both imagined and real punitive consequences in their interactions with law enforcement.

Ironically, the factors identified as undermining broad community mobilization are the same forces that create more reliance on St. Joseph Parish as a source of a particular form of social control. Given the diversity of interracial relationships between Latinos and African Americans throughout South LA, it becomes difficult to develop a comprehensive plan to address neighborhood violence. The high levels of poverty in the area make it a challenge to garner resources, and the undocumented status of Latinos further undermines community organization. Hence, neighborhood institutions such as St. Joseph's become increasingly significant for creating social order in poor multiracial neighborhoods such as those of South LA.

5

Street Justice

Gangs, the Informal Economy, and Neighborhood Residents

Throughout this work, I have argued that there is a disconnect between residents of South LA and the state. In response to the void created by this failed relationship, alternative governance has arisen.

The previous chapter highlighted the role of a specific Catholic church, St. Joseph's, in alternative governance. In this section, I provide a sketch of another key component of alternative governance rooted in the rules of the street and fear of law enforcement. Unlike St. Joseph's, as described in the previous chapter, the informal rules of the street draw their legitimacy from the informal economy, violence and fear.

In their classic work, *City Politics*, Edward C. Banfield and James Q. Wilson (1963) argue that the basic role of local government is to provide city services, such as sanitation and sewage, and to manage crime and conflict through law enforcement. Given the disconnect of local government in South Los Angeles, important questions arise: How do residents manage their day-to-day encounters with high levels of violence? What do they do when relations are strained with the police?

Within the urban sociological and criminological literature, the code of the street, as developed by Elijah Anderson, has been used to demonstrate the way in which social order is maintained among poor urban blacks. Several components underlie this concept. First, the code of the street is primarily based on an informal code of managing conflict, where retaliation is the core means of settling disputes (Anderson, 1999; Jacobs and Wright, 2006). Moreover, it is a central factor that fuels violence among poor urban blacks. Second, the code of the street is a framework in which individuals resort to either a street response or decent response to conflict. Those who display a "street" demeanor reject mainstream values and are more likely to use violence and retaliation. In contrast, the "decent" individual upholds the morals of middle class and mainstream society and is less likely to use retaliation and violence. It is important to note that in Anderson's framework, individuals often "code switch," alternating between street and conventional values. Thus, Anderson's code of the street is a binary framework, albeit one that focuses on violence as the primary means of dealing with conflict.

Finally, Anderson implies that the code of the street is exclusive to poor urban black communities. Few studies have explored whether it is shared by other racial groups in poor urban settings, such as Latinos. More importantly, few studies have explored multiracial settings where African Americans share their neighborhoods with Latinos.

The code of the street provides an important framework to understand how residents respond to violence. While Anderson is correct in noting that poor urban residents do manage conflict through a framework that can be both street and decent, his conceptual framework does not map neatly onto the way in which conflict is managed in large urban areas such as South LA.

This chapter builds on Anderson's framework and outlines an alternative framework to understand the way in which perceived danger and violence shape how conflict is managed outside the law. I suggest that South LA residents respond to danger through what I refer to as "street justice," a concept rooted in the constant danger residents face in their interactions with law enforcement and street violence. My argument is that fear of the police and street violence produces the constant perception of danger, which leads to the use of formal and informal strategies for managing violence. In what follows, I spell out the structure of street justice and the implications it has for understanding how poor urban residents respond to the dual-headed threat of the street and law enforcement.

Jerome Skolnick's classic *Justice without Trial* (1966) provides some insight into the underpinnings of street justice. Skolnick uses the concept of the "working personality" of the police officer as a way to explain how occupational environments shape the outlook of individuals. He illustrates that, while on the job, police officers are exposed to violence at higher levels than those in other professions. As a result, danger and the potential for violence become police officers' primary preoccupation. This dominant framework not only defines the police officers perspective on the job, but their personal, domestic lives outside of work as well.

Police officers are, therefore, more likely to view situations outside the realm of work as potentially dangerous.

The exposure to violence has two important consequences. First, it fosters suspicion and distrust of others. Skolnick argues that the threats of violence and danger to which police are exposed create a default response to citizens based primarily on suspicion and distrust. Second, he argues that police suspicion and distrust has a direct effect on how they navigate in and out of the boundaries of the law in exercising their discretion, for instance, to use force and to what extent. In essence, police are more likely to push the boundaries of the law when they feel they are in danger or may face violence—personal safety trumps the rule of law.

Skolnick's framework is relevant for understanding how frequent exposure to violence shapes a collective group's outlook. Drawing on his analysis, it is reasonable to note that the high level of violence South LA residents are exposed to is similar in many ways to what police officers face. The threat of violence pervades many aspects of routine life, such as work, home and beyond, for South LA residents, creating a suspicion of outsiders. In many ways exposure to violence is more present for residents since they live in the neighborhoods where homicides are frequent.

There are, however, major differences between residents and the police. One key difference for residents is the collective shared distrust of law enforcement including the Los Angeles Police Department and the Los Angeles County Sheriff's Department. As outlined in earlier chapters, residents were as fearful of law enforcement as they were of street violence and crime.

The simultaneous threats of street violence and law enforcement form the basis of street justice, a collective outlook and general strategy for coping with perceived danger. The constant threat of danger forces residents to weave in and outside the legal system—much as police do in Skolnick's framework—and at times embrace alternative strategies to cope with law enforcement and street violence. The simultaneous fear of the streets and formal law opens a new space in which to consider how residents deal with the threat of violence, conceived of in broad terms.

A second key feature of street justice is that it consists of frameworks, "street" and "decent," that appear to be contradictory. However, these multiple frames are reconciled by a more pressing issue and associated framework: minimizing danger and threats. Unlike what happens in Anderson's framework, code switching is not necessary in the street justice framework since both the law and street represent the potential for exposure to danger and violence.

Harding (2010) suggests that many poor urban youths maintain contradictory cultural models at the same time, through a process he refers to as simultaneity. In essence, simultaneity is the copresence of two competing models, such as "street" and "decent," that shape the outlook of groups at the neighborhood level. He suggests that a diversity of competing and conflicting cultural models can coexist in urban poor neighborhoods. Similar to Harding's view, I suggest that neighborhoods with high levels of violence force South LA residents to navigate and manipulate multiple sources of cultural messages. The framework I am proposing is hardly new in this respect. However, unlike Harding, I do not view simultaneity exclusively as a source of criminal or deviant behavior. Street justice as a general strategy requires both formal and informal strategies to deal with the threat of violence and danger. Thus, street justice involves maintaining multiple cultural models at the same time.

In sum, street justice guides the perception of poor urban residents exposed to high levels of violence in a similar manner as police officers in two key ways. Just as law enforcement maintains suspicion of poor urban minorities, residents maintain a deep distrust of law enforcement and are likely to frame interactions with them with suspicion. They are, therefore, less likely to use the formal law to manage violence and conflict. As a result, residents are likely to exercise wide discretion in their adherence to the law, often navigating in and out. Just as the police exercise wide discretion, such as in the excessive use of force, residents use strategies that entail both alternative and formal legal approaches to deal with danger and violence.

I make two claims that build on the common wisdom of the code of the street. First, retaliation is not the primary means used to handle conflict. Rather, I show that conflict is handled through a continuum of various informal strategies and that retaliation is often the last resort. Second, the informal mechanism of street justice is not reducible to decent individuals and street individuals. Instead, street justice acts as a framework of conflict management that is shared by all residents, including ordinary citizens and individuals who are noncriminal. The negotiation process between gang and non-gang members is what unites the community under the shared informal public norms—namely, street justice.

Who Gets Drawn into Street Justice and Why?

Before outlining the concept of street justice, it is important to note who gets drawn into settling conflict and violence outside the law and why. Is street justice exclusive to those who are street oriented, such as criminals and gangs? I argue that a form of conflict management outside the law is found among criminal and noncriminal segments of the population. The answer to this question is important because it illustrates that something much more comprehensive is at play in settling conflict in urban areas than the account given in analyses based on the code of the street.

Bruce Jacobs and Richard Wright (2006) suggest that criminals do not resort to settling disputes outside the law simply because they would otherwise expose their own illicit activities. Instead, they argue that the law has lost its legitimacy for other reasons and has come to be seen as irrelevant to the resolution of daily conflicts. In particular, they argue that disrespect by the police, ineffective laws, incompetent policing, and the importance of self-reliance in handling disputes are the central factors that have led to conflict resolution through a code of the street, where retaliation is the central means of achieving this (Jacobs and Wright, 2006). Thus, for Jacobs and Wright, it is mostly criminals who embrace a code of the street outside the scope of the formal law.

During my time observing, interviewing, and living in South Los Angeles, I found that a significant number of noncriminal residents were also enmeshed in a subculture in which the formal law has lost its legitimacy. What is significant is that conflict management outside the law is not exclusive to the criminal underworld or to those who take a street orientation in their public life, as the code of the street would predict. In this section, I describe different segments of the community in South LA, who are not criminals per se, but are nevertheless drawn into a subculture of handling conflict outside the law, and I seek to explain their motivations for doing so. Several other factors, besides participating in the criminal underworld, play a central role in allowing street justice to take hold in public housing and other residential settings.

Ordinary Noncriminal Citizens and Conflict Management outside the Law

An interview with an LAPD officer assigned to the Gang Task Force, Aaron Algren, provides one perspective as to why street justice is pervasive among residents not involved in gangs or in the criminal world.

> CID: What accounts for the high levels of crime in the 77th?
>
> OFFICER ALGREN: I think people just learned that you solve problems with violence, by shooting, and this is part of the culture. Poverty is a factor. They solve problems through violence by shooting each other.
>
> CID: I have heard there is something like a "people's law," where people take the law into their own hands—a street justice. Do you think that something like street justice exists here?
>
> OFFICER ALGREN: There is a street justice. The court system here is a joke. I have arrested people with guns all the time. Many times the jury pool acquits the guy. The guys doing crimes down here— nothing happens to them. The law doesn't work. People get away with murder every single day down here; it's really amazing. People take care of things themselves. Imagine if someone commits a crime against you or someone in your family, and he gets out and is back in the neighborhood. What would you do? Probably take care of the problem yourself.
>
> CID: So, it's like two types of law operating here. How does it make your job?
>
> OFFICER ALGREN: There are two forms of law operating here. From my standpoint, it's really frustrating when you have 15 witnesses to a shooting. The shooting never gets solved. It happens over and over. I see it all the time.

Officer Algren's comments speak to how many residents regard the local government and courts as ineffective in punishing offenders and protecting the innocent. Given those perceived inadequacies, residents are more likely to settle disputes themselves without the involvement of the police, courts, and other formal legal institutions. Officer Algren's comments suggest that "hustling off the books" is not the only factor that promotes the informal public set of norms of street justice.

A general perception that law enforcement and the judicial system are ineffective may also contribute to residents resorting to alternative forms of justice. In order to provide a more developed view of "street justice" from the perspective of community members, I interviewed residents of public housing. Keith, an African American in his early 20s who lived and worked in the Jordan Downs Housing Projects, illustrates a common view among residents regarding the police and law enforcement.

> Most people think the police are all about bullshit. When there is real work to be done, they are not there. One day we were playing basketball in the projects. There was a shoot-out and the cops were parked right across the street. The police were just as scared as everyone else when the shooting was going on. They waited until after the shooting to do anything. These people are getting paid for this? People are dying in large numbers every summer, and there is not enough police protection. There is very poor protection by the police. The police are scared when they come into a neighborhood. People really don't like them, though. They are the most feared, the enemy—you know what I mean. They keep violence in the neighborhoods going by doing underhanded things to make gangs fight against each other. They can keep violence going in the neighborhood; they have the power to do that. There are over 107 gangs in Watts. When I was younger, I had to walk through three different gangs from my housing project to the high school near another project. How do you think kids feel just trying to go to school? You do what you have to without the police.

Keith's comments parallel the ideas expressed by Officer Algren, as both speak to a common view among residents that law enforcement and "the system" are ineffective. The comments by Keith speak to two important factors not expressed by Officer Algren, however. First, police are perceived as being unable to protect residents from violence endemic to many neighborhoods of South LA. Second, the police are viewed by residents as the enemy, who is to be feared. It was common knowledge that South LA residents viewed the police with distrust and as being racist. These factors eroded the legitimacy of formal channels of rational legal justice and law enforcement. The perceived distrust and ineffectiveness of law enforcement have all played a role in the emergence of handling conflicts and disputes outside the law through street justice.

Latino Noncitizens: Avoiding Law Enforcement

There is also an important incentive for Latinos to embrace a position similar to that of African Americans in terms of a reluctance to work with law enforcement to solve neighborhood problems and issues. Previous research that draws on the code of the street framework fails to recognize that many Latino immigrants who are not citizens avoid working with law enforcement. This is a major oversight by urban and criminology scholars, who have focused primarily on African Americans. One significant factor in this phenomenon is that Latino residents who were not citizens believed that going to the police for problems could result in the discovery of their status as noncitizens. Given the large number of recent immigrants from Mexico and Central America into South LA, this is not a trivial matter. Census data for 2000 indicates that Latino noncitizens comprise close to 30 percent of the population in South LA. For these people, going to the police for any issue could ultimately result in deportation from the United States back to Mexico or Central America. An LAPD officer from the Southwest Division shared his views on the issue:

> Latinos get victimized a lot down here in South LA by their own people and by African Americans. They get robbed a lot by African Americans. One reason Latinos are targeted by blacks is because they know that Latinos will not go to the police. You can rob somebody and not have to worry about being turned into the cops. They feel like they have to let it go or find another way to deal with it.

A similar sentiment was expressed in interviews with the LA County Sheriff's Department regarding Latinos being victimized and their unwillingness to report these occurrences to law enforcement. Having attended numerous Neighborhood Council Ad Hoc Public Safety Committee meetings, I learned from law enforcement how common it was for Latino immigrants to be preyed upon. Latino victimization and their unwillingness to report crime gained the attention of the Sheriff's Department when several Latinos were murdered near a metro station in the spring of 2004. In several Public Safety Committee meetings, Sheriff's Department representatives revealed that getting Latino immigrants to report crime was a major problem that needed to be addressed.

Latinos regularly voiced their fear of the police in South LA. At the time, in this community, several high profile raids were conducted by US Immigration and Customs Enforcement (ICE). The director of the Watts/Century Latino Organization had very strong views about the matter:

> You know Latino immigrants do not go to the police very often. They are afraid of being deported and it's not just that, they are fearful of the way they will be treated. Many of them have had very bad experiences with INS and LAPD. I hear this daily at WCLO.

A Latino male interviewee from Mexico in his late 40s who lived in Watts described his perception of the police:

> You never know what could happen to you in this community if you go to the police. The raids around here are scary. Many people are afraid that they will get deported and never get to see their families again. I could lose everything, just for going to the police. I avoid them and places where there could be problems. You know, try to keep a low profile, that's what most Mexicanos try to do, I think.

In sum, both Latinos and African Americans did not trust law enforcement and were therefore more likely to seek alternative means outside the law. These factors played a central role in promoting the pervasiveness of street justice.

The Underground Economy: Licit Activity and Avoidance of the Law

A third reason why noncriminal residents resort to conflict management outside the law has to do with their involvement in the underground economy. As in many poor communities, South LA residents often resort to hustling off the books to survive. On the surface this may seem like criminal behavior; however, residents view such practices as doing little social harm, and there is no consensus about the wrongfulness of such acts. Moreover, from a legal perspective, the goods often distributed in the informal economy are not illegal in themselves, such as food sold by street vendors. According to Manuel Castells and Alejandro Portes (1989), the distinction between informal and formal activities is largely determined by the manner in which goods are produced and exchanged, not in the final product. In this section, I focus on licit commodities— legal goods—the sale of which is considered illicit in formal legal terms because of their manner of distribution. Operating a street cart without a license is illegal, not the food that is sold.

The distinction between licit and illicit is important because it is not entirely accurate to depict all individuals involved in the informal economy, for instance street vendors, as "street" or criminal. Selling fruit or ice cream to children is hardly a criminal act by most standards. Nevertheless, these individuals' informal income-generating strategies, by default, criminalize them and force them to settle conflict outside the law. In what follows, I outline the various reasons why those involved in the informal economy do not have access to the formal law.

Licit Commodities, Unlicensed Sales in the Underground Economy

The underground economy in South LA is a vibrant and ubiquitous phenomenon that has involved many residents. Both African Americans and Latinos are involved in various forms of underground economy as an alternate means of generating revenue, from street vending and car mechanic street operations to hustlers selling stolen goods. Latino residents are actively involved in both marginally and unambiguously illicit forms of the underground economic activity in this area. Throughout the major corridors of South LA, it is not uncommon to see Latino street vendors selling a variety of goods. On one commercial corridor, Slauson Avenue, one can readily see Latino immigrants selling barbecued meats, with side fixings of beans, rice, and tortillas. In areas of South LA where large numbers of people congregate, such as in churches on weekends before and after mass, at public parks when soccer games are playing, or at public schools after school lets out, one can regularly find street vendors selling corn, candy, soda, and fruit. Both Latino males and females are actively involved in street vending, and found their way into it through a variety of circumstances. One immigrant Latina from Mexico who resided in South LA had her four-year-old son accompany her to sell goods, such as candy and fruit with Mexican seasoning, outside a public library. She explained the circumstances that led to her involvement in this illicit form of street vending:

> I used to work in a factory in the garment industry in downtown Los Angeles. The pay was really bad and I worked a lot of hours. I had no one to care for my children. I couldn't work and take care of my children, so I decided to go into this type of work. Here I can sell my stuff, and I can bring my children with me to work at the same time. It's the only real option I have.

Gaining initial access to this interviewee was not easy. As a street vendor, the respondent knew there was a constant risk of being raided by the police because—like nearly all similar vendors—she did not have the appropriate licenses and permits to operate her business. The respondent was thus suspicious about revealing information to me for fear of sanctions and repercussions. Not having a license from the city to operate, by default, made this type of street vending illegal. It was very common for street vendors to have their goods confiscated and their vending machines seized and/or destroyed. This creates a set of conditions in which street vendors are not regulated by official city laws. Instead, the exchange of goods are regulated between vendors and their customers. An example from another street vendor, whom I will call Adolfo, further illustrates the implications of economic life being regulated by community members, versus the official city guidelines and rules. Throughout my fieldwork, I noticed that street vendors could be regularly observed conducting business at elementary schools after school hours. Initially, Adolfo was hesitant to be interviewed for fear that I was associated with law enforcement and that he would get raided. He agreed to let me interview him after I informed him that I was a researcher and not involved with law enforcement. The following is the conversation that ensued.

CID: How often do you work here?

ADOLFO: I have to work six to seven days a week.

CID: Why so many days?

ADOLFO: I get raided, on average, once a week by the police. They take my stuff and dump it on the streets and sometimes they damage my vending machine. Many times they have smashed it right in front of my eyes. I have to work a lot of extra hours and days to make up for the loss. I have to keep on them all the time and watch for the police all the time. If it's not the police, sometimes I get robbed for my goods by local kids who want free stuff. Other times I have been robbed for my money. There is not much I can do when this happens either, because who am I going to call if I have a problem—call the police?

CID: How did you get involved in this type of work?

ADOLFO: I used to work in a factory in downtown LA producing materials for clothes. It was physically demanding, and I injured my fingers and hands. The pay wasn't that good, and I worked a lot of hours. I couldn't take it anymore, and I realized I could make more money doing this kind of work. This kind of work is better, I think. I can set my own schedule and work when I want to, and it doesn't take a toll on my body like working in the factories did.

Several points are worth noting here. First, for both Adolfo and the Latina interviewed, their marginal positions in the workplace played a significant factor in forcing them into the underground economy. Both respondents were exposed to the harsh conditions of the industrial manufacturing economy, rooted in the garment industry of LA. Second, the conditions of both respondents reflect the fact that they were essentially forced to operate underground, outside the auspices of local government, by operating without a license and not paying taxes for the goods exchanged for money. There are immense implications in moving from the legitimate economy to the underground economy. The first and foremost factor is that entrepreneurs and their customers are responsible for regulating what is considered fair exchange, and disputes and conflicts may emerge between the parties involved. In the case of Adolfo, calling the police for a dispute he may have had with local youth who stole goods and/or robbed him was not feasible given the potential harm that could come to him as a result of his unlicensed street vendor business. By default, calling the police would call attention to his informal activity. As a result, the underground economy forces individuals to resolve conflicts among themselves. In other words, residents involved with this economy must explore the process of resolving and regulating relationships on their own, rather than with the help of local government.

African Americans in South LA were also commonly involved in activities within the underground economy. Street vending was not as common among African Americans, but other types of informal work, such as auto repair, could regularly be seen throughout residential neighborhoods in South LA. In one neighborhood where I resided for several months, a crew of two middle-aged African American males in their mid-50s operated a full-time auto repair business on the street right in front of their home. They averaged between two and four customers each day, performing various repairs for cars from oil changes to flat tires to new brake pads—all common requests for their services. The mechanics were aware of the implications of their unlicensed activities, and, as a result, made efforts to accommodate residents who were affected by their business. For instance, working with neighbors to provide spaces to park, as the parking shortage in the neighborhood was an issue that affected all of the residents. Their auto repair business often required that cars be parked in front of, or near, their operation. This meant that it was common for two to three cars to be parked there daily. Rather than wait for conflict to emerge, they would ask me, for example, if I needed to park my car. This subtle form of negotiation was critical because it headed off issues that might have led to an angry resident calling the police and reporting them. On several occasions, these same mechanics serviced my car. Their work was satisfactory, and their prices were noticeably cheaper than those of a legitimate, licensed business. However, some issues were not easily negotiated between the street mechanics and neighborhood residents. On various occasions, the street mechanics would dump oil from the cars they serviced into the street. A Latino resident from the neighborhood, who worked as a schoolteacher, commented, "I think it looks really bad when they dump that stuff in the street. It doesn't look good and it's bad for the environment. It really bothers me, but I don't want to say anything and cause any trouble."

Although these examples of street vendors and street mechanics represent distinct kinds of activity in the underground economy, they are similar in the way that they shape neighborhood social interaction. First, the goal of the informal economic exchange process is to keep the police out of the neighborhood and keep the unlicensed businesses hidden. Second, the residents seek to keep informal exchange issues within the neighborhood, which often entails various forms of negotiation between residents. These two factors point to a deeper social process common to these types of neighborhoods—namely, that economic exchange is mediated by residents rather than by local government, the City of Los Angeles, or other formal legal institutions. Internal neighborhood mediation of economic exchange forms the basis of shared principles common to neighborhood residents. I refer to the shared principles of neighborhood mediation as street justice, to denote the social process by which issues surrounding economic exchange, such as fair exchange and enforcement of contracts, are carried out by residents. After all, in this scenario, it is residents involved in the underground economy who determine what is considered appropriate justice, rather than an outside government institution. This type of internal mediation of economic exchange also has the potential to spill over into other forms of dispute and conflict resolution, not limited to economic and underground economic activity. Given the possibility that illegal economic activity could be discovered through police involvement, jeopardizing the operation of their businesses, residents often resisted involving law enforcement in neighborhood disputes. In essence, the underground economic activity of residents sets the tone for a more general orientation toward the police, in which involving law enforcement in mundane social disputes was frowned upon and used only as a last resort.

The Illicit Economy, Gangs, and Community

A fourth reason why residents do not have access to the formal law revolves around the unambiguously illicit economy and gangs. It should be noted that the illicit economy shapes those who are not directly involved in criminal behavior. In economics the term "externalities" refers to an economic exchange that has unintended consequences for third parties, those not involved in the buying and selling. In many respects, noncriminal residents were affected by the illicit economy and forced to navigate in and out of the law.

It has been well established by researchers (Jacobs and Wright, 2006; Anderson, 1999) that individuals involved in the criminal world do not resort to the law simply because they would be exposing their own illicit activities. I suggest that because of the illicit nature of their activities, gangs resort to their own form of regulation of the illicit economy. In essence, gangs act as a form of police in many neighborhoods that are at odds with the formal law.

I confirmed through interviews with youths involved in gangs, with LAPD officers, and through observations from fieldwork in numerous neighborhoods in South LA, that gang members are frequently involved in drug sales. It should also be noted that gangs are not limited to the narrow task of narcotics sales. The primary role of gangs, both Latino and African American, is to regulate illicit activity in neighborhood settings, and there are distinct ways in which gangs do that in various South LA neighborhoods.

Based on interviews with youths involved in drug sales, several factors seemed distinctive about the regulation of illicit activity in the neighborhood. Explaining in an interview one way in which illicit activity is regulated at the neighborhood level, Bob Marley, a 17-year-old African American who lived in a neighborhood with frequent gang activity, said, "Gangs don't just sell dope in the neighborhood. They try to control everything in the neighborhood. You can't sell dope in the neighborhood unless you pay taxes." Billy Bob, a 17-year-old Belizean on parole for gang activity, commented regarding the role of gangs in the community, "Gangs have a purpose; they try to grow up territory, control what comes in their area, and also try to sell dope." The comments from these young people illustrate the idea that gangs not only seek to generate income from the illicit economy, but also seek to regulate and control other forms of enterprise in the underground economy. Given the illicit nature of narcotics sales and other goods exchanged and sold, gangs and non-gang members engage in a process of internal mediation and regulation. Here, the activity of those involved in the illicit economy parallels the unlicensed business activity of the informal economy. Gang and non-gang individuals involved in the illicit economy regulate the exchange of goods. Any conflicts or disputes that occur during this process are worked out among the parties themselves.

A negotiation process usually occurred between groups or individuals wishing to peddle illicit goods who were not affiliated with the gang controlling the area. The negotiation usually involved receiving permission from the controlling gang. This often entailed paying "taxes," a certain amount of money from drug or other illicit good sales, to the gang in control of a neighborhood. In some instances, drugs and other illicit goods being sold were given as a form of barter instead of cash for the right to conduct business. Other forms of exchange and negotiation occurred between gangs who controlled an area and parties interested in selling illicit goods.

This social dynamic may also have applied to street vendors. Several street vendors who sold illicit goods mentioned in interviews that they had to receive the consent of the controlling gang in order to sell their goods in the area. It was not an uncommon practice for gangs to extort street vendors. For example, near Downtown LA in MacArthur Park, gangs often extorted goods and money from street vendors. In several interviews, former city councilman Mike Hernandez, whose district encompassed MacArthur Park, stated that street vendors were frequently forced to provide payment to gangs who controlled the area. It is not unlikely that similar dynamics were at play in South LA.

Based on field observations, it was unclear whether car mechanics were subject to the same type of gang extortion practices. The African American and Latino car mechanics I observed were longtime residents who maintained positive relationships with their neighbors, including gang members who lived in the area. I never witnessed car mechanics being extorted, nor did they state that they were victims of such activities.

The gang in the area often determined what was considered a "fair exchange" for allowing business to occur on their turf. Interviews with several young people, who were involved in gangs or in the illicit economy in the two charter schools in South LA, confirmed this view. Latino and African American youths interviewed at these schools stated that there were clear negative sanctions when vendors attempted to sell goods without the permission and consent of gangs. Respondents from both groups stated that sometimes unlicensed vendors would be warned that they could not sell in the neighborhood without the approval of the local gang. People selling goods would often get robbed and beaten—or in extreme cases, killed—if local gangs were not consulted.

A second key point is that the distribution of illicit goods in neighborhoods was primarily based on gang affiliation. Once a gang had control of a given neighborhood or area, it had exclusive rights to determine who could deal in the neighborhood. In most instances, the gang that controlled an area reflected the ethnic makeup of the immediate area, but this was not always the case. For example, there were many immigrant neighborhoods where Latinos became the majority, but African American gangs kept control despite the demographic changes. In these types of neighborhoods, Latino immigrants had not resided for long, and therefore, Latino gangs had not yet taken root. Race also played an important role in regulating the underground economy. Often, though not always, gangs consisted of one racial group—either African American or Latino. Poor relations between African American and Latino gangs minimized exchange relations between both groups. In general, Latino and African American residents not directly involved in gang activity were divided at the neighborhood level, as well. The end result of poor relations between African Americans and Latinos was that illicit goods, such as drugs, were most often exchanged within the same racial and ethnic group. Interviews with LAPD officers and youths from both schools confirmed this. Observations in my place of residence also confirmed this view. Potential drug customers from various gang dealings in the area consisted of people almost exclusively of the same race. Members of a different race engaged in economic exchange in the illicit economy, but this type of activity was in general tightly bound by racial differences. Important implications existed for the racial division of the underground economy. The racial divisions of both groups at the neighborhood level manifested as two different underground economies existing side by side and occasionally intersecting. Despite the racial demarcation of these economies, they both operated by the same principle of street justice.

Finally, neighborhood affiliation played a central role in the distribution of illicit goods. Although race played a significant role in shaping the boundaries of the illicit economy, neighborhood affiliation often could override race and hinder the possibility of exchange. If the distributor of illicit goods was associated with a neighborhood that was controlled by rival gangs, then exchange would be minimized. Individuals associated with gangs and rival neighborhoods posed potential threats, and would-be customers would avoid dealing with them. The same dynamic also applied to vendors. Thus, the illicit activity of gang and non-gang members promoted two important principles of street justice. First, residents keep personal disputes within the neighborhood; the two forms of dispute resolution are negotiation and/or violence where people are beaten and/or killed. The second principle of street justice can be summarized in the phrase "don't rat," which means to avoid calling law enforcement officials into disputes regarding illicit exchange. Gang and non-gang members all implicitly understand these principles. Going to the police is frowned upon because it is essentially the same as telling on oneself for participating in crime within the underground economy. Those that provide information to the police are viewed as "rats" and are often punished by community members—both gang and non-gang members.

In the next section, I chronicle how this way of thinking affects both those involved in the informal economy and individuals in residential settings who have little or no affiliation with gangs or the underground economy. Street justice thus expands beyond the confines of the underground and provides a framework with which all the residents must contend, whether they wish to or not.

Street Justice: A Continuum of Conflict Management from Avoidance to Retaliation

It is often assumed that retaliation through violence is the primary means of handling conflict outside the law among poor urban residents (Anderson, 1999; Jacobs and Wright, 2006). This assumption is ubiquitous and largely unchallenged in the urban and criminology literature. The common wisdom of this view is that the code of the street fuels violence (Anderson, 1999). Recent work by Randall Collins (2008, p. 368), however, suggests that the code of the street should be reconsidered as an interaction structure that manages conflict and violence. According to Collins, ad hoc violence without the social rituals to manage conflict, such as the code of the street, is more likely to produce higher levels of violence. While Collins provides important insights into how violence is managed by social rituals, such as the code of the street, he takes for granted the specificity and other unique forms of informal rules used by residents in poor, urban, multiracial areas such as South LA. Are the variations in the social rituals used to manage violence in other poor urban areas different from the code of the street?

Drawing on Collins's notion that social rituals manage violence, I suggest that residents are able to manage violence by minimizing danger. Based on extensive fieldwork in South LA, I found that conflict is managed by a range of strategies that operate outside the law. At the core of these strategies is a continuum of social engagement levels that range from avoidance, toleration negotiation, and violence. In contrast to Anderson, I show that violence is one of many key strategies utilized when it comes to managing conflict, and that other equally important options are utilized. This framework for understanding how poor residents manage conflict requires a new conceptual approach. I refer to the informal strategies used outside the law as street justice. In what follows, I spell out the core structure of the concept of street justice.

"No Snitchin'": Toleration

The first central component of street justice involves not turning to the police to handle conflict, or as it is known among residents, the principle of "no snitchin.'" Indeed, my fieldwork revealed that no snitchin' is what unites the community in dealing with conflict outside the law. In contrast to other scholars, I suggest that no snitchin' is just as important as retaliation, since it keeps community residents from having access to the formal legal system.

Numerous interviews were conducted with homeowners to explore how common the notion of no snitchin' was. I found it to be pervasive among residents from a variety of backgrounds, ages, and races. Most importantly, it was common among many residents who were not involved in the criminal underworld.

A Latina resident in her mid-50s, whom I will call "Anna," lived in the Watts area for over 40 years. She shared her views with me regarding snitchin'. I became somewhat close to Anna since I lived in her home in Watts for several months while conducting fieldwork.

Anna informed me that her neighbors, who were heavily involved in a gang, used to operate a business of prostitution and heavy drug trafficking. According to Anna, this prostitution and drug house operated for a few years, but neighbors were reluctant to report the illegal activity to the police for a variety of reasons. Anna stated that most residents felt it was too dangerous to get involved in these types of issues. They feared the possibility of retaliation that could follow if gang members or individuals of the illicit economy were singled out by the police or other law enforcement officials.

There was a credible reason to fear retaliation from gangs. I observed an illustration of this possibility from my room one night:

> Three African American males, in their late 20s, approach a man watering his lawn in front of his house who has recently moved into the neighborhood. They tell him they need the car in back of his house because it's theirs. He states he can't give it to them because LAPD wants it for an investigation. They plead with him, then calmly tell him, "OK, we will be back." They turn and walk away.
>
> Later that night, I look out the window of my room and notice the neighbor's garage, where the car is parked, is on fire. The flames are high, and I am afraid the fire will jump to my house. As I look down the block, I see red lights flashing. Fire trucks are parked halfway down the street. I talk to A and she tells me she heard her dog barking and was certain someone was trespassing on the neighbor's property and that it was probably the parties involved in lighting the fire.
>
> In the morning, a homeless woman pushing a cart stops in front of my house. She asks me if I know what happened. I say I don't. She looks me straight in the eyes and says, "That's what happens when you snitch. He was going to the police." She grabs her cart and moves on.

Later, Anna told me people don't really pay too much attention to these things, or get too involved with the police, because of fear of retaliation.

The acceptance of criminal activity by noncriminal residents represents a form of conflict management based on both toleration and avoidance. Toleration involves recognizing behavior that is not acceptable, but nevertheless permitting it. Neighborhood homeowners and residents essentially accepted the illicit activity by not going to the police. At the same time, the prostitutes and drug dealers from the previous example tried to accommodate the neighbors by telling customers to keep the noise down, or by acknowledging the concerns of the neighborhood residents.

In another interview with a Latino homeowner, whom I will call "Felix," similar themes emerged as in the interview with Anna. Felix is 27 years old and has lived in Watts his entire life. His views further elaborate why residents are hesitant to get involved in neighborhood affairs.

> Gangs do nothing positive for the neighborhood, except hate on other people. People feel unsafe in their neighborhoods, and they will not get involved with the police to address gang problems. People are not just afraid for themselves but also for what could happen to their children or other family members and their ability to be protected from gangs. When a person gets involved with the police, they are jeopardizing the safety of children and other family members, and that is why people avoid working with law enforcement officials. Gangs in this neighborhood do not hesitate to shoot-up houses, so there is reason to be concerned.

Many African American residents echoed the views of Latino homeowners concerning gangs and the role of street justice. One African American interviewee in her mid-70s, Ms. Brown, described her experience with gangs in her neighborhood:

> The 99th Street Crips are active in my neighborhood and they have had a beef with Latino gangs from 97th Street. I was alarmed by the feud because my house was in crossfire when the gangs were involved in a shoot-out. I heard from people that the African American gangs were fighting over territory. The gangs mostly sell dope in the area. These kinds of things make people reluctant to get involved with police.

Interviews with both Latinos and African Americans illustrate that toleration and avoidance of criminals and gangs was key to managing nonconflictual relations. What is significant is that both Latinos and African Americans expressed that street justice was pervasive in residential homeowner settings in the form of no snitchin'. The interviews with both Latino and African American homeowners reflects a shared understanding between gang members, residents, and others involved in the underground economy regarding appropriate conduct in dealing with illicit neighborhood issues. The imminent threat of street violence pushed many residents to use strategies outside the law. Implicitly, residents were also fearful of the law since they understood they could do little to solve neighborhood problems and protect them from possible retaliation for working with the police. Thus, no snitchin' is central to keeping conflict and criminal activity outside the purview of the law and within the parameters of two other strategies that I take up next, namely, negotiation and retaliation.

No Snitchin' and Negotiation

No snitchin' is important because it forces residents to deal with conflict on their own terms in a way that is not random or ad hoc. Contrary to the code of the street as described by Anderson (1999), residents often first resort to some form of mediation or negotiation rather than retaliation. Thus, negotiation and mediation represent a second component on the continuum of what I call street justice.

The comments of Keith from the Jordan Downs Housing Projects illustrate one of the key elements of street justice and reflect a widespread view. I asked open-ended questions of respondents, initially to explore their willingness to work with one another and law enforcement to solve neighborhood problems.

> CID: What would residents here do if there were a murder? Would they go to the police?
>
> KEITH: If there is a murder, you don't say anything—got to keep the code of the streets. You betray the code of the street and it's like what did John Gotti do back in the day, ya all? Just think about that, you know what I am saying. A lot of rules that sometimes people don't take heed to. And when you violate those rules you get dealt with and there are consequences.
>
> CID: What happens?
>
> KEITH: The biggest thing is when you are marked a snitch, you are marked one forever. There are no five-year statute of limitations. Now this could endanger your whole family. In a neighborhood, you'll get killed; your mom could get killed. Or depends on the situation on what you did.

CID: Someone from the Imperial Courts projects told me that when they have a problem, like a shooting, they get a leader to work it out to keep the police out.

KEITH: That would be the first alternative, getting leaders. People talk about getting leaders. Those are about separate issues though. That is a neighborhood thing. If the Jordan Downs went and shot up the PJs [the Imperial Courts Housing Projects] or went [and] shot up Nickerson—now, to solve that problem I would have go get my leader or the leader of the gangs in the Jordans or to holler at the leaders in the gangs of the Nickersons to figure out what the hell happened and who the hell did it, because they know.

CID: They will try to keep the police out.

KEITH: Can't keep the police out. No way you can keep the police out because whenever they want to come, they can come.

CID: I was thinking in terms of information being exchanged.

KEITH: No information will be exchanged with the police, ever, unless you are a snitch. Other than that "code of the street," if you shot me, I am not going to tell police I got shot. I am no snitch. That makes me look soft to the street. I am going to handle it on the street. That is how it go.

CID: The law and the code of the street are not the same thing. How is it possible to have two different types of law?

KEITH: Take it back to the mafia, man. All the stuff that was happening in the 1920s. They didn't deal with no police like that. It was the law of the streets. If your ass is a snitch, you going to be dealt with like one. It don't really matter. The mafia exists. To be a snitch is to be dead.

These comments illustrate the existence of an alternative form of justice that operates outside the scope of formal legal law and is widely understood among public housing residents. Two central tenets of street justice are widely recognized by residents and gang members alike. First, no information regarding crime is reported to the police. To go to the police is to be viewed as a "rat," which carries with it severe sanctions— retaliation from gangs or other residents. Given the consequences of calling the police, residents created a social space outside the law to handle conflict that is not reducible to street or decent. Instead residents utilized a framework of negotiation that allowed them to deal with the perception of potential danger and violence of the streets.

Second, the alternative social space provided residents with a venue to handle disagreements through mediation, usually among neighborhood leaders. Many believe that informal rules of dispute fuel violence; however, Keith's comments clearly indicate that the first alternative to conflict is getting neighborhood leaders involved, not resorting to retaliation, as much of the sociological literature suggests. His comments suggest that violence is potentially mitigated by negotiation. Among the urban poor, conflict is as common as it is in middle-class settings, but conflict does not always turn into retaliation. The conversation with Keith shows that conflict can be headed off through negotiation rather than through retaliation and violence. Thus, ad hoc violence, without the social interaction structure of street justice, is likely to escalate and spiral out of control.

Retaliation

Thus far, I have highlighted three dimensions of street justice—no snitchin', avoidance, and toleration and negotiation—that represent the dominant strategies residents use to manage conflict. However, when these strategies fail, retaliation is often the last resort in managing disputes in the continuum of street justice. Retaliation is often the source of violence in South LA.

An interview with LBM, an African American in his early 20s, highlights the manner in which street justice plays out in the residential setting of another public housing project. His insights are valuable because he spent most of his life growing up and living in public housing. In addition, LBM worked as a caseworker for the City of Los Angeles, providing job training and other employment services to youths who resided in public housing in South LA. (I quoted briefly from this exchange in the introduction.)

> CID: What happens in the neighborhood when a person is murdered?
> LBM: If there is murder, people will not say anything. Eyes wide shut, you know. In general, in public housing a jacket is put on him, paperwork is sent in the community. If he is well connected in a

gang or a family member in a high enough position, nothing will happen to him. Snitches get to work. Depends on your status. If you are well connected to a family with status, you may get a pass. What's supposed to happen, though—a snitch is supposed to get a deal in an orderly fashion, meaning if you dealing in the world of organized crime, people hustle—a cat supposed to get killed.

CID: When people don't want the police involved, who handles the problem? Who handles the justice in public housing? How do people handle disagreements?

LBM: Usually throughout the '80s and '90s, and to now, random acts of violence, drive-bys. Even if it's in that particular community—two individuals got beef, something happened, someone got killed; it's handled in house, yeah. Those who have the means of handling the situation in their grasp, they handle it.

CID: It seems like there is street justice and legal justice. One is in the law and the other is unstated, and one just knows. Are there two types of law that operate here?

LBM: Definitely. The individual who was victimized would determine the punishment for the perpetrator. That's how it's done. But, yeah, there is definitely two types of laws, the street law: More of a "just us," it's street just us in comparison to the judicial system. You know, it's "just us" so we can do it with just us. No way a police officer is going to be able to relate to what's truly going on and have a full spectrum of what's going on. So we got to implement it. They do it and conceal it as much as possible.

CID: Mainstream society would have a hard time, and cannot understand how this can be. How can you have two kinds of laws? How can you have street justice and legal law? How did this come about?

LBM: Basically when you have these classes—"haves" and the "have-nots"—this creates the laws of the land. No amount of paperwork can actually finish what is going on in the streets if a life is taken—that's the end of it. What you all are talking about, we ain't feeling—meaning the government.

CID: Over here, you have people isolated in public housing, with separate structure, with a separate set of laws.

LBM: Basically, you get this structure where individuals don't have much whatever. You are going to work with whatever resources you have to make something happen. If you have less resources, you are going to make do with what you got—you are going to make means happen with those.

Similar to Keith's perspective, LBM's comments demonstrate the existence of an alternative form of justice that is extralegal and widely shared among residents. LBM refers to this alternative form of justice with a play on words: "just us." This refers to the idea that conflict is managed among community residents, separate from the legal system. However, it also implies the inability of the police to effectively enforce the rule of law, and it highlights the isolation of poor, urban residents from mainstream legal institutions. The ineffectiveness of law enforcement and area residents' disconnect from the system as highlighted by LBM's comments can only reinforce the perception among residents that the police and the legal system are unable to effectively mitigate threats of violence.

More importantly, however, LBM's comments illustrate two key points about retaliation as a response to threats of danger. First, not everyone has the means to utilize retaliation as a means of conflict management. Individuals who do not have the social ties in the community to effectively organize the use of violence are constrained. This point should not be underestimated, since retaliation is one part of street justice. In addition, the possibility of counterretaliation is always something residents must consider. Second, those who do have the means will resort to violence. This point should not be overgeneralized, however, without consideration of the other strategies outlined previously, namely, toleration and negotiation.

Thus, disputes or disagreements are settled through violence, wherein residents confront the offending parties. The comments of LBM highlight the role of drive-by shootings and other acts of violence as being derivative and structured by public norms rooted in street justice.

Conclusion

Norbert Elias argues that violence is at the core of the social organization of society. In this chapter, I have argued that perceived danger and violence play a major role in the establishment of an alternative set of informal strategies known as street justice. The perceived danger emanates from two sources: the street and law enforcement. The alternative strategies that form the backbone of street justice, no snitchin', negotiation, and retaliation, are responses to perceived danger and violence.

Street justice has important implications for understanding how violence shapes the outlook of the urban poor. In contrast to previous works, I have shown how street justice affects the outlook of both African Americans and Latinos. The code of the street has been used to explain the experience of African Americans and its application to other groups has been limited. Other works (e.g., Bourgois, 1995) have tried to explain the experience of Latinos by arguing that honor rather than money often motivates criminal behavior and the adoption of informal rules of the street. In contrast, this chapter has shown how exposure to violence shapes the outlook of both African Americans and Latinos.

Next, I have emphasized how street justice is not reducible to the binary categories of "street" or "decent." It does not necessarily require code switching. Instead, I suggest that contradictory frames can coexist and shape the outlook of collective groups in neighborhoods with high levels of poverty. I have argued that contradictory frameworks are reconciled by the fear of violence pervasive in South LA.

Finally, an examination of South LA through the lens of street justice reveals that residents utilize a myriad of strategies besides violence. Most of the urban and criminology literature has focused on the retaliatory side of the code of the streets. My work has tried to show that multiple strategies are utilized besides violence. Garot (2009) has persuasively demonstrated a similar idea; however, his work has focused mostly on troubled youths. In contrast, I have tried to show how street justice shapes the outlook of both criminal and noncriminal residents of South LA.

6

Responding to Violence, Keeping the Peace

Interracial Relations between Black and Latino Youth Gangs

(CO-AUTHORED WITH DOMINIC RIVERA)

One of the central themes developed in this book is the pivotal role that violence plays in creating social order. The sites analyzed for this chapter also reflect a high level of homicide: a total of 55 individuals were murdered within a one-mile radius of the two school sites where data was collected, as detailed in Table 6.1. According to the LAPD, in 2003 and 2004, 31 individuals were murdered within a one-mile radius of the first school site, McCalister, in the central part of South Los Angeles. In the same two-year period, 24 individuals were murdered within a one-mile radius of the second school site, Jefferson, located in the western part of South LA.

TABLE 6.1. Latino Share of Population and Homicides

	2003 Homicides	2004 Homicides	2003 & 2004 Total Homicides
McCalister 1mi radius	13	18	31
Jefferson 1mi radius	8	16	24

This chapter explores how black and Latino youths, many of whom have had some gang affiliation, respond to the high levels of violence. Given the diverse nature of the community, where Latinos have an increasing presence in South LA, I explore the relationship between black and Latino relations and high levels of violence. Understanding this relationship is important for researchers going forward because in many ways it reflects the new urban realities across the United States.

The news media have long highlighted the tensions between blacks and Latinos in South LA. In January 2007, an op-ed in the *Los Ange-*

les Times stated that "Latino ethnic cleansing of African Americans from multiracial neighborhoods" was an "increasingly common trend" (Hernandez, 2007). By highlighting the occasional eruption of black and Latino violence, the media create the perception of ongoing interracial violence. John Hipp, George Tita, and Lyndsay Boggess (2009) convincingly demonstrate that, in fact, there has been very little interracial violence committed between blacks and Latinos in Los Angeles. Instead, they found that intraracial violence—black on black and Latino on Latino—is more common. The central question I explore here is the following: what is the relationship between interracial relations and violence among Latino and African American youths?

This chapter adds yet another layer in understanding the social order of South LA, where violence and avoidance play a central role. Just as in the neighborhood settings, parallel worlds emerge in response to the high levels of violence. However, in this particular setting, the parallel worlds of blacks and Latinos were shaped by the context in which violence affected young people's lives, and in the immediate threats that this violence posed.

Interracial Gang Relations

While the findings of Hipp, Tita, and Boggess are convincing, their analysis provides little explanation as to why there has been minimal interracial violence. A more developed framework for understanding the social dynamics that underpin African American and Latino relations is needed. I suggest that the relationship between violence and interracial relations requires further investigation. The issues have been framed within two distinct approaches. The most common and dominant approach focuses on interracial relations as a source of violence and conflict. A second, less common and less developed, examines how violence shapes interracial relations. The later approach provides a promising avenue to further understand the link between interracial relations and violence in diverse settings such as South LA.

In the sociological literature, scholars have addressed interracial relations as a primary source of violence in four main ways. Three of these approaches focus on ethnic conflict: social disorganization theory, ethnic competition theory, and routine activities theory. A fourth view (Sanchez-Jankowski, 2008) highlights the role of neighborhood type in shaping interracial conflict or cooperation.

Social disorganization theory is often used to explain ethnic conflict. It begins with the idea that a diversity of racial and ethnic groups makes it difficult to develop consensus regarding the acceptance of values, norms, and behavior. The differences between groups regarding acceptable norms become the basis of conflict and violence. A shortcoming of this perspective is that it ignores the possibility that new informal norms can arise to mitigate conflict.

A second perspective highlights the role of competition over scarce resources as a source of conflict. This competition heightens ethnic identity boundaries. In turn, heightened identity boundaries increase social distance, thereby increasing ethnic conflict.

A third view focuses on routine activities as a source of interracial interaction. This perspective details how social structure and social integration shape the likelihood of intergroup contact (Blau, 1977). The frequency of intergroup association and contact is determined by the opportunities to do so. Thus, ethnic conflict is shaped by similar patterns of activities that bring diverse groups together.

While the above views make important contributions to the literature on interracial relations, they tend to focus exclusively on relations between blacks and whites, and most do not deal with young people who have had gang affiliations. More importantly, they highlight the sources of violence, not the mechanisms that mitigate the potential for either interracial violence or how individuals avoid violence altogether.

Recent work by Sanchez-Jankowski (2008) considers the role of neighborhood type in shaping interracial relations that goes beyond black-and-white relations. He argues that areas that undergo ethnic transformation are likely to become contested neighborhoods, characterized by hostility between groups and territorial separation. Sanchez-Jankowski introduces the concept of the "fragmented neighborhood" to denote the social and class divisions that emerge, based on length of residence in neighborhoods, origin of birth, citizenship, employment status, occupation, and gender. Sanchez-Jankowski's framework advances beyond the theories outlined earlier, by highlighting the role of neighborhood dynamics in providing a context of interaction that shapes relations among residents. He takes into account interracial dynamics between Latinos and African Americans in specific settings.

Previous work (Martinez and Rios, 2011) has shown that conflict is not always a dominant outcome in areas that have undergone ethnic change. My colleague Victor Rios and I have argued that multiracial urban marginal neighborhoods operate under a matrix of forms of social interaction that occur simultaneously. Thus, conflict, cooperation, and avoidance are all at play in social relations, but avoidance dominates. Relations among residents are structured in an unwritten consensus that regulates conduct.

Violence Shapes Interracial Relations

While many studies have focused on interracial relations as a source of potential violence and conflict, few works have considered how the opposite causal relationship may work: how does violence shape interracial relations? In beginning to consider this relationship, one must understand the role of group identity and the factors that play a role in its construction. Previous work suggests that violence plays a central role in the construction of group identity. Building on these frameworks, I suggest that the formation of group identities plays a crucial role in shaping interracial relations between African Americans and Latinos.

Several works have indirectly addressed the relationship between violence and identity. Elijah Anderson's (1999) work documents how exposure to poverty and violence creates two distinct types of identities: "street" and "decent." "Street" identities draw on the norms of violence and the rules of the street as being central; whereas "decent" folks adhere to mainstream conventional values that emphasize the rule of law rather than violence.

David Harding (2010) illustrates a more explicit relationship between poverty, violence, and identity. He argues that exposure to violence creates neighborhood identities that promote obligations and loyalty based on what he calls "cross-cohort socialization." As in Anderson's analysis, according to Harding, youths are able to code switch between multiple identities, some of which are mainstream, and others that are street, creating what he calls "cultural heterogeneity."

In a similar vein, Robert Garot (2009) demonstrates how gang identities are performed. Gang identities, in his view, are soft identities that individuals are able to weave in and out of. According to Garot, this gang-identity performance is utilized as needed, and becomes a resource to deal with the challenges of urban life, violence being one of them.

Victor Rios (2011) argues that identities are primarily a response to the criminalization of black and Latino youths. As a response to the increasingly pervasive and punitive role of the state, via what he calls the "youth control complex," youths resist their circumstances and attempt to regain dignity. One central way that they resist is through what Rios calls "hypermasculinity," an identity that promotes the exaggeration of masculine qualities, such as aggressiveness, and also an overly promiscuous male persona.

This chapter builds on previous works and addresses the relationship between violence and identity more explicitly. Unlike previous works, however, I focus on how violence shapes group boundaries and solidarity, which becomes the basis of identity. While previous works have shed crucial insights into this phenomenon, these works do not directly explore how violence creates identity, or how it shapes interracial relations between Latinos and African Americans—the two largest ethnic groups in urban America.

Thus, a central question I explore in this work is how the formation of group identity, forged in the face of violence, shapes interracial relations. Previous work (Martinez and Rios, 2011) provides a key insight into this matter, identifying avoidance as the primary and dominant relationship between Latinos and African Americans, rather than conflict and cooperation. In this work, I revisit the concept of avoidance and its relationship to violence, group identity, and interracial relations.

Where does avoidance fit into the picture? While my previous work provided some foundational insights into the role of avoidance in shaping interracial relations in daily interactions between black and Latino youths, I did not investigate the deeper structural forces at play. One key issue not explored in the study I conducted with Rios, is the genesis of avoidance. Stated differently: why does avoidance become the dominant relationship between Latinos and African Americans in South LA? A second related issue, also not examined previously, is the following: once avoidance takes hold, what are the factors that maintain group boundaries?

I suggest that many scholars have misunderstood the relationship between interracial relations and violence. This chapter unpacks the social underpinnings of avoidance, with a focus on how residents respond to violence. I suggest that violence promotes the formation of distinct group identities that serve as a wedge, promoting avoidance between groups. Few works have explored the role of avoidance as a primary response to violence. Researchers have focused, too often, on interracial relations and their effect on conflict and violence. Thus, this work fills an important gap in the literature: the role of violence in shaping interracial relations and identities.

Theoretical Explanations of Minimizing Group Violence

One of the most important contributions to the sociological understanding of individual and group violence is the work of Roger Gould (2003). What is most relevant is his framework for explaining under what circumstances group violence is rare. Gould suggests that violence, and particularly group violence, is rare when solidarity is strong among adversarial groups. In a sense, this is a primary response to the threat of potential violence. Violence is less likely to occur because two factors operate simultaneously. First, group solidarity communicates to others that the threat of violence is a real possibility. Second, individuals weigh their own potential risks and potential for harm. Thus, both individual and group forces play a role in minimizing violence. The key, however, to minimizing violence in this framework is the role of solidarity. The stronger the perception of solidarity among rivals, the less likely that group violence will occur.

I find Gould's framework to be a useful starting point for explaining the low level of violence between blacks and Latinos. As the findings in this chapter will demonstrate, Latinos and African Americans in South LA maintained strong group boundaries in the face of high levels of violence. In this work, I explore the relationship between the need for strong group solidarity and its relationship to violence. I examine how Gould's framework can shed light on the empirical findings of Hipp, Tita, and Boggess (2009), who have convincingly demonstrated that black and Latino violence is rare. Thus, I build on Gould's framework to understand how blacks and Latinos respond to the constant possibility of an eruption of violence.

Gould's framework has some limitations, however. First, it provides a limited view of how and why groups form. Instead, he focuses on how the varying levels of solidarity shape the likelihood for the emergence of violence. The stronger the perception of group solidarity is, the less likely is the emergence of violence. He leaves underdeveloped the mechanisms that produce group solidarity and boundaries, but does provide limited insight when he argues that group conflict presupposes three common factors that bring people together, as a basis of conflict: (1) interest, (2) identity, and (3) social organization. Interest brings people together, or causes conflict when there is competition for scarce resources. Identity spawns group violence, when it is motivated by the need for self-esteem, which then necessitates viewing others through negative categories to enhance one's personal and group identity. Finally, Gould suggests that social organization is founded on normative arrangements and durable social relations that bind people together into groups. Social organization becomes essential, in this view, when limited state institutions for peace building compel residents to perform and create order on their own.

This chapter reevaluates and contributes to the sociological understanding of the relationship between solidarity and violence. My work revisits two factors that Gould dismisses as playing a role in group conflict: (1) the role of identity, and (2) the role of social organization. A complex social process exists that precedes the social group solidarity that he describes. Stated differently, a crucial antecedent process prior to group solidarity is missing. This study begins to address this shortcoming by switching the causal process, with the following question: how does violence shape group solidarity? In other words, how does violence shape identity and social organization? However, unlike Gould, the data used for this study reveals that the perception of violence or the anticipation of violence is what motivates group behavior. Given the ever-present threats of violence at the school sites used for this study, I find that there is no single imminent threat of violence, but multiple unpredictable moments of potential violence, such as drive-by shootings, or getting assaulted and/or shot before, during, or after school.

Thus, the "anticipation of violence" is an ever-present, powerful force in creating identity.

Second, while Gould explains that the process of solidarity is partly based on appearance, this explanation is not well developed in his work. I suggest that solidarity is a dynamic process, with a performance element, that is constantly being negotiated and regulated.

I argue that the constant threat of violence forces young people to seek out those who are similar to obtain security and protection in the face of the ineffectiveness of the police and other law enforcement agencies. Belonging to a group and establishing solidarity, therefore, become critical for youths. I find that Latinos and blacks are not so much fearful of each other, as they are of violence in general. Consistent with Gould, I find that the strength solidarity brings becomes a key resource for responding to violence, and for minimizing future violence. However, I discover that there are many contradictions in youths' behavior, which suggests, in many instances, that group solidarity is weak. Many youths crossed over racial lines, and, yet, were still able to maintain the perception that group solidarity was strong. Therefore, I suggest that solidarity is an ambiguous process, in which blacks and Latinos must constantly create the perception that solidarity is strong, as a means to deter future violence.

One key consequence of the constant negotiation of solidarity is the avoidance of other groups. I demonstrate that avoidance plays a central role in the performative element of solidarity. The appearance of solidarity is the primary response to violence, which creates the conditions in which African American and Latino groups avoid one another.

The Schools

Both schools were run by a Catholic nonprofit organization and the demographics of their student bodies were similar, primarily African American and Latino males and females, ages 14–18. The schools, which drew students from throughout South Los Angeles, were established by a Catholic priest who recognized that few educational options were available for youths who had been dismissed from the Los Angeles Unified School District. Indeed, many of the youths I encountered had been dismissed from the Los Angeles Unified School District for behavioral issues. Over half of the youths were actively involved in gangs; many others were forced to associate with gangs, inside and outside of school. In addition, over half of the students, in both school sites, were also on probation with the County of Los Angeles.

As noted earlier, I began this study as a volunteer teaching assistant at the McCalister field site in the central part of South LA. The area is exclusively black and Latino, with Latinos holding a slight majority. It is one of the most violent parts of South LA,[1] and also has one of the highest levels of poverty. The police division that encompasses the school has the second highest level of homicides in Los Angeles. My second field site was in the western part of South LA. The police division here has the fourth highest homicide rate in the city. It has many of the same characteristics as the other site, but with two key differences. It still has a majority of African American residents, and a higher percentage of middle-class African Americans. Nevertheless, it still contains some of the highest levels of violence and pockets of extreme poverty in Los Angeles. The respective percentages of Latino and African American residents who reside in the areas where the fieldwork was conducted are illustrated in Maps 6.1–6.4. Maps 6.5 and 6.6 illustrate the percentage of residents who live in poverty.

I used my volunteer position to gain access to one of the sites. At the other site, I was hired as an employee and was able to gain entrance as a teaching assistant. Previous works have emphasized the importance of establishing a role when conducting ethnography fieldwork because roles shape the way subjects of a study respond to their settings. Implicitly, this affects the way subjects will respond to the presence of researchers. For the most part, students and staff at the schools understood my role to be that of a school employee or a volunteer. Using these identities, I used participant observation as my primary method of collecting data. In addition, I lived in a neighborhood in South LA that was a short driving distance from both schools, so I also had the role of area resident. Later, I discovered that two of the gangs in the schools were located near my residence. At the schools, my duties included helping with instruction during class and monitoring the young people in the morning, when they arrived for school. I would also monitor them during breaks and lunch, in order to make sure that their conduct was appropriate, and that they followed school rules. My role as a teaching assistant afforded

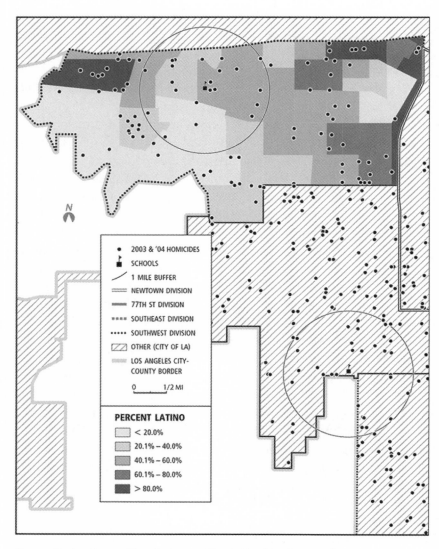

Map 6.1. Latino Share of Population and Homicides (Southwest LA)

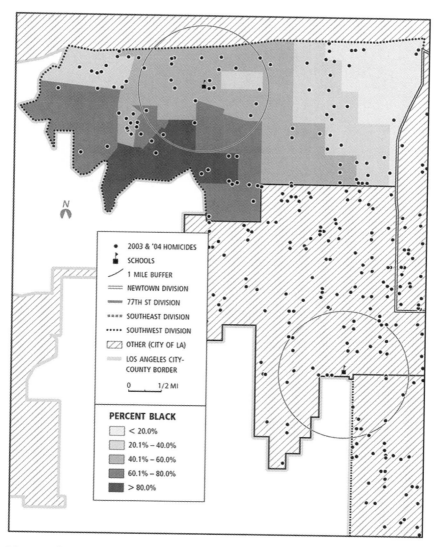

Map 6.2. Black Share of Population and Homicides (Southwest LA)

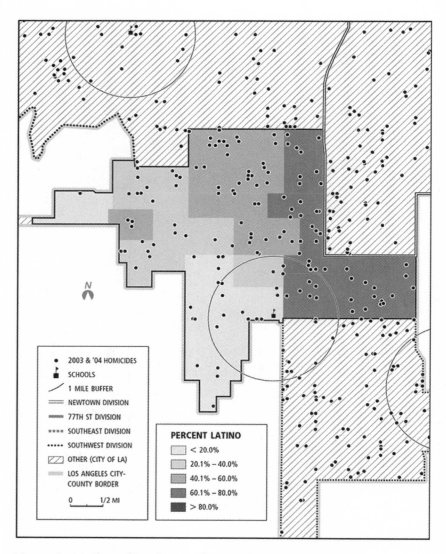

Map 6.3. Latino Share of Population and Homicides (Central South LA)

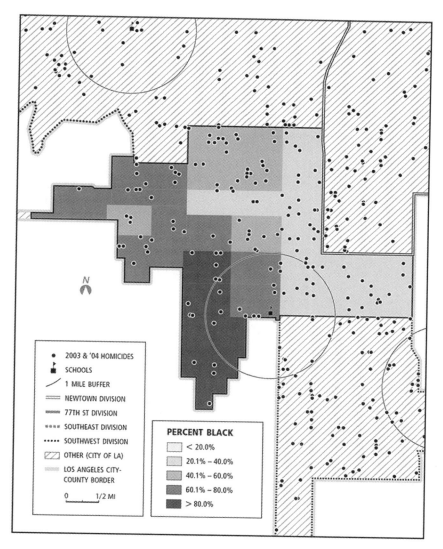

Map 6.4. Black Share of Population and Homicides (Central South LA)

Legend:
- 2003 & '04 HOMICIDES
- SCHOOLS
- 1 MILE BUFFER
- NEWTOWN DIVISION
- 77TH ST DIVISION
- SOUTHEAST DIVISION
- SOUTHWEST DIVISION
- OTHER (CITY OF LA)
- LOS ANGELES CITY-COUNTY BORDER

0   1/2 MI

PERCENT BLACK
- < 20.0%
- 20.1% – 40.0%
- 40.1% – 60.0%
- 60.1% – 80.0%
- > 80.0%

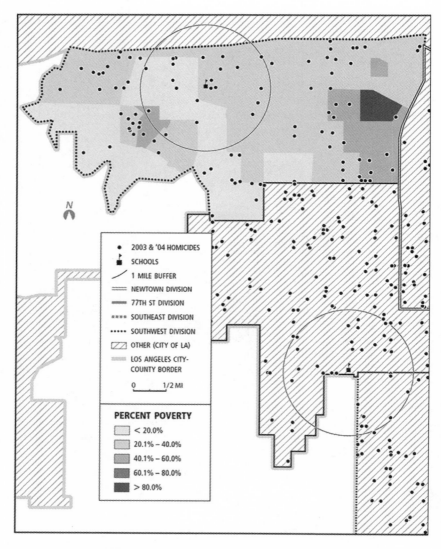

Map 6.5. Percentage of Population in Poverty and Homicides (Southwest LA)

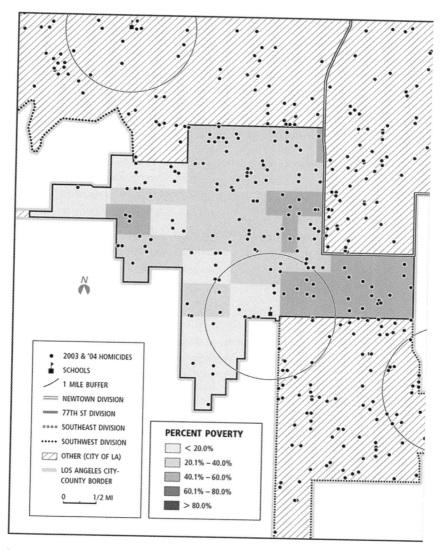

Map 6.6. Percentage of Population in Poverty and Homicides (Central South LA)

me many opportunities to directly observe the day-to-day routines of the students. Observing what people say and how they act often lends deeper insight into social phenomena than do interviews. Only at the end of the project, when I was exiting the field sites, did I interview subjects, after I had developed a rapport with them.

The Need for Protection

I found that school safety and protection was a major concern for the students, faculty, and administrators at the two school sites. During fieldwork at these sites, I witnessed a similar pattern regarding school safety. There was virtually nothing law enforcement or school officials could do to ensure the students' safety. A staff member from the school site in the core of South Central LA, told me on the first day of my volunteer work, "The area is hot both inside and outside the school. Many gangs surround the school area."

Given that many of the students were directly or indirectly involved with gangs, they were bound to have disputes in school, which followed them wherever they went. School officials, who did extensive interviews during the admission process, documented the gang activity of the young people to make sure that rival gang members did not attend school simultaneously, and thus, minimize violence in the school itself. However, these efforts could not keep disputes between the numerous gangs outside of the school from spilling onto the campus.

On many occasions, adults and youths who did not attend the school encircled the campus during breaks, lunchtime, and after school. In back of the school building, there was a chain-link fence approximately eight feet high that anyone could see through. Usually, these individuals would rev up their cars, music blasting, and stare at students in a menacing way. They often had shaved heads, wore white shirts, and were tattooed extensively. They would throw gang signs at the students behind the fence, and, at times, they would point their fingers at or flip off specific students. This process would go on for anywhere from 10 to 20 minutes.

These incidents were terrifying to the students and the staff. The students often communicated to me and other staff members that the people involved were from various gangs around their neighborhoods.

Many of the students acted tough, as if they were not scared, and would run to the fence and yell back. I had to tell students to "get away from the fence!" Everyone understood that, most of the time, the encircling cars were just a show to intimidate, but there was always the possibility that a shot could come through the fence and into the campus, when students were having lunch or breaks. In many instances, students were told that they had to go back inside the classrooms, and they were not allowed to go outside until the threatening drivers had left. Many staff members communicated to me, in private, that they were afraid that something was going to happen to them.

At least two to three times a week, I would call the police, for fear that someone would get shot. Every time I called, the dispatchers asked me if shots had been fired, or if a weapon had been seen. I told the police that no weapon had been seen or fired, and each time, I was told that there was nothing that the police could do.

The students thus ate their lunches and took their breaks in constant fear of being victimized. One, a 17-year-old Latino male, Damosque, who had taken a liking to me, asked, "Cid, did you call the police?" "Yeah, I called them," I answered. "They don't do shit, Cid. Everyone knows they can't help us. I know you trying to help, but they can't do anything for us."

These forms of intimidation were almost daily events at the school. While no one was shot during these drive-arounds, the situation produced and reaffirmed the students' fear and anxiety. Violence was a reality for many youths, both in their neighborhoods, and, especially, in the neighborhoods surrounding the school. As I previously described, during the time of my fieldwork, the school sites were located in the four Los Angeles police precincts with the highest levels of homicide. The *Los Angeles Times* ran a story about the area where one of the schools is located, referring to it as "Death Alley," because of the high number of homicides there.

As a result of the high levels of violence in the area, gang-intervention workers, who were contracted by the city government, would occasionally patrol the areas around the schools, and make regular contact with students and faculty at both field sites. They were allowed to visit classrooms and were given office space when they visited. On one occasion, their presence helped prevent a potential shooting.

One afternoon, when school was just about to let out in, I witnessed a group of three or four youths, about 17 to 19 years old, run out of an alley near the rear of the school. A gang intervention worker named Rico, whom I knew from doing fieldwork, seemed out of breath and excited, as he told me:

> RICO: Cid, you see them kids? They was packing and they were looking
> for someone on this campus; talkin' about how they were looking
> for so-and-so over here [the campus]. Cid, they did not know I was
> [a] gang worker. But, I saw their guns; they were all packing. I knew
> what was about to go down. I had to be slick, Cid, and I said, "You all
> better get the hell out of here. I saw the police in this alley, and they
> said they were looking for about four kids."
> CID: Were there police in the alley?
> RICO: Naw, man, I just told them that to scare them. I had to outsmart
> those kids, 'cause they woulda done something.

School officials were notified, the police were called, and, once again, even though the youths were seen carrying weapons, LAPD was unable to respond or follow up.

On several occasions, young people and adults were shot and killed around the campus sites. In 2003, just before I began volunteering at the school in the central part of South LA, a young girl was shot in the leg, right outside the school site. Luckily, she did not die. Students would occasionally reference this event when I talked to them about school safety. However, in my conversations with them, they seemed to have accepted this type of event as normal, or "no big deal." At the other school site, in the western part of South LA, a young man was murdered caddy-corner to the school, near a liquor store on a commercial corridor. These types of events, at both sites, marked the streets outside the school as dangerous social spaces.

During my research at the schools, I constantly heard the students talking about safety, and about how they were going to deal with it. I would often catch conversations about ongoing disputes with rival gangs in their neighborhoods, or about disputes with individuals that might jeopardize their safety. Many of the young people whom I observed and interviewed for this study consistently expressed the idea that police and law enforcement were ineffective in providing safety and protection. In addition, since many of them had identified as being gang members, or affiliated with gangs, they had strong reservations about going to the police.

Given the constant fear and possibility of violence, what were the young people to do? In the following section, I highlight the common responses and strategies that they utilized. One clear way that they responded to violence was in their organized approach to it.

Responses to Violence

In many respects, the observed routines of the youths reflected their organizational responses to violence. I witnessed some of the ways in which youths coped with the threat of violence.

During the morning, before class started at the school in the western part of South LA, I was instructed to stand in front of the building to observe the students and make sure they safely entered the school premises. The school building, which had an industrial look, was constructed of concrete and brick, and somewhat worn down. The Catholic nonprofit organization had purchased it from the Los Angeles Unified School District, and the building's architecture and condition suggested the previous owners had used it for quite some time. The staff was well aware of the potential for violence in the area, and the school instituted a policy wherein staff members were assigned to perform this front-guard role. Every day, from around 7:20 a.m. until 8:00 a.m., I watched students coming to school along the commercial corridor. Many would take the bus and get dropped off several blocks from the school. Others would get dropped off down the street from the school. A handful of the youths would walk to school or ride their bikes. Very few students were dropped off in front of the school. I observed a constant pattern among the students on their way to school. Latino and African American students made a concerted effort to organize racially bonded small groups, so that they could walk together with their own people. I asked some of them why did this.

"We're just looking out for each other," said one student.

"You never know want could happen out here," said another.

"You could get shot out here just because of how you look," said yet another.

The same pattern of social organization, based on race, was prevalent inside the school. During breaks and lunch, the social space of the school was divided between Latinos and African Americans. At both campuses in South LA, I observed the same pattern. At the central school site, five to eight Latino students would sit on a concrete slab. Mexican and Salvadoran students, wearing white T-shirts and baggy pants, would always sit in the area outside the rear entrance of the school. They rarely ventured away from this area. It was understood that black students did not sit in this location. Similarly, black students would stake claim to the area near the basketball courts, where bleachers were located. Latinos rarely went near this area, and almost never played basketball, unless instructed to do so by the physical education staff. I observed the same pattern at the west-side location, except Latinos laid claim to bleachers on one side of the campus, and blacks congregated near the entrance, where they sat on a concrete slab.

Inside the schools, there was more variation between the students in their interactions. Most classrooms had small tables that could seat three to four students. Most of the time, students would attempt to sit near people of the same race, unless there were no such seats available. In many instances, though, the teachers would move students, at their discretion, to manage school disruptions. For example, students were moved from tables to sit with other students, so that they could not talk to their friends.

Exposure to Violence outside the School

The organizational responses of the students to violence were shaped by their exposure to it outside the school, too. Gang membership and neighborhood loyalty have often been cited as the primary organizing forces for youths. To explore this issue, I later conducted interviews at both school sites. Many students revealed that gang affiliation was used as a primary resource to cope with the threat of violence and the need for safety. Furthermore, these responses were shaped by three factors: the need for protection, in general; gender; and the status of Latinos, as newcomers to South LA. These factors shaped the way in which violence forged distinct identities.

Gangs and Protection

African American and Latino students expressed similar views when asked why people in their neighborhoods joined gangs. Their responses focused, more generally, on the need for protection, a sense of family and obligations, reputation, stability, and order.

Frederick, an 18-year-old African American from the western part of South LA, shared his view regarding why people become involved in gangs in the area. Unlike many of the young people at the school sites, Frederick was not involved in a gang. His father worked as a coach for an afterschool program, but Frederick did not share any information about his mother.

> CID: Why do people join gangs?
> FREDERICK: They ask where you're from, and, then, keep messing with a person. They take advantage. Someone not in a gang, they can take advantage of them. A person might have a connection, from another gang; this sparks a war . . . can't avoid it. Anything can happen to them.

Sergio, a 15-year-old Latino male, who was actively involved with a gang in Watts, expressed a similar view. His father abandoned the family, and his mother was not employed. He explained that his father was from Guatemala and his mother was from El Salvador. "People join because their parents don't treat them right. Getting punked can be a reason why people join gangs."

Phatdaddy, an 18-year-old African American from the central part of South LA, expressed a similar perspective. Like Frederick, he was not actively involved in a gang. His mother was disabled and his father worked as a mechanic.

> CID: Why are youth involved in gangs around here?
> PHATDADDY: Gangs are retarded. But people join in my neighborhood for protection and money.

The interviews with Frederick, Sergio, and Phatdaddy illustrate that the need for protection from the threat of violence is the key reason that youths join gangs.

Other Latino males mentioned similar motivations for joining gangs. Creeper, a 15-year-old male of Mexican descent, was very explicit to school officials and other students about his gang involvement. He had two large tattoos, one on the left side of his neck, and one on the right side, each about six inches long. Each tattoo was a number from his gang. Many young people whom I came to know thought he would be shot soon, because he openly displayed the tattoos. "That fool is going to be shot and dead," another gang member, Damosque, said to me. As with many of the young people highlighted in this chapter, there were many strains placed on Creeper's family. His father was in jail, and his mother worked in a garment factory. Creeper explained why he joined his gang:

> CREEPER: I just grew up with it in the hood. My friends joined. Back up, make money, party, drink, kick it with girls. That's why. You're strapped up too, so no one messes with you.

Bob Marley, a 17-year-old African American from the western part of South LA, explained that both of his parents worked as security guards for different companies in Los Angeles.

> CID: Why do people join gangs?
> BOB MARLEY: They get pressured from people in the neighborhood. It's like a family, you know . . . it's tradition.

Marcus Taylor, a 14-year-old African American from the western part of South LA, added another key reason why people join gangs. Similar to other African American males interviewed, both of his parents worked as security guards.

> CID: Why do people get involved in gangs?
> MARCUS TAYLOR: They do it for sex, fame, and to get known. People want a reputation. But, it's stupid because you have to get up and do something . . . you know?
> CID: What do you mean?
> MARCUS TAYLOR: You have to prove yourself.

My interviews with Bob Marley and Marcus Taylor suggest that the exposure to the threat of violence also spurs pressure to join gangs and deal with the obligations that go along with membership. However, becoming involved in a gang also entails developing a reputation, as Marcus Taylor stated. Thus, the need for protection was a central factor in the social organization of peer groups outside school.

Gender and Gangs

Many female African Americans and Latinas voiced the same reasons as their male counterparts did for becoming involved in gangs. However, there were factors that made the females' situation different. Lady 8K, a 17-year-old African American, spoke with me about why she became actively involved with a gang. She said her mother had died when Lady 8K was young, and that she had no communication with her father.

> CID: Why do people get involved with gangs?
>
> LADY 8K: I got involved because my family was not around. My dad beat me, and then I got split up with my siblings. My mom died of AIDS, and my dad was involved with the Vermonts [a local gang]. That's what I observed growing up. I want to bail out, but it's hard. The street is where I get my guidance. That's where people get theirs . . . like stolen property, cars, shoes. But the main thing is the backup.

Giggles, a 17-year-old Latina whose mother cleaned houses and whose father was a mechanic, shared her view of gangs. "There is no one there for you. Homies are there for you, though. I was raised in a gang. I guess you do it for the money and protection."

An interview with Pop, a 17-year-old African American female, highlighted many of the same views. Like Lady 8K, neither parent was actively involved in her life. Her father died when she was young, and her mom was bed-ridden and ill.

> CID: Why were you involved with the gang?
>
> POP: Nobody cares about me. My peoples was involved . . . my brother. It became like family. Support group, basically.

Ms. Clowner, a 17-year-old Latina, had been actively involved in a gang, but recently transitioned out, due to a tragic event that had sent her uncle to prison for life, for murder. She explained why she became involved: "Parents weren't home to help me. I joined because Travisa asked me to join. But, then, you look for fights to show everyone who we are, so people don't mess with us."

My interviews with Lady 8K and Pop suggest that gangs provide an important element of protection, in the form of backup and support, and are an important resource for female gang members, in order to manage violence near their schools. The development of a reputation is important for young girls like Ms. Clowner, because it helps deter violence.

There is a third way in which gangs act as a resource for young African American and Latina girls. Being a volunteer in one school, and an employee in the other, my data was not limited to interviews. Through my observations, I also discovered that female gangs act as a resource to protect the girls from the sexist hostility of their male classmates. In many instances, I observed groups of girls standing up to boys who tried to belittle them with derogatory comments. I often heard males refer to girls as "bitches," "skanks," or "hood rats," and the girls were often told that they would be "dick-slapped." An interview with a classroom instructor showed he was well aware of this behavior.

> MR. K.: Boys often treat girls with disrespect. There is a lot of conflict between boys and girls. Girls, many of them are in gangs. They will not put up with it and will fight back.
> CID: So, they have their own gangs?
> MR. K.: Yes, they do, and two girls were recently suspended for beating the shit out of a boy.

Christine, a 16-year-old African American, shared her view on this issue. Her father was incarcerated, and her mom worked as a nurse. She was actively involved with an all-girls gang.

> CID: Why do young girls get involved in gangs?
> CHRISTINE: Gangs will have your back. Take care of you. No family, no one loves them. Have a lot of fun, get along. People care about me! And the girls' crew, nobody messes with us!
> CID: You mean boys?
> CHRISTINE: Yeah!

While African American girls and Latinas echoed many of the same reasons as boys for becoming involved in gangs—the need for protection from violence, in particular—there were two key differences: First, the girls tended to highlight the role of gangs as a form of support, whether emotional, financial, or for guidance. The boys also mentioned these factors, but not to the same extent as the girls. Second, membership in gangs served to protect girls from the derogatory and sexual hostility that some boys directed at them.

Latino Newcomers and Gangs

While many African American have resided in South LA for several generations, the area was increasingly becoming Latinoized, with a large influx of Mexican and Central American (primarily Salvadoran) immigrants. Their ethnic identity and status as newcomers played important roles in how violence shaped their new social identities. Many of these families and their adolescent children were not familiar with the informal social mechanisms that residents utilized to deal with conflict and violence, such as not calling the police or "no snitchin.'" In addition, over 30 percent of Latino residents in South LA were not US citizens, according to 2000 census figures. Thus, utilizing third parties, such as the police, was not an option. Latinos and their families eventually learned that there were alternative ways to deal with neighborhood conflict and violence.

In such situations, they looked to others who were similar in language, ethnicity, and culture for protection and aid. Given the high level of violence in the area, it was difficult for Latinos to develop trust with other residents, such as African Americans. Many African Americans expressed to me in interviews that Latinos never reached out to them, and, mostly, avoided them. My observations in various South LA neighborhoods verified the empirical data that Hipp, Tita, and Boggess collected indicating that interracial violence between Latinos and blacks was rare. Members of these two groups mostly avoided one another.

However, there were instances in which African Americans preyed on Latinos, usually for robbery. Several LAPD officers mentioned this phenomenon in interviews.[2] The result of these experiences was that both Latinos and African Americans mostly looked to members of their own ethnic groups in response to violence. Latino young people from these neighborhoods described how they learned to deal with neighborhood violence, and how it translated into how they dealt with the threat of violence in the school setting. A young Latino gang member, whom I will call Victor, explained his experience.

> VICTOR: On my block, we were picked on by blacks. They harassed us. So, Mexicans and Salvadorans formed a gang called HTO, "Hispanics Taking Over."
> CID: How do Salvadorans and Mexicans get along?
> VICTOR: There is no problem. We are in the same gangs!

Damosque explained his view:

> DAMOSQUE: Uh, I guess man, they think we're not gonna do shit about something. You know? They try to fucking push me, push us, you know, push us around, and shit, they can't do that shit. You know they don't like Mexicans, immigrants and shit.
> CID: That happens when you see a lot of immigrants getting robbed and picked on?
> DAMOSQUE: Yeah, man, getting punked and shit, man . . . for those people that never did anything, you know?
> CID: What kind of things, like getting robbed or what?
> DAMOSQUE: Robbed, punked, getting punked.

Eventually, as young people became familiar with South LA's high level of violence and how difficult it was to trust law enforcement and others who were different, they sought out means to deter violence and protect themselves. Latinos responded by forming coalitions with those who looked and acted most similar to them, as indicated by Mafioso:

> CID: What would you say, why do people join gangs?
> MAFIOSO: Because they feel like they need protection or something. Sometime, there be bitch-ass fools. When they was young, they used to get bullied, punked, and beat up, and, now, they feel like they grown up now, and they ain't trying to be bitches no more. They

think by going into the neighborhood, they are gonna have backup from the neighborhood.

In a separate interview, Skeloe built on this topic, when asked about newly established immigrants in South Los Angeles:

CID: So, there are a lot of like, people, like, who just . . . whose parents just came from Mexico or El Salvador . . .

SKELOE: And, they join gangs. You know what I'm saying? Exactly, that's what I'm talking about in the neighborhood. In the neighborhood, you know, you live there for so long, and you associate with them, so, then, it's like you have to be. You know what I'm saying? And, sometimes it's just for protection, you know, your backup support.

In conclusion, violence shaped group identity based on three factors: the general need for protection, gender, and the ethnic and newcomer status of Latinos. In distinct ways, these factors shaped group formation and the use of gangs as a resource outside the school. The next section illustrates how violence creates multiple-group identities, which are not simply reducible to the concept of a gang. Indeed, the use of gangs for identity building is documented in the literature, but there are multiple ways in which identities are created that go beyond gang membership, which involve factors such as gender, ethnicity, and newcomer status.

It is tempting to think of these group identities as fixed. The findings from this study suggest that violence is a powerful force in the creation of these identities. However, in the next section I demonstrate that, as the context of violence shifts, so to do the group identities.

Back in School: Racial Solidarity?

As outlined earlier, the threat of violence at the schools that I used for this study was constant. Given the context in which youths faced violence in the school settings, the group boundaries shifted to adapt to the needs specific to the schools. This setting, therefore, became significant in that it structured a microcosm of interactions. Observations in both school settings revealed how identities, based on the general need for protection, occasionally crossed interracial boundaries, and gender gave way to race and ethnicity. This is not to say that these group identities were not significant, but, in the context of violence in the schools, they became less salient. While neighborhood issues of safety compelled many young people to use gangs as a resource for protection, the daily threat of violence, in the school settings, solidified interracial boundaries, as a way to cope with the violence. One question, which requires further explanation, is why some of these organizing forces became trumped by race, as the central organizing feature, when youths entered the school setting. In this section, I illustrate how the threat of violence gives rise to new types of social solidarity, based primarily on race. Thus, racial solidarity becomes the primary response to daily threats. As a result of increased racial solidarity, interracial relations between African Americans and Latinos were predominantly structured through a general strategy of avoidance.

While individuals may naively believe that there is always strength in numbers, Gould (2003) argues that the strength lies in the solidarity of the group. Simply being a member of a large group does not necessarily ensure protection; rather, protection begins to develop when a group can *portray* an image of brotherhood, in which all members are intricately intertwined. It is much more difficult to target a victim if you believe that you will unintentionally be targeting his or her whole group, as an all-inclusive package, rather than just that one individual. Drawing from Damosque's comments quoted above, being caught alone puts individuals at an increased risk of victimization, and thus, portraying an image of solidarity is pivotal in deterring future violence for residents in South LA. However, analogous to the metaphor of dogs that are "all bark and no bite," when some groups' image of solidarity and toughness are tested, they are exposed as merely phony and weak. Skeloe discussed how he initially joined a gang for protection, only to be disappointed later, when his gang did not stand up for him or provide the protection he expected.

> CID: So, yea, if you're hooked up with somebody like this gang then, then that's protection right?
> SKELOE: People, you know, that's what they try to say, but you know you're more of a coward, to me, when you go in with a gang. You

know, I got in a crew because I thought they were gonna have my back, but they didn't have my back; the person that had my back was the person standing next to me, that's when I stopped being in crews, you know. I'm a Warner, you know what I'm saying? I tag, I tag my own name, and I represent myself. No one else.

Mafioso was also aware of the idea of perceived weakness of both African Americans and Latinos. When asked how Latinos perceive blacks in South LA, he replied:

The thing about blacks is them think they hard, like some of they think they crazy and stuff, that what some black people think. They think they all macho, and this and that. That's how they be thinking. We be like, those fools think they crazy and shit, but he ain't gonna do nothing.

Mafioso was also asked how African Americans think about Latinos:

MAFIOSO: Some of them think that some Latinos are bitches and shit, 'cuz some Latinos be putting themselves out there by showing them fear. . . . Some of the Latino kids, they're punks. Once they find out you're a punk, they come after you. They gonna keep on messing with you, if they see fear.

CID: Do you see a lot of that?

MAFIOSO: I used to. I used to see a lot of them [Latinos] acting like a little punk, and stuff. They need to know they're not punk, homie, they breathe the same air that you breathe.

The comments from Skeloe, Mafioso, and Damosque all suggest that the perception of group solidarity is critical as a response to violence. Both Latino and African American youths understood that they had to demonstrate that they were willing to fight and use violence, when necessary.

As I described at the outset of this book, my first day on the job, during lunch, I witnessed firsthand both groups demonstrating that they would back each other up when they needed to. The eating area was outdoors, in the back of the school. It consisted of long tables and a set of benches, placed next to each other on black asphalt and covered with a light aluminum roof for shade. The heat of a sunny day heightened the smell of the asphalt.

Someone had thrown a milk carton, which had hit a Latino boy on the head. Two male youths, one African American and the other Latino, each around 17 years old, and, like the other boys, wearing Dockers khaki pants and white polo shirts (the dress code at LA charter schools), started an altercation. The Latino male confronted the African American and asked him why he had hit the other boy with the milk carton. The confrontation escalated into an angry verbal exchange. In a flash, the two boys jumped up from their chairs, and circled around one another, swinging their fists, as a mob of mostly Latino and African American youths cheered them on. The scene got louder and louder, as the mob of students yelled: "Fuck him up," "Kick that punk's ass," "Get that fucking puto." I attempted to separate the two boys, but they kept darting into the crowd, and the other students obstructed me. Finally, a female schoolteacher, who was on yard duty, waded in and caught one by the leg. I was then able to restrain the other. Even though the fistfight was broken up, it had already sparked group conflict, as Latino and African American youths began to divide along racial lines in the lunch area. They yelled back and forth, and at moments it seemed like the situation might turn into a riot.

After the boys were separated, they were quickly brought to the principal's office, but the racial divide carried over into the classrooms. In my room, black and Latino students noticeably avoided each other, sitting apart and not speaking; occasionally one would stare blankly at another. Finally, during class, two boys, one African American and the other Latino, sat down in a corner and began talking dispassionately as if they were having a business meeting. Later, I learned that the Latino youth, Skeloe, was the leader of one of the Latino gangs on campus; the African American was the leader of a black gang. Their classroom parley was a negotiation.

Damosque, second in charge of the Latino gang, who would subsequently become my close friend, explained:

> "They worked it out, Cid. The school couldn't do shit. We just told them what they wanted to hear, but we were going to handle it ourselves."
>
> "Is that what Skeloe was doing?" I asked.
>
> "Yeah, he handled it with the black dude."

Although the school had tried to mediate the conflict by bringing in counselors to talk with the students, none of the boys would say anything. One of the teachers asked the class that I was in, "What is wrong with you guys? We are trying to help you guys, but nobody says anything." Both black and Latino youths understood that there were informal rules for handling disputes, which kept the violence from escalating.

Victor, an 18-year-old Latino whom I have previously quoted, shared his view regarding how solidarity is important: "Latino gangs regulate their own shit and so do blacks, they don't fuck with each other." Victor's comment illustrates how conflict is mediated and regulated by each racial group.

There was a perception shared by both groups that maintaining a strong sense of identity is key to keeping the peace. The contextualization of violence by the school setting created the conditions in which youths looked to those whom they felt most comfortable with, thereby promoting racial solidarity. As a result, the interracial boundaries that emerged from the threat of violence promoted a relationship between African Americans and Latinos that can best be described as avoidance.

The Contradictions of Group Solidarity

Thus far, I have argued that the imminent threat of violence forced many Latinos and blacks to stick with their own racial groups for safety and protection. The previous section highlights that racial solidarity was an important tool that the youths utilized to achieve this goal. However, another question that emerges from the previous section is: what keeps the interracial boundaries between African Americans and Latinos in play? Stated differently: why does avoidance become the default relationship between the two groups?

The answer to these questions is somewhat puzzling. I found, in many instances, that young people crossed over racial, gang, and neighborhood boundaries. Despite crossing over, they still used race as the primary means of building solidarity. Thus, they weaved in and out of racial, gang, and neighborhood associations. These contradictory findings seem to fly in the face of my findings, at first glance. Yet, I suggest that that crossing over reveals an important insight into the performative dimension of group solidarity. This section examines how crossing over was regulated so that group solidarity could be maintained.

Crossing over occurred in a variety of ways, one of which was interracial dating. Crossing demarcated social space showed a general recognition that both groups were in a similar situation regarding violence and poverty. Overwhelmingly, the most common form of interracial dating was among Latinas and African American males. I often observed the reactions of Latino males, who seemed uncomfortable with this. I asked several Latinas what it was like to date black boys.

> LILIA: For me, I don't care if the guy is black. But I get a lot of shit from the [Latino] guys when I date a black guy.
> CID: What do they say to you?
> LILIA: Oh, you know, stuff like, what's wrong with you? How come you kick it with that black guy; he's not one of us. Um . . . that I need to kick it with my own people and it doesn't look good. They mostly make fun with me and talk shit and laugh at me.

Although much less common, I occasionally noticed Latinos dating African American girls. I asked Latinos what their views about dating black girls were. The leader of the Latino gang, Skeloe, shared his experience with me.

> CID: Do you date black girls?
> SKELOE: Me? I don't date them.
> CID: Have you dated them in the past?
> SKELOE: Yes, I had a black girlfriend in the past. They're some fine ones that are cool. We moved on though, you know . . .
> CID: What do other Latinos say about this?
> SKELOE: They talk shit and give you hard time. You know, that we should be with Raza only. But, I noticed that's staring to change.
> CID: Do you see more Latino guys dating black girls?
> SKELOE: "It's starting to become okay. In the past, not too long ago, you would get a lot of shit, and it wasn't as common. I noticed that it's changing. So, people don' trip as much."

Frederick stated his view.

CID: What do you think about dating Latinas?

FREDERICK: Dating . . . it's open to any race here. People accept whatever they can comes to them [laughing]. Guys [other black males]
wouldn't say anything.

CID: What would black girls say?

FREDERICK: "Oh, why is he with her? He should be with a sister."

CID: What would Latino males say about it?

FREDERICK: I don't know . . . nothing.

Lady 8K, who was involved in a gang and on probation, expressed a
similar view regarding interracial dating.

CID: Do you date Latinos or have you in the past?

LADY 8K: Oh, yeah.

CID: What do African American males say about this at the school?

LADY 8K: They don't say anything.

CID: What about African American girls?

LADY 8K: "He's cute!"

CID: How about Latino males and females? What would they say about
the dating on campus here?

LADY 8K: "Oh, they whisper stuff behind your back, and say things
like, "What is it with them [Latino males]?" Mexican girls wouldn't
say anything at all.

Despite the racial boundaries and avoidance between the two groups,
which dominated social interaction, interracial dating was common, as
the interviews suggest. However, in my observations, I noticed that such
dating was often met with ridicule, mostly from other boys, both Latino
and African American. The ridicule was important, because it was a way
of shaming members of each group, which informed individuals about
the boundaries of group identity.

The Use of School Space and Friendship

As outlined earlier, the use of space was clearly demarcated at the school,
a result of group identities forged out of the need for protection. Both
black and Latino youths understood where they were supposed to go. A

staff member at the school site in the central part of South LA told me, "Black kids tell Latinos they can't play basketball if they are not black. Latino kids want to play, but they can't."

However, as already stated, there were many instances in which individuals would cross over. It was not uncommon for both Latinos and blacks to occasionally navigate in and out of each other's spaces. Marvin, an African American student, who was good friends with a member of the Latino clique, Mafioso, would occasionally sit with him on what was known to be the Latino bench. I asked Mafioso why Marvin was the only black kid to hang out with Latinos. "He cool, Cid," Mafioso replied. "I know him from my neighborhood. So Raza don't trip. We go back . . ."

Marvin would sit with Mafioso and talk, frequently. Occasionally, I noticed Marvin being marginalized by his own people, who would laugh at him or shun him when he went back to them. The Latinos who were part of Mafioso's peer group did the same. Mafioso's primary group consisted of Latinos who were on probation and who were actively involved in a variety of different gangs. The ridicule was a reminder that he could cross over, but that there were boundaries. In this example, neighborhood affiliations often created friendship ties between youths, and served as a force in crossing racial boundaries. However, in the public setting of the school, the use of social space was clearly defined.

Yvette, a 17-year-old Latina from the central part of South LA, stated her view of crossing over and the social boundaries associated with it:

> School relations are the same as in the neighborhood. We just talk to people when we need something. I know where to hang out. If I hang out with black people, they [other Latinos] say, "She trying to be black." But, you know, some of them are fun.

Yvette's comments suggest the subtle ways in which in-group dynamics shaped the use of space. Behavior could be regulated through the use of shame and criticism. In many instances, I observed Yvette interacting with African Americans; however, she was constantly reminded of the limitations on doing so. One of the most common responses that Latinas and Latinos experienced was that, if they spent too much time with

African Americans, they were "acting black." This form of shaming was a message to youths that they were crossing the boundaries of acceptable group membership.

Myra, a 17-year-old African American female from the western part of South LA, expressed a view similar to Yvette's:

> Black and Latino gangs hate each other in my neighborhood. In the school, it's a little different. The school is trying to make us build relations, making us interact. Mexicans stick with their own race . . . blacks with blacks. They are trying not to turn on their own race.

Myra's comments illustrate how neighborhood gang dynamics affect interracial relations. In her description, poor gang relations between blacks and Latinos spilled over into the school, creating the distance between the two groups. Myra illustrated how loyalty to one racial group is important to maintain. The perception that one could be "turning on their race" was viewed as a negative thing, and it limited the potential for crossing over. Despite this, the school made a concerted effort to integrate Latinos and blacks. This was particularly visible in the classroom, where interracial interactions were most common.

Marcus Taylor echoed the prevailing peer group view, but with a slightly more communal perspective:

> Right now, in the neighborhoods, there is a war between the F13 Latino gang and the Rolling Crips. In the school, it's a little different. Both groups do separate themselves; Latinos want to help each other out . . . back up, and all that. But we will help them, as well. In the end, we all want the same thing.

Similar to Myra, Marcus expressed that neighborhood gang relations shaped the likelihood of interracial interaction and the potential for crossing over. In many instances, students and staff at the school informed me that neighborhood gang rivalries determine who "your enemy" is. Interracial friendship and the use of space were shaped by these background factors. However, Marcus's comments reflect the idea that African Americans want the same thing as Latinos, namely, support and backup in the face of risk. His comments suggest that there is an underlying motivation to cross over, despite the reinforcing messages the youths received from their respective peer groups.

The comments and insights from the students illuminate many ways in which youths crossed over their racial boundaries. The interviews reflect another phenomenon, however. They shed light on the way in which students had to perform their identities within the group. Interracial relations between blacks and Latinos were managed and regulated in a variety of ways. As the interviews illustrate, when youths crossed over they were met with several strategies meant to maintain racial boundaries, which included the charges of "acting black" or "turning on your race," and being ridiculed, shamed, and shunned. These techniques were utilized to keep the appearance of social solidarity.

My observations also reveal how interracial relations were shaped by neighborhood association, gang affiliation, being on probation, and the interventions by the school to integrate the two populations. These factors were significant as organizing forces in shaping group boundaries, but were not as salient as race and violence were.

Factors Associated with Crossing Over and Racial Boundaries

Several factors at play here that promoted crossing over deserve more attention. Crossing over was shaped by gang ties, neighborhood loyalties, being on probation (discussed in the following chapter), and the general fear throughout the school. While these factors appear to be independent, they have one thing in common—they are underpinned by violence. More specifically, they are forged in the face of the need for protection.

According to students and staff members at the schools, neighborhood gang relations played a key role in shaping black and Latino relationships and maintaining interracial boundaries. Mr. Krystal, a school official and teacher, who had worked at the school for several years, told me:

> Sometimes neighborhood stuff spills over into racial rivalries. Sometimes blacks will say, "Why do Latinos get this?" or "Why do blacks get this?" They try to make it racial and mobilize people. Latinos will do the same thing, as well.

Gang affiliation could also promote turning on a member of the same race. Both Latino and black students stated that gang affiliation can determine if two people will get along, regardless of race. Victor stated his view on race relations between blacks and Latinos, "It's not just about race, but if someone is our enemy. If you're our enemy, then it doesn't matter if they are black or Hispanic, fuck it!" Victor's comments reflect the idea that, in many instances, being an enemy, referring to gang affiliation, trumps race as a factor in determining whether one can associate with a certain person.

Often, however, as noted in the previous section, these neighborhood gang affiliations were suspended, and youths, both female and male, would cross over their neighborhood and gang affiliations, and organize along racial lines. On the other hand, one of the factors that enabled youths to loosen their ties with neighborhood gangs was a direct result of deliberate school strategies. Interviews with several staff members, security, and the city gang reduction team that patrolled the school site revealed specific strategies utilized to minimize the potential for violence. A schoolteacher and administrator told me,

> We try to identify the leaders and bosses of gangs and remove them from the school site. We keep track of whom the leaders are, and remove them from the school site. The staff does this by looking for people who exchange notes for things like drugs and money. Members from Florencia [a local Latino gang] were recently removed because their leaders were causing a lot of racial problems.

Teachers and administrators explained to me that cliques were another type of street affiliation common between both Latino and black youths. These were looser associations, not organized at the same level as the gangs. According to staff members, most students stay within their own cliques, but these cliques tended to be more integrated than gangs.

The school strategy for removing leaders and bosses is significant because, according to school administrators and the city gang prevention staff, 70 percent of the kids in the school were identified as having some form of gang affiliation.

In principle, targeting gang leaders would minimize the potential for interracial divisions and hostility. In a clear majority of cases at the school, gangs were racially homogenous, which further promoted inter-racial boundaries if the gang leaders sought to reinforce them. There is no question that this strategy decreased the likelihood of violence, both inside and beyond the school premises. More importantly, it may have played a role in promoting crossing over.

In addition, the schools enacted a policy that encouraged interracial integration inside the classroom, so that students of different races were forced to interact with each other. In the classrooms where I worked, I observed that teachers made it a deliberate point to move students around the room, in order to break up the racial divisions. Moreover, there was less disruption, because students tended to talk to their friends, who were usually of the same race, if they were seated together.

While the schools' policy was effective inside the classroom, it was not as successful outside of the school, where, in many instances, the students would go right back to their rigid racial boundaries. The same can also be said about gang affiliation. In many instances, being from a rival gang did trump race relations, but in my observations at the school, black and Latino students tended to strictly associate with others of the same race, keeping sharp racial boundaries. When trying to make sense of interracial group boundaries, this becomes an enigma.

Whether or not gangs promoted racial boundaries, or promoted crossing over, is not clear, but violence, as a more general organizing principle, was at play in either case. Many students used racial solidarity as a tool to deal with potential violence. Gangs were utilized in a similar fashion, as a form of protection by students; but they also entailed cross-ing over, regularly, from the gangs into racial groups that were exclu-sively Latino or black. In essence, the gang issue is really about the larger issue of protection from violence. However, gang affiliation was not the only factor that shaped interracial relations between blacks and Latinos.

Probation and Racial Boundaries

Probation status was another factor that had the potential to shape racial boundaries. According to school officials, at least 50 percent of students were on probation. As one staff member told me, "This school is the middle link between probation camps and the Los Angeles Unified School District." Probation officers frequently met with teachers and school officials to monitor students' progress. Five patterns emerged when exploring the link between violence, probation, and interracial relations.

First, over half of the 40 students I interviewed stated that probation played an important part in their weekly routines. This was common among Latinos and African Americans, males and females alike. Lady 8K, on probation for second-degree burglary for one and a half years, shared her views about being on probation and racial boundaries:

> LADY 8K: Probation is a big part of life. They check on me in school and drug test me once a month. The school is like a jail that is hooked in with probation.
> CID: How does it affect relations between blacks and Latinos here?
> LADY 8K: In junior prison [i.e., the school], it's not an issue. There is no connection.

Pop, on probation for two years for assault and battery, voiced a similar view.

> POP: Probation is in all my business. I have to stay in school, stay out of trouble, can't leave town, and my PO [parole officer] is at school all the time.
> CID: What about being locked up? Does that affect the way blacks and Latinos relate?
> POP: In prison, people come out with a segregated mentality. The hood regulates itself, though. The school is the same as the hood. People talk to each other if they want to.

A second, related theme that emerges from the interviews is the separation of neighborhood life from probation and prison life in shaping race relations. For many students, probation had a big impact on their lives, but, as the interviews suggest, neighborhood life was regulated by a different set of rules. Giggles, who was previously on probation, shared her views.

> GIGGLES: I was on probation and they were in my business. They actually did help me though. I got a job and it changed my life.

CID: How does probation, or getting locked up, shape relations between blacks and Latinos here?

GIGGLES: Prison does have an impact on race in the hood. It gets more racist. My brother was locked up and he said, "Don't hang with blacks." The neighborhood has its own rules that are different.

CID: What do you mean?

GIGGLES: I think the longer people have been locked up will affect you [in terms of racial perceptions].

Sergio, who was on probation, gave his view about incarceration and its relationship to race, "In the pen, it's separate between blacks and Mexicans. Young people don't think its true; they don't follow that. It's not a big issue."

Sergio's and Giggles's comments bring to light a third point, namely that older neighborhood peers, one's family, and the length of time on probation may all shape interracial attitudes between blacks and Latinos. However, their views also demonstrate that neighborhoods tend to be regulated by a different set of rules than the rules of those on probation. Overall, their views illustrate that the length of time on probation and the involvement with the criminal justice system may play a role in determining the extent to which young people embody racist ideas. But, given that all the students who were interviewed were 18 or younger, their exposure to the criminal justice system was limited and they may, therefore, be less likely to subscribe to the views of interracial boundaries held by adults in the neighborhood.

The comments made by Maurice Robinson, an 18-year-old African American male on probation for breaking and entering, show how probation affected neighborhood life and its connection with school.

MAURICE: Probation is a big part of my life. They tell me where I can hang out, can't hang out with friends, who I can talk to, who I can't talk to. They force me to go to school.

CID: Does that affect who you can talk to in school? Like, if you can talk to only blacks or Latinos?

MAURICE: The hood determines the problem. If you're cool, or if you have a problem with someone. School relations between blacks and Mexicans are more like the hood. Some get along, some don't.

Maurice's interview captures a fourth pattern: the link between probation, neighborhoods, and school. From his perspective, racial boundaries in the school tend to be more like those in the neighborhoods, rather than like the racial boundaries of probation.

Although these interviews suggest that there were many similarities between neighborhood life and life in the schools used for this study, there were important differences. Phatdaddy, previously on probation, shared his views about this relationship:

> PHATDADDY: In my neighborhood, blacks and Latinos get along. A lot of the people in gangs grew up together—they get along. Taggers cause most of the division in my opinion, cause there are racist gangs, too. T-Flats [a Latino gang] are racists; Florencia [a Latino gang] is racist. Different in the school though. More beef outside than inside the school.
>
> CID: What do you mean?
>
> PHATDADDY: The schools regulate themselves differently, just like the streets regulate themselves differently.

Frederick expressed a similar view of the link between neighborhoods, probation, and schools in shaping racial boundaries, "In jail, people talk about sticking together by race. Black for black, Latino for Latino. People do bring it to the streets. But, it is a different story in the school."

The interviews with Frederick and Phatdaddy illustrate that, despite the influence of different contextual settings, such as life on probation and neighborhood life, the schools utilized for this study were regulated by a separate set of rules and served as social spaces that played a powerful role in shaping racial boundaries between blacks and Latinos. The interviews also suggest that there are unique factors at play that force the reconfiguration of group identity from one based on neighborhood, gang affiliation, and/or probation to one overwhelmingly based on race. Thus, youths wove in and out of these different group identities that shaped their racial boundaries.

Finally, it should be noted that Latino and black males and females overwhelmingly expressed similar views regarding the role of probation and its effect on black and Latino relations. Thus, the cases utilized for this study highlight the common views of young people across race and gender lines.

Some important conclusions may be drawn from focusing on the role of probation. First, regarding violence and racial boundaries, many of the students I interviewed were socialized in juvenile camps, and probation deeply penetrated their lives. Many students discussed how the length of time one spent on probation had an influence on interracial relations. Moreover, they expressed how peers who had been incarcerated could potentially influence the views of younger adolescents. Overwhelmingly, however, they stressed how interracial relations were different in the school settings.

Second, the students' behavior was monitored by probation visits in the school settings, and there were consequences for their conduct. I witnessed the constant interaction of probation officers with students in the schools. If the students were dismissed or suspended for fighting or for drug violations, for instance, they would violate the terms of their probation and be subject to further punishment. Thus, the potential consequences of probation violation may have provided an added incentive for students to get along with people whom they may otherwise have viewed as problematic, including those from rival gangs or different racial groups.

In the end, the effects of probation were overshadowed by a more important and pressing demand—the need for safety.

Conclusion

I have provided a framework for understanding the relationship between violence and black and Latino relations. Following a long line of previous studies, this chapter demonstrates the centrality of violence in creating group identities. Interracial relations are mitigated by several factors: school, gangs, neighborhoods, and probation. The central questions I address are: Why are interracial relations unique in the schools? How and why did other group identities traverse and transform into a new identity? The basic answer I present is straightforward: the need for protection and the fear of violence. While gangs, neighborhoods, and probation-based identities may seem unrelated, what these factors have in common is that they are underpinned by violence. The exposure to different settings, where violence takes on a variety of unique forms, plays a central role in the creation of multiple identities.

First, my findings have important implications for the substantive literature on black and Latino relations, violence and identity. Contrary to the standard literature, I find that violence shapes interracial relations. In contrast, much of the previous literature has focused on cultural differences or competition over resources as the key to racial conflict.

Another set of literature addresses the link between violence and identity, such as Anderson's analysis of the code of the street, through which violence creates "street" and "decent" identities. Harding's work highlights the role of neighborhood violence and identity, as well. The key contribution of my findings is how group identities, forged in the face of violence, also create group boundaries.

The work of Norbert Elias (1969[1939]) emphasizes the link between violence and the creation of social order. In many ways, my findings illustrate the way in which violence produces order. My work underscores that, in examining black and Latino relations, it must be understood that group boundaries promote a type of interaction where avoidance becomes the primary means of interaction, not just because of racial prejudice, but also out of the perception that there is a daily necessity for protection. Racial avoidance creates parallel worlds of black and Latino youths, and becomes the primary basis of social order in response to violence.

Why do these parallel worlds emerge and what role does violence play in their creation? The answer lies in the contextual factors at play. In particular, the failure of municipal government to provide for the safety and protection of youths from violence becomes a critical contextual force, shaping interracial relations. Previous chapters in this book highlight how the distrust of police and weak ties to mainstream institutions such as Neighborhood Councils contribute to the creation of these parallel worlds.

The idea that violence shapes group identity and social order also has implications for revisiting Gould's theory of group solidarity and violence. His framework is premised on the idea that the appearance of group solidarity minimizes violence, because rival groups perceive the possibility of a credible threat in response. However, I suggest that violence plays a role in shaping group identity. In essence, this is the step that precedes Gould's analysis. For groups to form, they must first be exposed to potential violence. My analysis, therefore, complements Gould's analysis by providing insight into an overlooked precondition that shapes group identity. These group identities then take on lives of their own, where avoidance rather than confrontation becomes a less noticed means of responding to violence.

Second, this chapter has also demonstrated the fluidity by which youths weave in and out of different group settings. This point has important implications for Gould's work, as well, since the notion of identities becomes variable, based on exposure to violence. According to Gould, the perception of group solidarity is key to minimizing violence. My research adds to his framework by illustrating the ways in which solidarity is a dynamic and changing process. I show that, inside the schools, blacks and Latinos demonstrate the appearance of intragroup solidarity. However, outside the schools, the young people convincingly stated that gang and neighborhood ties determined who was a friend, a foe, or a stranger. I found that the differences and social ties outside the school were no longer as relevant inside the school. Instead, inside the school, the social groupings changed and were based almost exclusively on race and gender.

Third, my work adds to Gould's framework by demonstrating that although fluidity was common, the social boundaries were closely regulated. While Gould explains that the process of solidarity is partly based on appearance, this theory is not well developed in his work. I suggest that solidarity is a more dynamic process and that it is, in many respects, a performance that is constantly being negotiated and regulated. Crossing over, as conceptualized in this chapter, is a process that is regulated by strategies such as shame, shunning, and ridicule. In the schools I studied for this work, it was okay to traverse groups, but only up to a point. Creating the appearance of group solidarity is what both groups, especially in the face of danger or potential violence, demanded.

Finally, my research questions the role of probation and the broader relationship with the criminal justice system in shaping black and Latino relations. In the current criminology literature, this relationship is widely accepted as one of the most important features in shaping the behavior and attitudes of young people. While support exists for this view, it does not totally explain the dynamic manner by which blacks and Latinos cross group boundaries. Instead, we discover that there are several competing and informal norms that also shape group interaction, such as neighborhoods, gangs, and the school administration. One factor that all these elements share is that they are underpinned by violence. The context of violence is the most important underlying element.

Given the unique heterogeneous makeup of South LA, where Latinos comprise a majority of the population, a new vision of the social order must be considered that goes beyond the traditional black-and-white paradigm. This chapter provides insight into the new urban social order. The lack of social ties to the municipal government, along with the hypercriminalization of youths, produce two parallel worlds. These racially bounded worlds are based on racial and ethnic trust, safety, security, and protection from violence. In this respect, youths' responses to violence become a form of ritual that reconstitutes and reinforces the social order based on racial group boundaries and avoidance.

Conclusion

Revisiting Alternative Governance

Following my fieldwork in South LA, I have made it a point to stay in contact with many of the people with whom I formed friendships while conducting research. Every time I visit Los Angeles, I feel the necessity to catch up with old acquaintances. I find that these follow-up encounters often shed new light on my work, sometimes placing the fieldwork within a broader context. In the summer of 2012, I reconnected with a former field contact named Jerry who had helped me navigate City Hall while I was studying the Neighborhood Councils in South LA. He had worked with the LA Human Relations Commission and was often deeply involved with the same Neighborhood Councils I examined in my study.

On my most recent visit, Jerry thought it was important for me to see a particular room that is relevant to LA politics—the Tom Bradley Room, located on the 27th floor of City Hall. Bradley was the first African American mayor of Los Angeles, and he had strong ties to South LA during the early years of his political career. After seeing this room, we exited the building, and ran into an acquaintance of Jerry's who is one of Mayor Antonio Villaraigosa's top advisors: Larry Frank, a white male who stands about six foot six tall, and who was dressed formally in a suit and tie. We stood near the security checkpoint where the guard was screening people who came in and out of the building. It was late Friday afternoon, and there were few people in the area. Jerry informed Frank about my previous work in South LA, and he immediately showed a great deal of interest in knowing more about what I did. I told Frank that I study the intersection of politics, religion, and gangs.

Frank informed me that City Hall has struggled to forge relations with community members in South LA. "We've had a hard time connecting with local leaders and developing new leaders to work with us," he stated. "We're trying to develop and implement a new gang-intervention program in South LA, called GRID. Maybe you've heard of it?" I told him I had. He continued, "The way that these programs work is that they have to have community buy in, in addition to the resources. And you know we aren't getting the local leaders involved and aren't getting community residents involved, either. It makes it really hard to address the gang problem from a City Hall perspective. Maybe you have some perspective on this?"

I told him I had worked with Neighborhood Councils and had volunteered in the community, and that I had seen a lot of things. Frank then suggested one of the reasons why it is difficult to make connections in the community: "There's a lot of loyalty to the community in South LA, rather than to City Hall, and you can't blame residents." I replied, "Yeah, there were two big riots: Watts in 1965 and the South Central Riots in 1992. I don't think people trust City Hall."

"There is a big trust problem," he stated. "But, you know, three of the biggest drug dealers in LA's history have come out of the area." Frank rattled off the names of three people who he thought were the biggest drug dealers in LA over the past 30 years. Then he mentioned the name of a person whom I had frequently heard of in South LA, and had actually met, along with a member of his family. I had had several discussions with this family member. I was thrown off; I had met the individual whom Frank thought was one of the biggest drug dealers in South LA, and in LA at large. "People like that get a lot of respect in the community and the residents are loyal to them, or are afraid of them. Plus, they support the community in their own way, provide jobs, donate to causes in the community, you know. How can we compete with that?"

"I was also interested in black and Latino relations in South LA," I told him.

"Well, what did you find?" he asked. I told him violence was mostly black on black and Latino on Latino. He replied:

> It is, but the communities are pretty much divided. Occasionally when the violence is interracial they keep it to themselves, within their own communities. They listen to leaders from the streets or from the prisons to solve the problems. They don't look to the police or City Hall. There is a

conflict going on between blacks and Latinos now. And it's the guys from prison who are trying to make the calls about how it should be addressed.

Frank went on to explain that, in this particular instance, the leader of one of the ethnic groups was trying to escalate the conflict from prison.

This anecdote reflects the major challenges LA's municipal government continues to face in dealing with violence. The themes outlined throughout this book have direct implications for day-to-day policy and policymakers at the city level. The long history of poor relations between South LA and City Hall make it difficult for City Hall to connect with residents in order to provide beneficial programs and services. Distrust developed over long periods of history is difficult to overcome.

A second challenge LA's municipal government faces is the interracial divisions that have become the basis of social organization among South LA's poor residents. In the face of weak government, people look to those with whom they feel comfortable, and, in many instances, these are people of the same ethnicity, culture, and language. It's widely felt that such people are more likely to be trustworthy. As this work has shown, people frequently form communities based on similarities, often as a result of poor ties to local government. The growing diversity of LA's largest ghetto has implications for City Hall's ability to address violence. In essence, City Hall must be able to connect with two distinct communities, which, in theory at least, coexist in the same space.

Finally, the informal economy that many of LA's poor have resorted to as a means of subsistence has taken on a life of its own, often standing in opposition to City Hall. As Frank's comments suggest, residents feel loyalty to those who are able to provide for their material existence. Among residents who reject this way of life, the fear exists that there will be violent and dangerous consequences for those who work with the police or City Hall.

The anecdote above provides a window into the key concept of this work—alternative governance. In this study, I argue that, in response to the social ties and poor relations to formal government structures, residents have developed alternative means to resolve and manage violence.

During the course of my fieldwork, I discovered that it is not just the weak ties to the state that have alienated the poor from resources to address violence, but also the state's increasingly punitive role. One of the major reasons why Latinos do not feel that they can turn to local government and the police for help is their citizenship status. The federal government has also taken on a punitive role in the ghetto, via the Department of Homeland Security's Citizenship and Immigration Services and Immigration and Customs Enforcement agencies. Thus, the state has withered in some aspects, but has been emboldened in others, for example, its crackdown on Latinos who are not citizens.

The historically punitive role of law enforcement has also had a negative effect on relations with those who are US citizens. During my research, I discovered that there is a large and concentrated presence of federal, state, county and city law enforcement in South LA; some are undercover and others make it a point to be visible to residents. I learned from attending the Ad Hoc Public Safety Committees of the Neighborhood Councils, that DEA, ATF, FBI, CIA, Homeland Security, and other agencies associated with the Department of Justice are in constant surveillance of would-be criminals. Even accounting for the large levels of violence in the area, many residents feel they are unfairly overpoliced. Many African Americans in South LA have historically viewed the Los Angeles Police Department with distrust and suspicion. The clearest examples of this historically poor relationship can be seen in the 1965 Watts Riots, and, more recently, the 1992 Los Angeles riots, conflicts in which South Los Angeles was ground zero. Thus, poor relationships, weak ties, and the state's increasingly punitive responses have undermined government legitimacy and limited its ability to intervene in neighborhood violence.

Another important aspect of my argument in this book is that, as the state remains disconnected and withdrawn from South LA's poor Latinos and African Americans, alternative governance has arisen to fill the vacuum left behind. Alternative governance fulfills some of the basic needs of residents, although it is limited in its capacity to do so. One of the basic mandates of the state is to protect and ensure the rights of citizens. For reasons outlined earlier, the state is not able to ensure the protection of Latino immigrants and African Americans or guarantee their basic rights, and this constitutes a major failure on its part.

By protecting Latino immigrants, the Catholic Church acts as one of the pillars of alternative governance. The informal world of the local Catholic parish, St. Joseph's, contains several of the key components of a community response to violence that I have explored in this book. First, the church provides a social setting where Latino newcomers feel protected from the potential dangers associated with being a noncitizen, such as the constant threats of deportation and other sanctions. Second, the church acts as a sanctuary, creating a shared social space, fostering trust, and promoting a feeling of safety among parishioners who face daily threats from neighborhood and gang violence. In addition, the Catholic Church imbues parishioners with a set of public norms that act as a psychological motivation to confront repeated instances of neighborhood violence and the quite real possibility of death, all of which are endemic to the Watts area. Finally, the church proffers its own version of morality that is not reducible to that of the state or to that of the street.

In many ways, St. Joseph's mirrors interracial relations between blacks and Latinos in South LA. There are separate ministries and masses for blacks and Latinos—two separate worlds existing in one space. However, the parish leadership makes a concerted effort to bridge the different communities. Utilizing a common Catholic faith, the pastor is able to build social ties within the parish. Utilizing these interracial social ties, the parish is able to extend its relationships to the broader community—to Latino and black leaders and various community organizations in South LA. Thus, St. Joseph's is able to leverage its social ties to address violence with a form of "legitimacy" lacking in public institutions such as the LAPD and City Hall.

This book has also demonstrated how street life, or what I refer to as street justice, has taken on a central role in the social order of South LA. More importantly, street justice has become another primary response by residents to violence. As with the other settings explored in this book, street justice is heavily influenced by interethnic relationships between Latinos and African Americans. In many ways, interracial dynamics between gangs are at the core of these relationships. I suggest that avoidance and cooperation are the dominant forms of relationships between Latino and African American gangs. In contrast to the common perceptions of the media, I argue that race alone is not enough to foster interracial violence. Relationships between African Americans and Latinos are instead predicated on four factors: (1) territorial affiliation, (2) control of the illicit underground economy and the neighborhood, (3) gang affiliation, and (4) race. A combination of these factors leads to interracial cooperation, avoidance, or conflict. More importantly, shared notions of economic and social exchange between Latino and African American gangs play an important role in promoting cooperation. Violations of these precepts lead to interethnic conflict. This study has documented how street life has filled the void left by the state.

This book has also provided an account of how informal norms shape the interactions between gangs and their relationships with neighborhood residents. I provide empirical evidence that shows the existence of an informal world rooted in street life. I illustrate how African American and Latino residents negotiate the presence of street gangs and how they, in turn, are affected by neighborhood conflicts. I term these informal norms street justice.

The emergence of the new Latino immigrants into South LA challenges the notion of street justice, illustrating the importance of interracial relations in urban settings in understanding the violence. Findings from this study show that Latino immigrants are more likely to report illicit activities to law enforcement, whereas African Americans are less likely to do so. Latino newcomers are more likely to uphold the precepts of street justice the longer their length of residence in South LA. As the modern state has withdrawn from the urban poor, street justice has risen in its place. This framework complements the informal public norms outlined earlier in this study. Street justice forms the backbone of a second pillar of alternative governance, providing an informal means to manage conflict, a task typically handled by the modern state. Thus, alternative governance is key to understanding how urban poor institutions respond to and manage violence.

Theoretical Implications

The findings from this study have major implications for understanding how poor urban residents respond to high levels of crime, implications that have not been fully realized by urban scholars or criminologists. There is an important distinction to be made regarding how residents respond to violence and how they minimize and regulate the use of violence. My key contribution to the existing literature is the concept of alternative governance, which focuses on the response to violence. I suggest that this concept makes three major contributions to existent urban literature on violence and the urban poor. First, I introduce it in an attempt to move beyond the limitations of informal social control. Second, I go beyond the limitations of traditional research that have framed urban crime as a black-and-white phenomenon. Finally, my concept of alternative governance underscores the relational dynamics between core institutions and the way in which they shape how residents respond to violence. Indeed, few sociological works, including ethnographies, have examined the intersection of urban politics, the street, and religious institutions and their role in responding to violence.

To date, the only work to directly engage the intersection of religion and street life among the urban poor is Venkatesh's *Off the Books* (2006). Venkatesh demonstrates how the poor residents of Chicago are socially isolated from City Hall and the police. As poverty increases, gangs and the informal economy become one of the primary means by which residents generate income for survival. The fallout from the proliferation of gangs and this informal economy create the need for social order. The black church, utilizing its moral authority, then becomes an important source of informal social control. According to Venkatesh's model, social control operates in multiple domains—the church and the street mediate relations between residents, such as disputes about exchange and conflict in general. Also, the multidimensional form of informal social control mediates relations between residents and public institutions, for example, between police and residents. In essence, these types of informal social control operate as extralegal mechanisms.

My work also has shown that legitimacy among the urban poor exists in multiple forms of social control that are not reducible to the state or the street. In this respect, this book is an important advancement beyond previous works, and adds another layer to our understanding of how multiple forms of informal social control operate by outlining how they are culturally bound. My ethnography has shown how African American and Latino communities exist in two separate, yet culturally bound worlds. How do extralegal mechanisms operate in these diverse settings? While Venkatesh outlines the process by which these mechanisms function, he does not provide a framework for examining how they are shaped by interracial relations. My work attempts to address this gap by outlining the role of interracial relations between Latinos and African Americans in shaping extralegal mechanisms. I have tried to demonstrate that interracial relations are important for two reasons. First, race determines the social organization of the urban social space. Therefore, as alternative governance develops, it operates through racial and ethnic-bound social ties, leaders, and institutions. It is for this reason that most crimes in South LA tend to be between members of the same race: black on black or Latino on Latino. Second, when conflicts do emerge between the two groups, it is the established leadership within each ethnic group, utilizing the informal rules, who usually mediate disputes. This is clearly demonstrated in the chapters of this book on black and Latino gang youths and in the chapter on street justice. Thus, a careful examination of the increasingly multiracial landscape of urban America must be undertaken to fully appreciate the complexity of new forms of social organization and in what way these structures control how communities respond to violence.

What previous studies have ignored is how the social organization of urban America has been reshaped by the emergence of the Latino population. As urban America becomes more diverse and increasingly populated by Latinos, now the largest ethnic group in American cities as a whole, no analysis of the urban poor and violence can continue to ignore this population. Indeed, the emergence of the Latino population in America's largest urban areas presents a unique set of issues that are distinct from those of African Americans and yet are similar in many ways.

The noncitizen status of many Latinos has forced them into the shadows of society. Going underground is motivated not by a disdain for the law, but from fear of being criminalized. This way of thinking has a direct impact on immediate family members, especially children, and also on extended family members. It has a profound effect on the lifestyle of Latino immigrants who are forced to work in the underground economy, socialize only in safe spaces, and avoid public areas they deem dangerous because of either the state or the gangs. What I have discovered is that noncitizen Latinos must create alternative communities and spaces in order to feel safe. These alternative spaces, which have become the basis of social organization for many Latinos, often exist in the same physical spaces as those inhabited by African Americans. And it is the interrelationship of these alternative spaces, both black and Latino, that most scholars have overlooked. Such spaces are critical because they shape the way in which residents respond to violence.

Previous research has made significant inroads into understanding the role of Latino immigrant communities and violence, but the existing literature does not adequately explain the South LA case. A key concept in much of this literature is a particular view of how immigrant communities respond to violence, often referred to as "the Latino paradox." Sampson (2008) argues that immigrant communities have lower rates of crime due to cultural traits that emphasize conformity, solidarity, and community, and, therefore, effectively regulate deviant behavior. In addition, he stresses that selection bias brings only the best, brightest, and most motivated immigrants; therefore, they are less likely to commit crimes.

Other scholars emphasize that the cultural distinctiveness of immigrants can mitigate a culture of violence that is endemic to the United States. They demonstrate that the more assimilated immigrants become to American culture, the more likely they are to become deviant and commit violent crime. Thus, communities with higher concentrations of Latino immigrants and Spanish speakers are likely to have lower rates of violent crime. These findings run contrary to the popular view that immigrant culture is the cause of many social pathologies and of much of the crime in poor Latino communities.

Three major shortcomings exist within the Latino paradox perspective that make it inadequate for understanding the South Los Angeles case. First, proponents of this perspective have little to say about the role of institutions in immigrant communities and how these institutions may assuage violent crime. These scholars suggest that ethnic solidarity acts as a form of informal social control. However, none (or very few) of them have provided evidence concerning the institutional mechanisms and the systems by which these operate to minimize violent crime. These neighborhood mechanisms, which provide protection against violence, essentially constitute a black box of unknown social processes. In this work, I suggest that shared, informal neighborhood rules exist and that these rules structure the routines of residents and the ways in which they respond to violence. More importantly, however, I show how neighborhood institutions, such as the Catholic Church, have become a source of refuge from neighborhood violence and from the state.

A second shortcoming of the current literature is that it provides very little insight into immigrant communities with high levels of violent crime. Indeed, in the South LA area where my study was conducted, vio-lent crime is five times the national average. At the same time, the area has one of the largest concentrations of new Latino immigrant arrivals in all of LA within the last 20 years. While the Latino paradox scholars have much to say about how immigrant communities keep crime down, they have little to say about high-crime immigrant communities.

To date, the only study that has explored this problem is Kubrin and Ishizawa's (2012) comparative study of Chicago and Los Angeles. Examining large metropolitan areas, such as Chicago and LA, Kubrin and Ishizawa find that immigrant concentration tends to reduce crime. However, in areas with large concentrations of Latinos bordering high-poverty areas with large amounts of crime, immigrant neighborhoods have higher crime rates than those of nonimmigrant neighborhoods. The protective effect of immigrant neighborhoods is essentially trumped by other factors, which, so far, remain unknown to researchers.

These findings run contrary to the Latino paradox literature. Kubrin and Ishizawa suggest that the standard social disorganization explana-tions may account for the higher immigrant crime rates: residential mo-bility, generational status, and neighborhood structural disadvantage. They further speculate that immigrant communities may produce more crime because they are not anchored in the Americanized community, haven't learned the culture of honor,[1] or are relegated to disadvantaged neighborhoods rife with social pathologies. Neighborhood disadvan-tage, in this view, appears to be the most promising explanation for high rates of crime in immigrant neighborhoods; a substantial body of re-search shows that, after controlling for internal neighborhood condi-tions, three characteristics of proximate areas affect violent crime rates: (1) residential instability, (2) disadvantage, and (3) the relative preva-lence of white residents. My work has demonstrated how Latino immi-grant communities respond to violence in high-crime neighborhoods. To date, few studies address the problem using empirical data, and virtu-ally no ethnographic studies exist that explore this puzzle.

Finally, the Latino paradox literature misses a key element that is also absent from the standard urban sociological literature highlighted ear-lier in this section. The Latino paradox literature is limited in explaining crime in multiracial neighborhoods that are not exclusively Latino. This is an important point often overlooked by criminologists and sociologists who assume that immigrants live on isolated islands, when, in fact, urban areas have become more diverse.

I have demonstrated that in many neighborhoods in South LA, Latino immigrants and native-born residents live not in separated geographic spaces from African Americans, but often in the same neighborhoods. This is not a trivial point since, again, South LA is considered the largest ghetto west of the Mississippi. Thus, the Latino paradox lacks a sufficient framework for explaining violence in black and Latino neighborhoods, which are likely to be the archetypes for the rest of the country in the years to come. Alternative governance provides a window into the way in which Latino and African Americans respond to violence.

A final theoretical contribution of my work to the literature is how institutions structure the response to violence. Part of my argument is that, in the face of weak ties to the state—i.e., law enforcement and the local government—alternative sources of legitimate governance have arisen, which play a central role in the response to violence. The concept of legitimacy is important because it provides the basis for alternative social spaces where people trust one another, and it promotes the possibility of collective action to respond to violence. More importantly, however, the concept is significant because it explains how competing sources of social order arise in response to and in competition with the state.

In my study, I found that there are diverse sources of legitimacy that are based on moral authority, fear and violence, and the informal economy. According to Max Weber (1978[1922]), legitimacy is important in explaining why people submit to authority. Many studies of informal social control take for granted the basis of authority, and also conceive of it as a given. Legitimacy is a central precondition to informal social control and alternative governance—it is the potential collective power for establishing community and it shapes the norms of interaction.

Christopher Winship and Jenny Berrien (1999) argue that the moral standing of religious institutions plays a key role in establishing legitimacy. They highlight several factors. First, churches are some of the few anchoring institutions committed to the welfare of residents that exist in poor urban neighborhoods. Community members rely upon individuals within these anchoring institutions to provide leadership, which underscores the importance of ministering. Through religious messages of salvation that focus on the whole person, residents receive meaning in their lives that goes beyond the confines of law enforcement and the criminal justice system. Messages that resonate with residents, such as personal salvation and the sanctity of human life, help them develop trust with one another, and also help them to build a shared moral authority that makes community members accountable. Other forms of ministering, such as walking the neighborhoods at night and during the day, provide religious ministers with an understanding of street issues such as crime, gangs, and poverty. Thus, clerical status combined with street knowledge increases the moral standing of religious leaders and their churches. Winship and Berrien refer to the moral standing of churches in poor urban neighborhoods as the umbrella of legitimacy, a form of credibility that compels neighborhood residents to defer to church leadership in times of crisis.

In many ways, the concept of the umbrella of legitimacy applies to the neighborhood Catholic church described in this study. It is one of the few anchoring institutions in one of the poorest neighborhoods in South LA, and it provides a wide variety of services, including food, clothing, legal services, social services, and English training. In addition, the church maintains a K–6 elementary school and offers scholarships to many local youths. At the same time, the clergy engages in an active street ministry as priests regularly walk the streets and through public housing. Even more importantly, the church serves as a refuge from the state and the INS. In many ways, the legitimacy of St. Joseph's derives from its independence and the protection it provides from the state. All these factors give the church and its priests, and especially its pastor, a unique moral authority. As I note here, the church maintains an umbrella of legitimacy that neighborhood residents revere and trust. Many residents, both Latino and African American, feel safer in the church than they do with the LAPD.

The other source of legitimacy that I explore in this study is rooted in street life. In particular, legitimacy in the street is founded on two principles: (1) fear and (2) the economic incentives of the informal economy and the potential for sanctions from the state. Part of my argument is that the idea of street justice is not limited to those involved in the criminal underworld, in gangs, or in other forms of illicit activity. Noncriminal residents are also influenced by the precepts of street justice. Many residents, both African American and Latino, are afraid to go the police for fear of retaliation. While retaliation does not always occur, it happens often enough that residents are intimidated and come to believe that it is safer not to get involved with law enforcement or local government to address issues of violence. The passive attitude of residents in not reporting violent crime to law enforcement is the result of a type of rule in which legitimacy is based on violence, fear, and intimidation. In interviews, both Latinos and African Americans expressed fear of the consequences for their families if they worked with police and other city agencies. This passive acceptance of violent crime reaffirms the existence of alternative governance outside of the state.

A final dimension of legitimacy is rooted in the informal economy. According to many scholars, a frustration with social mobility in the economic sphere can be a source of cynicism about legal authority that leads the urban poor to embrace the code of the street. I do not disagree with previous findings on this matter. Here, I only want to emphasize that many of the urban poor are forced to resort to the underground economy to generate income for basic subsistence. Given that that economic exchange is illegal, it is not possible to utilize the police to settle disagreements. A person would be calling attention to their illegal work or other associates' illegal work in the informal economy. Thus, a need to operate outside the law emerges. Although people may work within the illicit economy, this does not mean there is no order. Business transactions and other forms of interactions necessitate the reduction of risk. Therefore, informal rules emerge as the primary means by which residents regulate exchange and manage conflict.

Thus, my argument makes an important theoretical contribution to the literature by highlighting the existence of multiple forms of governance, the role of institutions in Latino immigrant neighborhoods, and the role of legitimacy in shaping the ways in which residents respond to violence. I have introduced the concept of alternative governance to overcome the shortcomings of existing frameworks.

Policy Implications

Recent policy recommendations by academics and law enforcement officials reflect the need to address the proliferation of an alternative street culture in urban areas that emphasizes noncooperation with the police and violent retaliation as the primary strategy for conflict management. The strategies for addressing alternative street justice are significant and useful; however, I suggest that they do not go far enough.

Both academics and law enforcement agree that addressing the issue of "snitches" is significant. Jacobs and Wright (2006) argue there are several steps that can be taken to reduce what they call "street justice"—in their usage, the term refers to a subculture among the urban poor in which violent retaliation is the primary means of conflict management for street criminals. Addressing the issue of "stop snitchin'" is significant because it allows for the existence of street-based conflict management that operates outside the scope of the law. They suggest that snitches— informants who work with the police—should be protected. This is a justifiable recommendation, but it would be very costly for law enforcement and local government to protect regular citizens from potential retaliation for cooperating with the police.[2]

A second common recommendation is to improve relations between law enforcement and poor urban communities. According to a Police Executive Research Forum report (PERF, 2009) published by the US Justice Department's Office of Community Oriented Policing, local law enforcement officials must communicate with residents of such communities and acknowledge their lack of trust in police and the criminal justice system in general. Law enforcement personnel must address the fact that they are often perceived as abusive toward residents. Moreover, they must work to change the perception that they do not care about the safety or well being of black and Latino residents. Finally, law enforcement officials must demonstrate that they can effectively protect residents who cooperate with the police.

Jacobs and Wright (2006, p. 130) share a similar view regarding the importance of improving community relations. They state that hatred for the police is woven into the fabric of street culture. What is crucial, in their perspective, is to improve access to legal resources to facilitate community residents' development of a "legal conscience," which would ostensibly reduce reliance on informal social control. They recommend a localized form of dispute resolution to bring street-oriented criminals into the legal system.

Finally, scholars and many law enforcement officials believe that it is important to have community involvement in addressing issues related to the counterculture of "stop snitchin'" and retaliation, a conclusion also reached by the Police Executive Research Forum. They emphasize the importance of law enforcement officials' meeting with neighborhood associations, working with clergy members and local churches, recruiting local leaders, and increasing police presence in high-crime areas where the stop-snitching ethos is prevalent.

Other scholars argue that it is difficult to get community institutions and leaders involved because the "old heads"—original gangsters—no longer have the influence they once had and their power has become diffused. In the past, these gangsters were able to manage conflict because of their street experience and the respect shown to them (Jacobs and Wright, 2006, p. 131). According to this perspective, the crack epidemic, deindustrialization, and social disorganization have all contributed to the original gangsters' loss of power. Furthermore, according to this perspective, nothing has emerged to replace the old heads; nothing has filled the void in the community control of poor urban neighborhoods, thus enabling the escalation of violence.

These scholars have made significant contributions to the literature, but they are out of step with contemporary forms of urban marginality as witnessed in the South LA case. Without an adequate understanding of the contemporary forms of urban marginality, it is difficult to adequately address violence. In many ways, South LA is a window into future urban trends in America, and can inform us about upcoming challenges and solutions in other urban areas throughout the country.

The first thing to recognize, contrary to the findings of Jacobs and Wright, is that the decline of the old heads did not mark a decline in the social order of the urban poor. Instead, I argue that, in fact, multiple forms of alternative governance have arisen to fill the void left by the state, and, to some extent, that left by the street. Thus, there is a dynamic relationship between alternative governance and the state.[3]

Alternative governance weakens when the state reintegrates its residents. When residents view the state as legitimate, they are more likely to use formal legal channels to resolve disputes, minimizing the violence that often stems from informal street rules. I suggest that connecting residents to the state is one of the most important ways to address violence among the urban poor. The first step is to give residents the tools to participate in local government. Local city government officials must make a concerted effort to leverage resources for residents, including training residents in civic participation and designating beat patrol officers who are accountable to residents. The goal is to help build residents' capacity to be actively involved in addressing violent crime in their community. Many residents have been left out of the process and have not been given the opportunity to participate in a meaningful way in order to learn the necessary skills to address issues such as neighborhood violence.

More importantly, however, City Hall must utilize decentralized government so that residents are not passive participants in policing policy. Instead, they must have an equal voice at the table when policies and strategies are developed. This calls for a major overhaul in the way municipal government structures police and community relations. It is not enough for beat officers to meet with residents and educate them about crime in the community. Nor is it enough for law enforcement officers to participate in Neighborhood Council meetings and demand that residents state their problems and give up the names of would-be criminals. (These types of practices were common when I conducted my fieldwork in the Neighborhood Councils of South LA.) Instead, local governments must be willing to entrust local groups, citizens, and professionals to develop their own agendas and to set their own goals. What is needed is what Fung refers to as "deliberative practices" (2004, p. 13) that institutionalize direct avenues of communication and oversight between local officials and the citizens they are meant to serve.

Institutionalized avenues of communication must extend beyond the level of law enforcement; they must reach the level of the City Council and the mayor's office. Ultimately, policing policies are forged, developed, and debated at the city and county level of municipal government. For residents to truly have a voice in policy, they must have access to political actors and institutions that have real power to shape policing practices.

Equally important, residents must have the power to make law enforcement officials accountable. This means giving residents more advisory power to hire and fire city officials. At first glance, this approach may appear to be extreme, but as Fung (2004) points out, the City of Chicago successfully implemented a program in which residents were given a say in the retention of law enforcement officials. When city officials are held accountable by community members, they are more likely to be effective and efficient in their response to issues such as violent crime.

Those who are familiar with recent developments in Los Angeles might respond that there have been great improvements in the relationships between the Los Angeles Police Department and residents of South LA, so why is anything else needed? Indeed, beginning with Chief of Police William Bratton, the city has made a concerted effort to improve its relations with residents and to utilize a statistics-driven form of policing that targets high-crime areas. Bratton's replacement, Chief Charlie Beck, has continued the tradition of improving relations with residents. A *New York Times* article (Nagourney, 2011) suggests that the LAPD, once viewed as racist and corrupt, is now viewed more positively by most people in the city, including blacks and Hispanics. The article highlights a 2009 *Los Angeles Times* poll that found a majority of voters strongly or somewhat approved of the police department's performance, with 76 percent of Latinos and 68 percent of blacks giving the agency positive grades. These developments are promising; however, more research is needed to thoroughly understand current community and police relations in Los Angeles.

Recent events, however, suggest that many people in South LA still view the police with suspicion, and this lack of trust continues to be an issue despite the improved efforts of the city and Chief Beck. The murders committed in 2013 by former LAPD officer Christopher Dorner highlight the significance of this issue. Dorner shot and killed four police officers as a form of payback for what he believed to be unfair treatment by the LAPD. More importantly, he claimed that the LAPD was still deeply racist, and that officers in the department continued to routinely abuse African American and Latino residents, and even other police officers. To be clear, many of Dorner's claims were unsubstantiated. However, his claims, made public by the media, raise the possibility that racism and corruption continue in the LAPD, and conjure up a long history of bad memories for Latinos and African Americans in South LA. As a result, area residents have demanded meetings with the police to find out if Dorner's allegations are correct, for example, that police officers with a history of abuse still work on the force.

As long as African Americans and Latinos continue to have a marginal role in the decision-making processes around policing, lack of trust and suspicion will persist. Many in South LA continue to view the police as a colonizing force. When people are not directly involved in decision-making processes that directly impact their daily lives, they will speculate about motivation, and they may resort to default perceptions of the LAPD based on a history of abusive behavior. Therefore, one effective way to build trust between the LAPD and residents of South LA is to further open channels of communication at the higher levels of City Hall, and, by doing so, give residents the real power to hold their officials accountable.

Another policy consideration whose significance most scholars and law enforcement officials have failed to recognize is the necessity of moving beyond the black-and-white paradigm of policing to fight violent crime. I have illustrated that many people, for many reasons, are forced to live in the shadows of formal government and to manage conflict outside the scope of the state. Because of police abuse, ineffective laws, and ineffective policing, both Latinos and African Americans must deal with neighborhood issues, like violence, on their own without state resources. The experience of Latino immigrants in urban America adds a new layer of issues because many are not citizens and therefore believe they must act outside the scope of government.

While Latinos are now the largest minority group living in urban America, there has been little discussion of the issue of noncitizenship among urban sociologists and criminologists. Increasingly, Latinos have been criminalized for being "illegal." Immigration and Customs Enforcement has aggressively begun treating Latino immigrants as criminals, imposing harsher sentences for crossing the border without legal documentation. These highly militarized policing policies have had the unintended effect of creating a whole class of Latinos hidden in segments of the urban ghetto. This has created what I have referred to as a parallel world, separate from mainstream institutions, and, to a large extent, isolated from African American institutions. One of the consequences of this has been the production of fear and distrust of local government and law enforcement. Distrust of law enforcement by Latinos has two effects: community members (1) do not report violent crime and (2) must engage in alternative means to address conflict. The end result is the creation of an alternative, parallel world that it is likely to produce more violent crime by eroding the protective elements of Latino immigrant communities.

Thus, the federal government must find ways to provide access to the law for noncitizen immigrants. This will serve as a major challenge given the noncitizen status of many Latino immigrants. Policy efforts that focus on human rights may make further inroads into addressing this issue.

Finally, a stronger human relations approach by the Los Angeles municipal government would help to mitigate violence in South LA. Given the municipal government's historical weakness in building ties with the community, and the alternatively punitive reputation it has developed, residents have created their own forms of alternative social organization based on identifiable similarities such race, ethnicity, language, and culture. South LA, like other parts of the city, has developed two distinct communities: one African American and the other Latino. One of the key findings in this study is that avoidance defines relations between Latinos and African Americans. Avoidance is problematic because residents are not likely to develop interracial social ties that would enable them to work together to minimize violent crime. A stronger presence by the city of LA within the community can facilitate improved interracial relations between the two groups.

Previous studies have shown that a lack of community consensus can often breed weak social controls, whereas strong ones are necessary to combat violence. What is needed, then, is a way of putting the community back together. City outreach programs can help foster interracial social ties between key institutions and community leaders. Furthermore, a more developed human relations presence can help to improve relations between City Hall and residents of South LA. In chapter 2, I argue that it is difficult for residents to overcome the collective memory of abuse and neglect by the LAPD and City Hall. A well-developed human relations agenda would strive to facilitate dialogue and enhance avenues of communication between City Hall and residents of South LA. Communication based on real dialogue will help to overcome the historically poor image of City Hall and enhance its legitimacy. This suggestion is similar to the one outlined earlier regarding policy; however, the emphasis here is on strategies that focus exclusively on improving relations.

At first glance, many may feel that these policy recommendations leave out one key factor: inequality. Many studies have illustrated that legal cynicism, a perspective in which formal legal channels are not viewed as legitimate, can lead to informal governance, such as the code of the street (Anderson, 1999). Previous research by Sampson and Bartusch (1998) suggests that legal cynicism is a result of neighborhood disadvantage. They argue that blocked opportunities and social isolation breed cynicism toward mainstream institutions, potentially producing violent crime (Kirk and Papachristos, 2011).

The implications of these findings are that, until inequality is addressed, legal cynicism will continue to exist. I believe this claim to be true; however, it is also true that policing efforts, and, thereby, the role of local government, can play an important role in mitigating legal cynicism and its role in producing violence. Recent work by Zimring (2012) suggests that the monumental decline in crime in New York City is due to several factors, some still unidentified. However, he argues that one factor, preventive policing, has had a demonstrable, significant effect on the decline of crime. To quote Zimring, "Police matter and they matter a lot more than many experts thought as recently as 20 years ago" (p. 158). In New York, the police were able to decrease crime by taking down drug markets and, thus, abating drug violence. According to Zimring, these findings fly in the face of conventional social science wisdom, which has traditionally viewed policing as playing a minimal role in the reduction of crime.

In many cities in America, police operate under the direction and guidance of local government; in LA they are accountable to City Hall. It is unlikely that the United States will make dramatic shifts in most policies that affect the urban poor. Policymakers and academics cannot wait until another "War on Poverty" is launched. Instead, academics and policymakers should focus on what can be done immediately. If local policing matters, then local government matters even more in addressing violence. The old adage, that local government has the largest effect on most matters affecting people, also applies to efforts addressing violent crime.

NOTES

INTRODUCTION

1 To protect the privacy of subjects, places and names have been changed. However, some of the names and places that involve public events and pertain to the
   official business of the City of Los Angeles municipal government have not been
   changed. Official public events sponsored by the City of Los Angeles are not
   subject to the same privacy standards according to the Institutional Review Board
   guidelines.

2 For more information on this perspective, see Hirschman (2004).

CHAPTER 1. NEIGHBORHOOD COUNCILS

1 LA PATH is a pseudonym I created to protect the privacy of individuals associated with the agency responsible for gang intervention. It should not be confused
   with the City of Los Angeles program People Assisting the Homeless (PATH),
   which is that different agency's actual name.

2 Fung (2004) argues that there are at least three models of municipal governance:
   top-down bureaucratic, market oriented, and decentralized. However, even within
   decentralized forms of governance elements of top-down bureaucratic management can remain within the structure.

CHAPTER 2. ALTERNATIVE GOVERNANCE

1 Sally Engle Merry (1981) argues that urban communities that lack institutions that
   crosscut interracial lines utilize race and kinship as the basis of social order. I use
   this idea in a different way by emphasizing how the disconnect of municipal government creates a vacuum where residents rely on race and the rules of the street
   as the primary basis for connecting with each other.

2 Two key points that I have tried to illustrate in this chapter are the idea that alternative governance challenged and often trumped the rule of law that City Hall
   tried to impose via the Neighborhood Councils. Instead, race, kinship, and the
   rules of the street became fused together and formed the glue of social organization in South LA.

3 By supermajority, I am referring to neighborhoods that are over 80 percent Latino.

4 As the Latino population continues to increase, African Americans have begun to
   cluster in the western part of South LA, near Crenshaw Avenue.

CHAPTER 3. NEIGHBORHOOD INSTITUTIONS

1 I borrow the concept of a larger conceptual framework that goes beyond racial identities from Delores Hayden's *The Power of Place* (1995).

CHAPTER 4. FAITH IS THE OPPOSITE OF FEAR

1 In Spanish, the word for "hope" is *esperanza*. Interestingly, it denotes waiting for things to improve; it thus has a temporal dimension of hopeful waiting.

2 After the 1965 Watts Riots, the Los Angeles HRC was formed to improve community relations and facilitate community dialogue and cooperation to address neighborhood issues.

3 A ritual celebrated mostly by Mexicans and based on the Bible. It begins December 16 and goes to December 24.

4 In all fairness, St. Joseph's and WCLO had more Latino members than any other institutions in the local area. They were arguably the most influential community institutions in this section of South LA, where violence tended to be concentrated.

5 According to 2000 census estimates, Latinos comprise 60 percent of the population in the area. Many community members, including parish clergy, believe the actual share to be higher.

CHAPTER 6. RESPONDING TO VIOLENCE, KEEPING THE PEACE

1 By most violent, I am referring to the number of homicides in the City of Los Angeles. There are four police divisions in South LA. During 2003–2004, these four precincts had the highest homicide figures in the city.

2 I found it difficult to find statistics on this phenomenon. However, Los Angeles Police Department officers often told me in interviews that many Latino immigrants were victims of robbery and that African Americans targeted them. Latinos were considered easy targets, because they were not US citizens and would not report incidents to the police. I was able to find police statistics on robberies at a housing project near one of the school sites. According to these, 86 gang-related robberies were committed from January 2002 to June 2002 within the project. Seventy-six of the 86 victims were Hispanic, while the suspects in 85 of the 86 cases were black.

CONCLUSION

1 The culture of honor refers to an honor-based type of society where status and reputation are paramount. The use of retaliatory violence is often employed in such a society to enhance an individual's status.

2 The Police Executive Research Forum report (PERF, 2009) referenced in the following paragraphs also underscores the importance of breaking the code of silence associated with the "stop snitchin'" sentiment common in many poor urban areas. The report recommends witness protection programs.

3 By "state," in this context, I mean to refer to both the local government, including local law enforcement, and federal law enforcement agencies—in particular, US Immigration and Customs Enforcement (ICE).

REFERENCES

Abu-Lughod, Janet. 2007. *Race, Space, and Riots in Chicago, New York, and Los Angeles*. New York: Oxford University Press.

Anderson, Elijah. 1999. *Code of the Street: Decency, Violence, and the Moral Life of the Inner City*. New York: W. W. Norton.

Banfield, Edward C., and James Q. Wilson. 1963. *City Politics*. Cambridge, MA: Harvard University Press.

Berrien, Jenny, and Omar McRoberts. 2000. "Religion and the Boston Miracle: The Effect of Black Ministry on Youth Violence." In *Who Will Provide? The Changing Role of Religion in American Social Welfare*, edited by Mary Jo Bane, Brent Coffin, and Ronald Thiemann. Boulder, CO: Westview Press.

Berry, Jerry, Kent E. Portney, and Ken Thomson. 1993. *The Rebirth of Urban Democracy*. Washington, DC: Brookings Institution Press.

Blau, Peter M. 1977. *Inequality and Heterogeneity: A Primitive Theory of Social Structure*. New York: Free Press.

Bourgois, Philippe. 1995. *In Search of Respect: Selling Crack in El Barrio*. Cambridge, UK: Cambridge University Press.

Bridges, Amy. 1997. *Morning Glories: Municipal Reform in the Southwest*. Princeton, NJ: Princeton University Press.

Bursik, Robert J., and Harold G. Grasmick. 1993. *Neighborhoods and Crime*. New York: Lexington.

Carr, Patrick J. 2005. *Clean Streets: Controlling Crime, Maintaining Order, and Building Community Activism*. New York: New York University Press.

Castells, Manuel, and Alejandro Portes. 1989. "World Underneath: The Origins, Dynamics, and Effects of the Informal Economy." In *The Informal Economy: Studies in Advanced and Less Developed Countries*, edited by Alejandro Portes, Manuel Castells, and Lauren A. Benton. Baltimore: John Hopkins University Press.

Colebrook, Claire. 2002. *Gilles Deleuze*. New York: Routledge.

Collins, Randall. 2008. *Violence: A Micro-Sociological Theory*. Princeton, NJ: Princeton University Press.

Drake, St. Clair, and Horace R. Cayton. 1993[1945]. *Black Metropolis: A Study of Negro Life in a Northern City*. Chicago: University of Chicago Press.

Elias, Norbert. 1969[1939]. *The Civilizing Process: The History of Manners*. New York: Urizen.

Fung, Archon. 2004. *Empowered Participation: Reinventing Urban Democracy*. Princeton, NJ: Princeton University Press.

Garot, Robert. 2009. "Reconsidering Retaliation: Structural Inhibitions, Emotive Dissonance, and the Acceptance of Ambivalence among Inner-City Young Men." *Ethnography* 10(1): 63–90.

Garrison, Jessica. 2000. "New Mural Wraps Watts Church in Its Colorful History." *Los Angeles Times*, June 12. Retrieved from http://articles.latimes.com/2000/jun/12/local/me-40123.

Gould, Roger. 2003. *Collision of Wills: How Ambiguity about Social Rank Breeds Conflict*. Chicago: University of Chicago Press.

Harding, David. 2010. *Living the Drama: Community, Conflict, and Culture among Inner-City Boys*. Chicago: University of Chicago Press.

Hayden, Dolores. 1995. *The Power of Place: Urban Landscapes as Public History*. Cambridge, MA: MIT Press.

Hernandez, Tanya K. 2007. "Roots of Latino/Black Anger." *Los Angeles Times*, January 7. Retrieved from http://www.latimes.com/news/la-op-hernandez7jan07-story.html#page=1.

Hipp, John, George Tita, and Lyndsay Boggess. 2009. "Inter- and Intra-Group Violence: Is Violent Crime an Expression of Group Conflict or Social Disorganization?" *Criminology* 47(2): 521–564.

Hirschman, Charles. 2004. "The Role of Religion in the Origins and Adaptation of Immigrant Groups in the United States." *International Migration Review* 38(3): 1206–1233.

Hunter, Albert D. 1985. "Private, Parochial and Public Social Orders: The Problem of Crime and Incivility in Urban Communities." In *The Challenge of Social Control: Citizenship and Institution Building in Modern Society*, edited by Gerald D. Suttles and Mayer N. Zald. Norwood, NJ: Ablex.

Jacobs, Bruce, and Richard Wright. 2006. *Street Justice: Retaliation in the Criminal Underworld*. New York: Cambridge University Press.

Keller, Suzanne. 1968. *The Urban Neighborhood: A Sociological Perspective*. New York: Random House.

Kirk, David S., and Andrew V. Papachristos. 2011. "Cultural Mechanisms and the Persistence of Neighborhood Violence." *American Journal of Sociology* 116(4): 1190–1233.

Kornhauser, Ruth. 1978. *Social Sources of Delinquency*. Chicago: University of Chicago Press.

Kubrin, Charis E., and Hiromi Ishizawa. 2012. "Why Some Immigrant Neighborhoods Are Safer than Others: Divergent Findings from Los Angeles and Chicago." *Annals of the American Academy of Political and Social Science* 641(1): 148–173.

Lyons, Christopher J. 2007. "Community (Dis)Organization and Racially Motivated Crime." *American Journal of Sociology* 113(3): 815–863.

Martinez, Cid Gregory, and Victor Rios. 2011. "Black/Latino Gangs and Neighborhoods in California: A Comparative Study of South Los Angeles and East Oakland."

In *Just Neighbors? Research on African American and Latino Relations in the U.S.*, edited by Edward Telles, Mark Sawyer, and Gaspar Rivera-Salgado. New York: Russell Sage.

Martinez, Ramiro, Jr., and Abel Valenzuela, Jr. 2006. *Immigration and Crime: Race, Ethnicity, and Violence*. New York: New York University Press.

McRoberts, Omar M. 2004. *Streets of Glory: Church and Community in a Black Urban Neighborhood*. Chicago: University of Chicago Press.

Merry, Sally E. 1981. *Urban Danger: Life in a Neighborhood of Strangers*. Philadelphia: Temple University Press.

Messner, Steven F., and Scott J. South. 1992. "Interracial Homicide: A Macrostructural Opportunity Perspective." *Sociological Forum* 7(3): 517–536.

Monea, Emily, and Isabel Sawhill. 2009. "Simulating the Effects of the 'Great Recession' on Poverty." Brookings Institution. Retrieved from http://www.brookings.edu/papers/2009/0910_poverty_monea_sawhill.aspx.

Muniz, Ana. 2014. "Maintaining Racial Boundaries: Criminalization, Neighborhood Context, and the Origins of Gang Injunctions." *Social Problems* 6(2): 216–236.

Murr, Andrew. 2007. "Racial 'Cleansing' in L.A." *Newsweek*, October 24.

Nagourney, Adam. 2011. "A Troubled Police Force Has Been Transformed in Los Angeles." *New York Times*, August 13, p. A11.

Olzak, Susan. 1990. "The Political Context of Competition: Lynching and Urban Racial Violence, 1882–1914." *Social Forces* 69(2): 395–421.

Pattillo-McCoy, Mary. 1998. "Church Culture as a Strategy of Action in the Black Community." *American Sociological Review* 63(6): 767–784.

PERF (Police Executive Research Forum). 2009. *Stop Snitching Phenomenon: Breaking the Code of Silence*. Washington, DC: Office of Community Oriented Policing Services (COPS), US Department of Justice. Retrieved from https://www.ncjrs.gov/App/Publications/abstract.aspx?ID=248880.

Rios, Victor. 2011. *Punished: Policing the Lives of Black and Latino Inner-City Boys*. New York: New York University Press.

Sanchez-Jankowski, Martin. 2008. *Cracks in the Pavement, Social Change and Resilience in Poor Neighborhoods*. Berkeley: University of California Press.

Santa Cruz, Nicole and Ken Shwencke. 2014. "South Vermont Ave: LA County's Death Alley." *Los Angeles Times*, January 19. Retrieved from http://homicide.latimes.com/post/westmont-homicides.

Sampson, Robert J. 2008. "Rethinking Crime and Immigration." *Contexts* 7: 28–33.

Sampson, Robert J., and Dawn Jeglum Bartusch. 1998. "Legal Cynicism and (Subcultural?) Tolerance of Deviance: The Neighborhood Context of Racial Differences." *Law and Society Review* 32: 777–804.

Sampson, Robert J., and Lydia Bean. 2006. "Cultural Mechanisms and Killing Fields: A Revised Theory of Community-Level Racial Inequality." In *The Many Colors of Crime: Inequalities of Race, Ethnicity and Crime in America*, edited by Ruth Peterson, Lauren Krivo, and John Hagan. New York: New York University Press.

Sampson, Robert J., Jeffrey D. Morenoff, and Thomas Gannon-Rowley. 2002. "Assessing 'Neighborhood Effects': Social Processes and New Directions in Research." *Annual Review of Sociology* 28: 443–478.

Shaw, Clifford R., and Henry D. McKay. 1942. *Juvenile Delinquency in Urban Areas*. Chicago: University of Chicago Press.

Skolnick, Jerome. 1966. *Justice without Trial: Law Enforcement in a Democratic Society*. New York: John Wiley & Sons.

Small, Mario L. 2007. "Is There Such a Thing as 'The Ghetto'? The Perils of Assuming That the South Side of Chicago Represents Poor Black Neighborhoods." *City* 11(3): 413–421.

Suttles, Gerald. 1968. *The Social Construction of Communities*. Chicago: University of Chicago Press.

U. S. Census Bureau. 2000. *American FactFinder Fact Sheet: Los Angeles County, CA*. Washington, DC: US Census Bureau.

Venkatesh, Sudhir A. 2006. *Off the Books: The Underground Economy of the Urban Poor*. Cambridge, MA: Harvard University Press.

Vigil, James Diego. 2011. "Ethnic Succession and Ethnic Conflict." In *Just Neighbors? Research on African American and Latino Relations*, edited by Edward Telles, Mark Sawyer, and Gaspar Rivera-Salgado. New York: Russell Sage Foundation.

Wacquant, Loïc J. D. 1997. "Three Pernicious Premises in the Study of the American Ghetto." *International Journal of Urban and Regional Research* 21(2): 341–353.

Weber, Max. 1978[1922]. *Economy and Society*. New York: Free Press.

Whyte, William Foote. 1943. *Street Corner Society: Social Structure of an Italian Slum*. Chicago: University of Chicago Press.

Wilson, William Julius. 1987. *The Truly Disadvantaged*. Chicago: University of Chicago Press.

Winship, Christopher, and Jenny Berrien. 1999. "Boston Cops and Black Churches." *Public Interest* 136: 52–68.

Zimring, Frank. 2012. *The City That Became Safe: New York's Lesson for Urban Crime and Its Social Control*. New York: Oxford University Press.

INDEX

abuse, by police and law enforcement, 26–27, 76, 78, 232, 235–36

accountability: of city officials, 42–47; of police and law enforcement, 42–47, 77, 129, 234–35

African Americans: Catholics, 102–3; church and, 101; civic institutions of, 83; cognitive-maps of, 80; criminalization of, 53, 78; gangs, 54–55, 79; GTF and, 140; homeowners, 72; Latinos *versus*, 1–2; parishioners, 111–12; participation of, 82; police and law enforcement and, 79–80, 152, 224; population and homicides, *24, 89, 183, 185*; shootings and, 140; St. Joseph's Parish and, 91; in underground economy, 157

afterlife, 122–23

alcoholism, 68–69

Algren, Aaron, 150

alternative governance, 29, 60; Catholic Church as, 117–18; City Hall and, 85; components of, 53; emergence of, 53, 145; interracial relations and, 73–74, 225–26; state and, 234; violence and, 8–12, 17–18, 84, 221, 229. *See also* street justice

Anthony, Reggie, 34

anti-tax sentiment, 10

assault, 69

attachment, integration and, 115

authority: of gangs, 63–64, 126; legitimacy and, 229–30; of Neighborhood Councils, 33; traditional types of, 62

avoidance. *See* interracial avoidance

Beaumont Neighborhood Council, 47–48

Beck, Charlie, 235

bilingualism in church, 113–14

bottom-up governance, 74

Bradley, Tom, 26

Bratton, William, 235

Catholic Church, 2–3, 5, 6, 17, 91; African Americans in, 102–3; as alternative governance, 117–18; as alternative social space, 117; interracial conflict mediation of, 99; Latino immigrants and, 94–95, 222–23; Latinos in, 103–5; legitimacy and, 230; role of, 145; social organization of, 92

Catholic Welfare Bureau (CWB), 109–10

Catholic Youth Organizations (CYO), 109–10

CBOs. *See* community-based organizations

Census Demographic Profile, U.S., 92

Center Court Neighborhood Council, 82

Center Town: community in, 75–76; crime and violence in, 75; description of, 74–75; gangs in, 75; interracial relations in, 75, 78; Neighborhood Council, 74–78; Public Safety Committee, 76–77; Safety Fair, 77

Central North Neighborhood Public Safety Committee, 57–58

charter schools, gangs in, 7

Chavez, Cesar, 106, 107

Chicago, 225, 228

children. *See* youth

ABOUT THE AUTHOR

Cid Gregory Martinez is Assistant Professor of Sociology at the University of San Diego. He received his BA, MA, and PhD from the University of California at Berkeley.